ON YOUR CASE

ON YOUR CASE

A Comprehensive, Compassionate
(and Only Slightly Bossy)
Legal Guide for Every Stage
of a Woman's Life

LISA GREEN

wm
WILLIAM MORROW
An Imprint of HarperCollins*Publishers*

HarperCollins books may be purchased for educational, business, or sales promotional use. For information please e-mail the Special Markets Department at SPsales@harpercollins.com.

FIRST EDITION

Designed by Jamie Lynn Kerner

Gavel icon copyright © by Evgin/Shutterstock, Inc.

Library of Congress Cataloging-in-Publication Data has been applied for.

ISBN 978-0-06-230799-6

15 16 17 18 19   OV/RRD   10 9 8 7 6 5 4 3 2 1

For Claire and Andrew

CONTENTS

THE CAVEAT PAGE

Void where prohibited. Your mileage may vary. Professional driver on closed course.

Lawyers love conditions. So here are some, from me to you.

I am a lawyer, but I am not your lawyer.

After all, even if I could be your lawyer, you'd still need a lawyer.

Why? Let's start with where you live. The answers to so many legal questions that matter to us, including those related to marriage, divorce, and estate planning, are going to depend on very specific, and sometimes puzzlingly quirky, state laws. Before you talk to a local lawyer, read the relevant chapter of this book, then consult the resource section for more specific information; armed with that knowledge, your meeting will be more cost-efficient and productive.

Even if you read this book and then decide to engage in some do-it-yourself legal work, you'll probably want a lawyer to review your handiwork. Laws are seldom imprecise, so even an innocent mistake on a prenup or will could render the entire document useless. Fixing that mistake could cost you multiples of any lawyer's fee.

What's more, while law may seem set in stone, that stone is time-soluble. In other words, laws change in response to societal and political shifts, and that means no book about legal advice can be permanently up to date. A perfect example of a time-sensitive legal issue is our nation's dramatic embrace of same-sex marriage, with related state and federal law shifting as I type. (For updates on this and other fast-developing legal issues, I invite you to visit my companion website, lisagreenlaw.com.)

For all those reasons, think of this book not as legal advice, but as a start—I would say, the head start—to identifying and coping with legal issues that come your way.

Before we proceed, one more note. This book features a lot of disputes. In some instances the combatants' names have been changed; their cases were never well publicized and there's no need to start now. In all instances, the stories are true.

INTRODUCTION: YOUR FRIEND
AT THE BAR

I know we've just met, but I recognize you. Like me, you are an expert.

Please, no need to feign humility on my account. You're at home, half watching that awards show and second-guessing that starlet. Her gown: what was she thinking? She's too thin, the width of a pipe cleaner. Or maybe a paper clip. Who told her pixie cuts look good?

You're at the coffee shop. I see you there every weekday, holding court with the moms in the back, pontificating (and not quietly) about the president's budget speech, the mayor's education decision, that appalling reality show catfight you all admit you watched, squealing with the collective pleasure of indulging in cable instead of reading or paying attention to your husbands. Or you are ahead of me in the supermarket checkout line, extolling the superiority of that particular brand of yogurt.

Admit it. You hold unimpeachable opinions about just about everything: hemlines, tutors, men. So what if you aren't an "expert"? Who needs to be formally trained to be right? You know how to read advice books and websites, and you know how to pick up the phone and ask for help. Your friends insist on your two cents before they act, and they consider calling you before dialing 911 in an emergency. Even your kids occasionally admit you have a point. That's why for almost any matter—what to wear, what to see, whom to hire—you usually sit pretty. When you have a problem, you just consult yourself (with the occasional call to treasured gal pals, Mom for big-ticket items, or your cousin the psychologist in case a decision could hurt a family member's feelings, heaven forbid) and then steer the big ship of needy friends and relatives to the correct result.

But I bet there's a big exception to your expertise.

It's the law.

Women and the law have long had a rocky relationship. Sure, today women are Supreme Court justices, partners at prestigious law firms, chairwomen of major law enforcement agencies. Then again, a woman wasn't named partner at a United States law firm until 1937, when the intriguingly named Soia Mentschikoff got the nod at the intimidatingly titled Spence, Hotchkiss, Parker & Duryee. Not a single woman graduated from Harvard Law School until 1953. Recent strides aside, we are still catching up professionally from a very late start.

While you may be only vaguely aware of the status of women in the legal profession, I guarantee you are an avid consumer of law stories. Who can resist that idle flip through an afternoon's cable offerings until you hear the familiar *da-dum* and settle into the guilty pleasure of some *Law & Order* reruns? Did you watch any coverage of the lurid Casey Anthony murder trial? Read a legal thriller? Thought so.

So here's what I don't understand: if some of us are advancing professionally as lawyers, and all of us are enthralled by the law, why are women reliably dumbfounded when they have a legal problem?

It pains me to bring it up, but it's true: legal problems are as predictable as bad weather, and somehow, though we are otherwise often immaculately attired, we never carry appropriate umbrellas.

Consider three dire emergencies I heard about in a recent two-week stretch. Each happened to a friend of mine who told me her story, unsolicited.

1. A registered nurse and mother of two wonderful children, happily married and enjoying an idyllic, outdoorsy life, learns that her husband has spent sixteen of their twenty-three married years in a secret relationship with another woman.

2. Another mom, a successful film industry professional, encourages her son (enrolled in a leading liberal arts college) to go outside and take some fresh air, advice he understands to mean "walk outdoors, and bring a joint." The New York City police come calling soon after.

3. Still another successful working mother with affluent parents who live, independently and well, in another state discovers they have lost a substantial chunk of their savings to a fraudulent financial adviser. He gained her parents' trust after he was able to impress them with his knowledge of family information he had gleaned from a rudimentary Google search.

Smart women? Yes. Generally clued in to the best approach to professional and personal problems? Absolutely. Clueless about how to respond to these life-altering problems? Utterly.

Have these types of unnerving emergencies happened to you? There are only two possible answers: no, and not yet.

If you are still skeptical, let's try this pop quiz. It's pass-fail, and just between us, so be honest.

Question 1: If you are married, are you maintaining separate credit accounts, and do you understand that you are fully liable for debt your spouse rings up in any joint accounts, even if you eventually were to divorce?

Question 2: If you have children, have you designated a guardian in case something happens to you?

Question 3: Whether or not you have children, or even a spouse or partner, have you signed an advance medical directive and identified someone you trust to look after your finances in case you take ill?

If you answered "no" to any of these questions, welcome to one of America's largest, unheralded demographics: women who think laws related to child care, money, illness, and death somehow don't apply to them.

I'm going to try not to raise my voice, but there's something I want you to understand: You don't get to decide when your luck will run out or your fortunes take a turn for the worse. Nor do you get a vote about whether your contractor will abandon your job, whether your boss will hit on you, or whether your doctor will commit malpractice.

Ladies, it's time we acknowledge an essential truth of modern life. Whether or not you invite it into your life, the law will find you. When it does, will you be ready to respond? If you are prepared, you have increased your odds that you can properly answer these predictable questions: Should you sign that prenup? Remarry? Read the incomprehensible lease for your son's first apartment before you cosign?

I wrote this book so you can understand the legal issues that will fall inevitably (and just like our jawlines) into the most carefully protected lives.

I'm a lawyer who worked at a leading New York firm for several years and helped clients with a wide range of problems, from children who needed to be legally emancipated from their harmful parent so they could be adopted by a loving foster family to major media companies who wanted to assert their intellectual property rights in the digital age. In addition to having personal experience with legal issues, ranging from my own divorce to dilemmas about real estate and employment contracts, I also explain them on television, which means I can separate fact from speculation and direct your attention to the key issues you really need to know. Think of me as your aide de camp: the relative with a law degree that your family failed to produce. In short, let me help you.

Together, we'll look at the legal issues that arise in each phase of a woman's life, from that first serious move-in relationship to the workplace, babies, kids, teens, spouses, exes, aging parents, and (sorry, but it's inevitable) aging you.

On Your Case is organized chronologically, to make it as easy as possible to find the guidance you need at your current stage of life, to read ahead and plan for future issues, or to look back to give the best possible advice to family and friends.

Stick with me, and together we'll face tough situations and improve your odds for success. I cannot repair a leak, identify a zone defense, or self-administer a manicure, but thanks to my training and research, I can stand my ground when I see a dense contract or hear yet another tale of legal woe.

By the time we're done, you'll wonder why you forgot to think about the legal implications that pop up in matters of love, work, and family. Then you'll stop worrying and perform the act that reliably banishes worry. No, not binge-watching reruns. Taking informed action.

So: Confidence up. Posture straight. Spanx on. Let's go.

PART ONE

RELATIONSHIPS AND THE LAW

LAUNCHING A RELATIONSHIP: WHEN IS ONLINE OVER THE LINE?

OPENING STATEMENT

Jeanne McCarthy, a writer and devoted volunteer for Habitat for Humanity, wanted companionship, and needed help finding it. She hired the Two of Us dating service, paying $7,000 for help finding a man, age fifty-eight to sixty-seven, with an active lifestyle like hers.

Unfortunately, we can glean details of Jeanne's dating service experience not from a triumphant wedding announcement, but from court papers. Her lawyer recounted Jeanne's situation in order to sue Two of Us, claiming that in five months, the aptly named site offered Jeanne just two introductions. Only one of the two yielded a date: a man with an outstanding criminal warrant. A spokesman for the agency said the incident was isolated, and that the company guaranteed introductions, not dates.

Do lawsuits bring relief when a dating experience goes south? More on that in a moment. First, though, let's take a brief look at current dating trends in the Internet age.

Alarming dispatches from the usual sources suggest that the way we date now has changed, and not for the better. To illustrate this tired Style section trope, let's check in with a reliable source for trends that induce hand-wringing: National Public Radio.

For a feature on "How Young People Date Today," NPR conducted an earnest interview with an entrepreneur who insisted that the word *date* was passé, and that the better term for a social get-together would be *grouper*. Conveniently, that was also the name of his online dating website, which encouraged daters, I mean groupers, to assemble an entourage, go out together, and, inevitably, post self-referential photos of the evening.

Why ditch dating for grouping? The Grouper CEO observed that young people in the "hashtag generation" need a new approach to dating in part because they can't tolerate the possibility of date failure. As he told NPR: "For a generation of people who grew up with participation trophies, rejection is a hard thing."

I don't doubt that today's daters have fragile egos. That would surely explain why my own young adult children refuse to disclose even rudimentary information about their romantic partners to me.

But the notion that the essential emotion that dating invokes—profound insecurity—has changed over time because of evolving gender roles, smartphones, or start-ups is nonsensical. Dating is and will always be an awkward activity fraught with anxiety and rejection-infused dread.

And it remains that way throughout life.

My experience with Dating: The AARP Years may be representative. In middle age, I carried the same fear of rejection, plus the added disappointment of meeting suitors who, like me, were falling apart and often burdened with either actual excess weight and/or the weight of unfulfilling jobs, irksome ex-spouses, and hapless children. In midlife, daters suffer the same neuroses and dashed hopes of our younger counterparts, but with a twist: absolutely everyone looks younger in their profile photo than in person, and at our age, that's not a positive thing.

In short, dating hasn't really changed. It's a rehearsal for a more serious relationship, so it tends toward the tentative, hope-dashing, and usually terrible.

Since dating can lead to disappointment, and disappointment equals suffering, and pain and suffering is a category for which people often seek legal recourse . . . well, you can see where this is going.

Not that I mean to encourage anyone unlucky in love to sue: the opportunities for compensation are limited. After all, have you ever heard of a firm specializing in matchmaking law? Nonetheless, unhappy suitors have tried to recoup their investment, and sometimes even damages, when their dates have gone awry, looking to persuade a court that they were promised happiness but got something else entirely. That's when both sides of the dispute take a closer look at the contract to see what, if anything, the brokenhearted plaintiff can claim.

IT'S THE LAW

To understand how much you can legally depend on a matchmaker or dating site to introduce you to the attractive, successful, and nonhomicidal partner of your dreams, let's look at that enemy of romance: fine print, specifically the fine print for OkCupid.com.

OkCupid has a perky, user-friendly, and altogether upbeat-looking website. How upbeat? The service is run by a company called Humor Rainbow Inc. When it comes to the lawyerly fine print, however, its terms and conditions are humor-free. Want a sense of how relaxed OkCupid wants you to feel about embarking on your online dating adventures? Consider this caveat. The capital letters are theirs.

HUMOR RAINBOW STRONGLY ADVISES YOU TO USE EXTREME CAUTION BEFORE SHARING PERSONALLY IDENTIFIABLE INFORMATION WITH OTHER USERS ON ITS WEBSITE. HUMOR RAINBOW DOES NOT CONDUCT CRIMINAL BACKGROUND CHECKS ON ITS USERS.

You may be thinking: "Dating is tough enough. The last thing I need is discouraging boilerplate from the people who are suggesting that they can help me meet my match." But I applaud OkCupid for its candor. These sites are clearinghouses, not old-fashioned matchmakers or your friend with the (usually misguided) hunch that you would adore her husband's law partner, the one whose wife dumped him on the grounds of first-degree marital boredom.

At the heart of this legal language lies a practical bit of advice: it's important to be realistic about people you meet online.

Consider the case of New York lawyer John Friedland, who claimed the matchmaking firm Amy Laurent International promised "the ultimate experience in high-end dating" but delivered a sub-ultimate experience to him. According to Friedland, Laurent failed to live up to her vow to pair him with three appropriate dates each month and then refused to refund his fee. The case was settled out of court.

Friedland is hardly alone, at least in the legal sense. Joan Cooke of Florida sued the matchmaking company Kelleher & Associates after it paired her with men she found unsuitable (including a Republican; Joan's a Democrat). The service called the lawsuit baseless and it was ultimately dismissed.

Match.com spent four years fighting a proposed class-action

lawsuit brought by clients who claimed that the site left millions of expired profiles online and served up fake ones, too. Those lawsuits in California, New York, and Texas federal courts all failed, with Match reminding the courts that its terms of use protect the site from liability.

These stories get nationwide, sometimes worldwide attention, and the prospect of that publicity surely helps reduce the number of claims. After all, while the suing suitor can reach an out-of-court settlement that presumably includes some cash, she first has to endure tabloid scorn as a hapless loser, or victim, in love.

Sometimes, though, an online date ends so horribly you might think compensation would be in order. But is it?

EXHIBIT 1: WORST-CASE SCENARIO

Mary Kay Beckman had a catastrophic dating problem. The Nevada woman met Wade Ridley on Match.com in 2010. After a handful of dates, she decided to break it off. Surely Mary Kay imagined that Wade would go quietly. Instead, Ridley hid in Mary Kay's garage with a knife and surprised her, stabbing her ten times until the knife broke, then stomping on her head. Incredibly, Mary Kay survived, though she required multiple surgeries. Ridley was later arrested for murdering another woman; he committed suicide in prison before he could be tried.

Mary Kay sued Match.com for negligence, deceptive trade, failure to warn, and negligent infliction of emotional distress. Match reportedly responded that while what happened to Mary Kay was "awful," the lawsuit was "absurd"—the site could not be held responsible for the behavior of its members and the behavior of one individual with no prior criminal record did not reflect the community of Match .com users. There's no public report of the outcome of the lawsuit, but chances are that Match.com's lawyers had the better argument: that users, including Mary Kay, agreed to terms of use that protected Match from liability.

Is this story representative of the typical online dating experience? Of course not. But it's a cautionary tale of what can go wrong when you meet a stranger online for a date, something Match.com says 40 million Americans have tried. Connectivity has revolutionized the way singles meet, but it's also introduced a fresh new crop of potential dangers.

Leaving liability aside, how can we protect ourselves when we head out of the safety of our homes and into the company of someone we may know only from photographs or a voice on the phone?

In 2012, Match.com (along with two other prominent dating sites) pledged to check their users against online sex offender registries, but a Match executive acknowledged that daters need to exercise "common sense and prudence" when meeting someone new.

FOR MORE INFORMATION

Plenty of websites, including Match and its competitors, as well as organizations like AARP, offer thoughtful guidance about safe dating so you can meet new friends and make sure you get home in one piece.

I like the following advice from an unexpected but logical source: a university filled with young people who are wading into the dating pool, largely unsupervised. These tips, aimed at female students but useful for women of any age, are excerpted from a helpful list published by Johns Hopkins University:

◆   Always tell someone where you are going with your date and when you are expected to return.

◆ Check out a first date or a blind date with friends. Meet in and go to public places. Carry money for a taxi or take your own car in case you need to cut the date short.

◆ Pay attention to what your date says about himself or herself. If you detect discrepancies, this should raise a flag.

◆ Trust your instincts. If a place or the way your date acts makes you nervous or uneasy, get away from the situation.

◆ When out with friends, keep together and try not to get separated. Do not leave a social event with someone you have just met or do not know well.

◆ Be careful not to let alcohol or other drugs decrease your ability to take care of yourself and make sensible decisions.

◆ Do not accept beverages from someone you do not know or trust. Always watch your drink and never leave it unattended.

Beyond that, if you are looking for dating advice, I suggest you look for another book. My dating experiences have all fit in the narrow range between the awkward and the appalling, and through it all I seem to have learned nothing other than the veracity of the frog-to-prince ratio.

2

COHABITATION: DOES PRACTICE MAKE PERFECT?

OPENING STATEMENT

Objection.

I'm a lawyer, not a linguist, but I have a problem with the word *cohabitation* on the ground that it is just . . . cold. Couldn't we substitute a more appealing term for a couple who live together, often happily and unencumbered by societal constraints or a contract?

To my ear, *cohabitation* sounds faintly zoological, or like the situation forced upon a group of meek, captured scientists by a malevolent genius who has imprisoned them in a windowless tower until they invent the death-dealing superweapon of his dreams. The B-movie dialogue nearly writes itself: "That's right, you will all cohabitate, without hot meals or premium cable, until you develop the device that will let me rule . . . the . . . world . . . mwah-ha-ha. . . ."

Semantics aside, for many couples the decision to cohabitate is a welcome compromise, and, of course, often serves as a practice round for marriage. More couples are choosing to cohabitate, and they are remaining together as unmarried couples for longer periods of time. According to the 2006 to 2010 National Survey of Family Growth, almost half of the women surveyed cohabited, rather than married, as their first union with a partner. The duration of those relationships rose to twenty-two months from thirteen months in 1995. And couples are not rushing to marry once they have children; the survey found 23 percent of births to women ages 15 to 44 occurring while the women were living with (rather than married to) their mate, up from 14 percent in 2003.

But while these relationships may be longer lasting, they hardly guarantee a stable, lifelong partnership. The survey reported that one-half of these first cohabitations from 1997 to 2001 led to marriage, but one-third ended within five years. Is that a big deal? Yes, if property and, more significant, kids are involved.

Enter the law. Can it stabilize these popular, sometimes fragile relationships? More specifically, should you consider a cohabitation agreement?

IT'S THE LAW

It's decidedly unromantic. And you may think the very reason to cohabitate, rather than marry, is to avoid the burdensome responsibilities that a marriage imposes. But before you scoff, ask yourself: Will you be sharing rent or the cost of maintaining a home? Buying a pet together? Is anyone pregnant? Have either of you socked away savings?

As you live together, if things go well, you will start to accumulate assets and debts, and maybe dependents. You will have a relationship that resembles a marriage but lacks its protections if you split up. Is this the most sensible way to proceed? Or would it make sense to plan for a worst-case scenario before it might arise?

A cohabitation agreement needn't be complicated, and if it makes things easier, we can give it the adorable nickname that appeared in a British newspaper: a "no nup."

If you live in a state that recognizes cohabitation agreements, and almost all do, what can your "no nup" include? The American Bar Association offers these prospective deal points:

- *Expenses.* From rent or mortgage to the weekly grocery bill, you can agree in writing to divide the bills, or assign percentages for who pays what.
- *Debts.* You can confirm that you will not be responsible for the other's separate debts and can decide how you will share responsibility for jointly held debt (though keep in mind that to your creditor, you are both responsible for joint debt).
- *Assets.* You can agree that neither one of you has the right to assets the other holds, whether it's real estate, pensions or retirement accounts, or a business one partner is building. You can agree that if one partner helps pay a home mortgage, that partner can have the right to share in any increase in the home's value if you split. If you buy assets together, you can agree on how they would be divided.
- *Support.* Is one partner supporting the other? We'll take a closer look at palimony below, but a cohabitation agreement is the right place to decide whether to offer support or waive any rights to collect.
- *Estate planning.* You can agree not to try to claim any share of an estate if your partner dies and that is your mutual plan. Of

course, if you are taking my advice, you will make your beneficiaries clear in a will or trust; still, it never hurts to reiterate
your posthumous intentions.

◆ *Children.* Cohabitation (and other) agreements have limited power to determine parenting issues, such as custody
and child support. Why? Because courts take a strong interest in protecting children's rights, so they are loath to
let couples make private decisions that might harm kids.
In other words, while it's prudent to include your shared
thoughts about the care of your kids if you split up, a judge
will retain the right (if prodded by an unhappy parent) to
supersede the agreement with a ruling she thinks is better
for the children.

Another consideration for unmarried couples: paternity. When a
married couple has a baby, the husband is presumed to be the father.
This presumption doesn't exist for unmarried partners, so consider
having the father sign a statement acknowledging paternity.

Even if you are squeamish about an agreement, consider whether
you should at least identify your partner as your health care proxy. If
you aren't married, and you take ill, you want to be sure your partner
has the necessary permission to visit you, and the right to make decisions about your care. Separately, you may want to grant your partner
power of attorney to manage your finances. (You can read much more
about these documents in chapter 26.)

If you decide to sign a cohabitation agreement, even one you draft
yourself using an online form as a starting point, I recommend you
review it with a lawyer familiar with your state's law so you know
whether it's enforceable in court. Make that two lawyers. Each partner should be represented separately; even if you like your partner's
lawyer, you need your own. For one thing, you want to be sure the
agreement is fair to both partners. Also, the two-lawyer review pro-

tects each partner should the other complain she was strong-armed into signing something she didn't understand. This comes up a lot in prenups, as we'll see later.

EXHIBIT 2: THE PATHBREAKING PALIMONY CASE

Are you pleasantly surprised that you can create a legally enforceable agreement with your live-in partner about critical issues like money and property even though you are not married? Then take a moment to thank Michelle Marvin, whose blockbuster lawsuit paved the way.

Before Michelle's landmark legal action, cohabitation agreements were essentially unenforceable. They were considered distasteful, sex-for-money deals that served no public policy purpose. In California, cohabitators were said to be parties to a "meretricious union."

The events that would shift Californian and then national opinion about cohabitation were set in motion in October 1964, when Michelle Triola moved in with debonair, gray-haired, and still-married actor Lee Marvin. Over the next seven years, Lee got a divorce, while Michelle changed her last name to Marvin. Along the way, Michelle claimed she gave up her "lucrative career as an entertainer [and] singer" to devote herself full-time to his care "as a companion, homemaker, housekeeper and cook" (weren't the sixties charming?) in exchange for what she said was an oral agreement that promised her lifetime support. They split up in May 1970, and Lee paid her $800 a month in support until November 1971. When Lee stopped paying, Michelle sued for half the property accrued in his name while they were together.

Michelle's case was dismissed by a lower court, but on appeal the

Supreme Court of California ruled palimony contracts like the one she described (that's *pal* + *alimony;* clever) could be enforced as long as the agreement didn't contemplate an exchange of services, or money, for sex.

Michelle secured a resounding victory for cohabitating partners who could hereafter have their agreements enforced. But in a case of winning the battle but losing the war, Michelle was not able to prove that she and Lee had made a cohabitation agreement, so she never won the share of property she sought. She was able to secure a judgment for $104,000 after a trial, but that award was overturned on appeal two years later.

As an interesting coda, Michelle eventually lived with Dick Van Dyke for thirty years, until she died in 2009.

While Michele's legal battle was pathbreaking, take care not to misread its effects: it remains much harder to secure financial help from your ex if you do not get married. Cohabitation is simply less secure, especially for the partner with less money and fewer assets. That's fine if you want the flexibility to change your mind about your mate without a divorce. That's not fine if you want to rely on your partner for financial help. The next story is an interesting, and rare, exception to the rule.

CELEBRITY LAW LESSON:
SESAME STREET EDITION

This story is brought to you by the letter *D,* which in this case stands for "Do not read this court case to mean that you can count on palimony without something in writing." That said, every once in a while a judge will hear a plea for payment and find a way to make it so, ruling for the jilted partner with no paperwork.

That was the result New Jersey Superior Court judge Ned Rosenberg delivered to Sharon Joiner-Orman, who spent thirty-nine years as the unmarried companion to Roscoe Orman. (Sharon sometimes used Roscoe's last name, including on deeds to property they owned together.) You would recognize Roscoe: he is the actor who played Gordon Robinson for decades on *Sesame Street,* with time-outs along the way for appearances on *Law & Order, Law & Order SVU, Sex and the City,* and *The Wire.*

During their time together, Sharon stayed home and took care of the couple's four children while Roscoe built his career. Then, in 2010, Roscoe left Sharon. While he sent her $3,600 a month in support payments, Roscoe also encouraged Sharon to move to a smaller home. Sharon stayed put. Roscoe married and stopped writing checks to Sharon. Sharon sued Roscoe for palimony, claiming he had promised to look after her for the rest of her life. Even though they had no written palimony agreement (required under New Jersey law), Judge Rosenberg found in Sharon's favor. Because Sharon relied on Roscoe's unwritten promise, it would be unfair ("inequitable," in court terms) to fail to enforce that promise, said the judge.

Roscoe's lawyer vowed to appeal and some Garden State court watchers thought the ruling was vulnerable. Perhaps the couple settled out of court. No matter the outcome, the battle illustrates that cohabitation is no ordinary business relationship, even as courts and lawmakers strain to routinize the rules of engagement.

FOR MORE INFORMATION

Unmarried Equality, an advocacy group that works toward "fairness and equal treatment of all people," offers additional tips on living together at unmarried.org.

Nolo publishes of a series of well-regarded do-it-yourself legal books and online resources, including *Living Together: A Legal Guide for Unmarried Couples*.

3

MARRIAGE BASICS

OPENING STATEMENT

He was so . . . reassuring.

Dark hair, tailored suit; perfectly comfortable in the spotlight next to the rabbi. As I stood before him, extravagantly coiffed and precisely powdered, in my dream-come-true designer bridal gown, we gazed at each other, mindful of the importance of the moment, respectful of its long-term consequences.

Deeply apprehensive, I sought his wordless guidance. What could I expect? What would the future bring? What about my doubts: Were they the "reasonable" doubts lawyers love, the ones that mean you can't convict, or, in this case, commit? Or were they the last-minute jitters of a neurotic law student who had studied Edith Wharton all too well, knowing that a woman who fails to make a timely marital match will end up like a modern-day Lily Bart, forced into the twentieth-century equivalent of sewing, incompetently, for a milliner and developing a fatal addiction to chloral hydrate?

He never spoke directly to me, but his calm look and the well-modulated sound of his voice sent a strong message: just do it.

That man wasn't my future husband. He was the cantor, stationed alongside the rabbi to chant the traditional songs and blessings that accompany a Jewish wedding. Long after the ceremony, I wondered: If I had asked the handsome clergyman for advice about my wedding-day jitters, what would he have suggested? If he'd told me to pay attention to my ambivalence and stop the proceedings, would I have listened?

One marriage, one divorce, two grown kids, and many years later, I can tell you this: I love marriage. I am glad I got married. I'm not even sorry I married the man who later became my ex. Our divorce had its very rough spots, but today we are friendly, our kids are wonderful, and I still sneak a look at the wedding album from time to time, mostly to remember relatives who have passed and to marvel at our youth, not to mention the time capsule outfits and hair.

Whether you are a feminist, postfeminist, or feign neutrality on the issue of women's rights, you were conditioned to love the grandeur of marriage: the gown, the reception playlist, the ability to stealth-torture your girlfriends with bridesmaid costumes, and those charming, romantic proposals.

Marriage is at the very heart of the Western ideal of family and culture, and despite the institution's perennial lack of success, it remains wildly popular. The law, at least when it comes to heterosexual couples (though thanks to advances in marriage equality, that distinction is disappearing), does its part by making it very easy to get legally hitched.

In chapter 4 we will look at common-law marriage, which in a few states is the by-product of little more than living together with the proper intent. In most states, however, if you want to be wed, you will need to do a little legal planning.

IT'S THE LAW

Your marriage ceremony will be legal if you follow these laughably easy steps:

1. Obtain a marriage license from the county clerk's office in the state where you will be married and wait the number of days your state requires you to hold off before you wed. Don't wait too long, though, or the license will expire. If it does, buy some socks, because I suspect your feet are cold.
2. Secure a judge, justice, or court clerk to perform your civil ceremony or a clergy member to perform your religious ceremony. They may need permission to officiate, depending on where you wed. A few states (notably Pennsylvania, where Quaker tradition took root) allow couples to marry without an officiant.
3. During the ceremony, whether you insist on writing your own vows, reading doggerel, or pulling time-tested text from the Bible or off the web, you probably should state your mutual intention to be wed—but there are no set rules. Designated witnesses are not required in every state, but they can't hurt.
4. Have your officiant file a marriage certificate in the appropriate county office. A fun fact for future reference: if you lose your marriage certificate, you can get information about how to contact your home state for a replacement from the Centers for Disease Control and Prevention's website: www.cdc.gov.

That's it! It's harder to set up a streaming video account.

Oh, wait: there are minimum age requirements for marriage, but they can be as young as fourteen for young men and thirteen for young women, and parental consent can reduce that minimum age.

A few states offer covenant marriage, which was designed to make it more difficult both to marry and to split. Covenant couples agree to undergo premarital counseling, to engage in still more counseling should they contemplate divorce, and to tougher conditions for divorce if they decide to break up.

What if you get married abroad? The U.S. Department of State's guide to overseas marriage notes that while the United States is happy to authenticate your foreign marriage document, and surely wishes the best for you and your beloved, in order to get married abroad you will need to follow the host country's rules. These may include residency requirements, proof in writing that you have the legal capacity to marry, and even blood tests, depending on your destination. Generally speaking, your overseas marriage will be recognized here, but you'll want to check your state's law to be sure.

IS THIS MARRIAGE FOR REAL?

Did you know your former college roommate, work acquaintance, or Pilates pal can perform your wedding ceremony as a minister, without enrolling in a seminary for formal training?

That's the premise of the Universal Life Church. Curious? Fire up your mobile phone and take a look at ulc.net. The church says it's ordained 20 million people worldwide. That number may seem unbelievable, but consider this: if you have two minutes and a working Internet connection, you can join their ranks.

Are you wondering if a Universal Life minister can really marry a couple legally? So did a groom we'll call D.S., who was married in 2005 by a Universal Life Church minister and later sued, claiming the marriage couldn't be valid. (He also challenged the validity of the postnup he and his wife, R.S., signed three days later.) The judge agreed with D.S., but the woman who thought she was his legal wife appealed, and the appeals court reversed the decision. Said the judges, "It is not the role of the courts to question the ULC's membership requirements or the method by which it selects its ministers."

Despite its growth and popularity, the ecclesiastical authority of the ULC may have its limits. When New York clothing designer Anya Ponorovskaya wanted a divorce from her husband, lawyer Wylie Stecklow, Stecklow was able to persuade the judge that the marriage was never valid. Why? Because Wylie and Anya "wed" at a resort in Tulum, Mexico, in a ceremony performed by Stecklow's cousin, a dentist who was ordained as—you guessed it—a Universal Life Church minister. While the then-happy couple incorporated elements of a traditional Jewish wedding into their ULC proceedings, their ceremony failed to follow Mexican law. Nor did the couple bother to secure a license in New York. The judge could not excuse these oversights, concluded that the marriage was void, and dismissed Anya's request for a divorce.

EXHIBIT 3: THE INNOCENT SPOUSE RULE

While the barriers to entry are low, the consequences of marriage are serious. Marriage launches you and your spouse into a hopeful, romantic start-up, a merger of conjoined finances and feelings. How does this starry-eyed business venture work? Let's look at taxes.

When you marry, you will have the less-than-romantic opportunity to decide whether to file taxes one of two ways: married filing jointly or married filing separately. Your tax adviser can go over the pros and cons of each, but one consequence of joint filing is that you will be responsible for the entire tax bill you both owe, and for any fraudulent statements your spouse makes.

This becomes a problem when one spouse takes charge of the tax return and the other signs off without review, or after a well-meaning but ill-fated attempt to read it first. If you've done that, don't be ashamed. I've tried, and failed, to understand my own 1040. Unlike you, I have good reason to feel guilty about my incompetence: I loved tax law in law school. I suspect that even the author of my beloved tax law casebook, Professor Michael Graetz, the eminent tax scholar and former Treasury Department official, might sympathize with the challenge of comprehending a tax return. After all, he wrote *100 Million Unnecessary Returns*, a book calling for a simplified U.S. tax plan.

No matter how compelling Graetz's argument, or mine, any hope of meaningful tax reform seems faint. In the meantime, the Internal Revenue Service will continue to exercise its enforcement prerogatives. In other words, if one spouse cheats on taxes, the signing-without-checking spouse may find herself caught in the IRS's crosshairs.

If that happens, what should the unknowing spouse do? Carol Joynt could advise. Her husband, Howard Joynt, owned and ran Nathans, a popular bar and restaurant in the Georgetown section of Washington, D.C. As Carol recounted in her memoir, together they enjoyed "good schools, good doctors, serene vacations, beautiful homes, excellent services, and a world of agreeable people who more often than not enjoyed similarly comfortable lives."

Carol was a television news producer, smart and naturally curious, but when it came to money, she did what women so often have done, and let Howard take the lead.

The kicker? When Howard died unexpectedly in 1997, Carol discovered her husband had been under investigation for criminal tax fraud, and left behind an almost $3 million tax bill that was now her sole responsibility.

With the help of a well-chosen tax lawyer, who, as an IRS commissioner, had helped write the provision, Carol invoked the "innocent spouse" rule. The rule allows a spouse to try to prove to the IRS that he or she didn't know, or have any reason to know, that a spouse was committing tax fraud. Thanks to the rule, Carol was able to settle her tax bill with the IRS for far less than the government had sought. (However, as a knowing friend and matrimonial lawyer told me, the agency is less likely to forgive a spouse who makes the innocence argument after she led a "very good life." It is not, after all, the Incurious Spouse rule.)

As you might expect, the IRS doesn't exactly specialize in the merciful resolution of fiscal quandaries. One estimate showed the agency received more than fifty thousand innocent spouse applications a year and granted fewer than half. But that was before the agency abolished its requirement that spouses ask for help within two years from the time the agency sent its collection notice, or else lose out on any chance for relief. The deadline was a problem for spouses who only learned of their dire situation years after a divorce or death. To its credit, the IRS also is more forgiving about incorrect taxes for a spouse who was a victim of abuse, even if that spouse knew the return was incorrect.

How can you avoid this tax nightmare? It's not foolproof, but an early emphasis on sharing financial information can help establish a relationship that makes money a joint effort. The more you know, the less likely you are to be fooled. See the section at the end of this chapter for organizations that offer advice about how you and your spouse can start a conversation about finances.

EXHIBIT 4: SAME-SEX MARRIAGE

The history of our nation's courts encompasses epic battles over social issues, with a legacy of decisions both admirable and unforgivable. That history encompasses landmark decisions about civil rights, including those that tried to right the shameful legacy of segregation. Beginning in the 1970s, the U.S. Supreme Court handed down abortion decisions that still inflame debate. Today, courts are tackling same-sex marriage. The rapid pace of change in this area, both in the courts and before state legislatures, has astonished even longtime proponents of equal rights for same-sex couples.

How quickly has the legality of same-sex marriage spread? In March 2013, when the U.S. Supreme Court heard arguments in two important same-sex marriage cases, nine states and the District of Columbia permitted same-sex marriage. By the end of that year, soon after the Supreme Court held that same-sex married couples were entitled under the Constitution to federal benefits, that number had doubled to eighteen.

How quickly will these rights become available to couples in other states? Change may come slowly in states with bans on same-sex marriage; those states often also require that any change in the law has to be approved by popular vote. (Those bans, however, are themselves under legal attack.) On the other hand, it's highly likely that before too long, the U.S. Supreme Court will determine whether our Constitution grants same-sex couples the right to marry in every state.

The ability of same-sex couples to marry in some states, and not others, during a time of dynamic political, legal, and social change means that keeping up with the law in this area requires up-to-the-minute advice. You can find some of it from the organizations I list on page 33, and more on my website, lisagreenlaw.com.

BOSSES OF THE BAR:
MARGARET MARSHALL

Long before television—usually a leading indicator of cultural change—introduced delighted viewers to an adorable Cameron and Mitchell on *Modern Family,* much less married them off, a state court judge issued a stirring opinion in a decision that revolutionized marriage rights in America.

In 2003, Margaret H. Marshall, then chief justice of the Massachusetts Supreme Judicial Court, wrote the majority opinion (a 4–3 squeaker) in *Goodridge v. Department of Public Health,* ruling same-sex marriage legal under the state's constitution. A native of South Africa, where she'd fought apartheid, Margaret was the first woman to serve as the state's chief justice and brought a lifelong devotion to civil rights—and a resonant writing style—to the task. The language of the *Goodridge* decision is so inspiring that it's been incorporated into wedding ceremonies by both same-sex and heterosexual couples. Here's an excerpt:

Civil marriage is at once a deeply personal commitment to another human being and a highly public celebration of the ideals of mutuality, companionship, intimacy, fidelity, and family. . . . Because it fulfills yearnings for security, safe haven, and connection that express our common humanity, civil marriage is an esteemed institution, and the decision whether and whom to marry is among life's momentous acts of self-definition.

FOR MORE INFORMATION

Sure, by all accounts almost half of marriages end in ruin. But I'm an optimist, and I can't in good conscience discourage a wedding. If you are so inclined to marry, here are some useful repositories of advice.

The Internet is stuffed with sensible questions engaged couples or newlyweds should ask each other (sadly, it seems that information is available in inverse proportion to the number of couples who use it). One useful place to look is twoofus.org, a project of the National Healthy Marriage Resource Center, an information clearinghouse about all sorts of marriage issues (including those unique to blended and military families) that is underwritten by the federal government and various foundations.

Freedom to Marry (freedomtomarry.org) and the Human Rights Campaign (hrc.org) offer advice for same-sex couples. The IRS offers tips on same-sex marriage tax issues at irs.gov.

For a comprehensive and user-friendly checklist of documents to help with finance, tax, and legal issues facing same-sex couples, go to nerdwallet.com.

4

COMMON-LAW MARRIAGE

OPENING STATEMENT

A few years ago, my boyfriend arrived in New York from Boulder, Colorado, home of thin air, thinner people, and a surplus of new-age thinking. After he and his wife split up (she's lovely, and all is amicable), my soon-to-be-boyfriend headed northeast toward a new life. Two of our liveliest and most discerning mutual friends engineered a blind date, and it worked: midway through dinner, I stole off to the ladies' room and triumphantly texted our friends, congratulating them on their matchmaking prowess.

One day, as we were sitting around his kitchen table, chatting about errands and schedules as carefree, emotionally committed, but legally single adults are wont to do, my boyfriend mentioned that he and his purportedly ex-wife had been married in a common-law ceremony. (I didn't want to pry, but I suspect the festivities involved plumes of fragrant smoke, Sanskrit chants, and something called "essential botanical oils.") Perhaps the elevated Colorado altitude clouded their analytic skills, but apparently they never researched the legal consequences of their common-law marriage; in other words, my beloved told me, they never bothered with a divorce.

The poor, sweet man. Upon hearing this news, the contours of my face changed, from happy-couple calm to something akin to horror.

He wasn't aware of the central principle of common-law marriage. To wit: it's a real marriage. For it to be over, legally, it is not enough to inform the shamans, ultramarathoners, and yogis who witnessed the ceremony. It must end with an actual, court-sanctioned divorce.

A few months, a little nagging, and only the slightest threat of an ultimatum later, problem solved.

I will not, of course, let this happen to you.

IT'S THE LAW

The common-law marriage made sense at a time when it was harder, especially in our newer frontier states, to rustle up a justice or minister who could make your union legal. But now that your cousin can be ordained by the Universal Life Church and legally marry you soon after, common-law marriage is considered anachronistic, and most states don't allow it. As of this writing, nine states and the District of Columbia permit a couple to agree, without contracts or ceremony, to hold themselves out as husband and wife. (Curious? The states are Alabama, Colorado, Iowa, Kansas, Montana, Oklahoma, Rhode Island, South Carolina, and Texas.)

If you are a common-law married couple whose union is legal in your state, your marriage will be recognized in all fifty.

What's required? To summarize, you are in a common-law marriage if you

1. cohabitate; and
2. hold yourself out as a married couple. This can happen when, for example, a woman takes her common-law husband's surname.

Requirements vary by state, but in general, common-law marriage is born of intent, not from staying together for a set period of time. Since a legitimate common-law marriage can have such an informal foundation, problems arise when one member of the couple changes her mind but the other wants to persuade a court that a marriage still exists. It's easy enough to prove that you cohabitated, but what if the person you think is your spouse disagrees?

That was the problem faced by a woman who sued her partner for divorce, alimony, and equitable distribution of their property after they split up, even though they were never married.

According to court records, the couple, who first moved in together in Texas, purchased rings together after the man reassured his apprehensive partner that in Texas, common-law marriage was legitimate. True enough. However, over time, evidence of their commitment to a common-law marriage grew ambiguous. The couple, who had moved to North Carolina, told friends they were husband and wife, but filed some legal papers, like deeds, that stated they were unmarried. That was all it took for the court to deny the woman her divorce and the money and property she sought. As far as the North Carolina court was concerned, no common-law marriage existed. The lesson, as is so often the case in law: if you want to enforce a commitment, get it in writing.

FOR MORE INFORMATION

Still interested in common-law marriage? Unmarried Equality (unmarried.org) offers a fact sheet on common-law marriage, including a list of states where it remains available and guidance about what it takes to be considered a married couple.

5

CIVIL UNIONS AND DOMESTIC PARTNERSHIPS

OPENING STATEMENT

If you are going steady with a man but don't want to get married, that's entirely your choice; who am I to judge? (If you are going steady with a woman, I feel the same way, though if your bar to marriage is a legal one, I hope that impediment is removed ASAP.)

But you should know that a few states offer alternatives to marriage, called civil unions and domestic partnerships. If you are an unmarried couple (same sex or opposite sex) and would like to take advantage of state government or workplace benefits, some significant, without a march down the aisle, these alternatives are worth a look. If you do, remember that the availability of these options is in flux, and that they do not offer the considerable federal benefits available to married couples.

IT'S THE LAW

What are civil unions and domestic partnerships, and why did states introduce these marriage alternatives?

Generally (as always, the scope of these options varies by state), a civil union provides couples with legal recognition of their partnership, and rights similar to those available to married couples. Domestic partnerships are generally (but not always) weaker, providing some state-level rights to unmarried couples.

These options were clumsy solutions state legislatures launched in response to a rising sense of unfairness about the limits of marriage. Take Vermont. In 1999, the state's supreme court held that same-sex couples were entitled to the benefits of marriage, but did not necessarily have the legal right to get married. The court then directed lawmakers to figure out how to make those marriage-like rights available, and lawmakers decided that couples who entered into a civil union could enjoy those rights. These legal contortions ended when Vermont approved same-sex marriage in 2009.

Some states, including Vermont, Connecticut, and New Hampshire, dropped these options once same-sex marriage became legal. On the other hand, Colorado, where same-sex marriage had not been legal, approved civil unions in 2013 after two failed attempts.

As more states allow same-sex marriage, the utility of domestic partnerships will wane, though not in Hawaii, where something called the Reciprocal Beneficiaries law allows friends, or even siblings, to enjoy certain rights to property, hospital visits, and inheritance without a will.

Meanwhile, as the right to marry expands, we are certain to see more changes to the availability of these marriage alternatives. Employers will reconsider whether to offer domestic partner benefits to couples who could wed instead.

EXHIBIT 5: UNDOING CIVIL UNIONS AND DOMESTIC PARTNERSHIPS

I thought divorce was difficult (and if you get a divorce, believe me, you will, too). But at least the legal logistics of divorce are well established in all fifty states.

With civil unions and domestic partnerships, the situation is far murkier. If a couple in a civil union breaks up, must they make it official? Can one partner demand alimony or other support?

I'm sorry to say the answers are not entirely clear. For one thing, only a few states offer these partnerships; fewer still will legally recognize a partnership forged in another state. That means a couple who partnered, then moved, might need to return to their partnership state to split up. Once there, though, another problem presents itself: many states have residency requirements for couples who split; you can't simply waltz back and break up. (Lately, a few states have made it possible for couples to get a divorce without adhering to residency requirements.)

All this may make it tempting to simply walk away from a civil union or domestic partnership. Not so fast. Consider the situation faced by two men in New England. (I know, they are not women, but their cautionary tale is worth sharing.)

They married in Massachusetts. M. (we'll use initials here) filed for divorce. His spouse, F., then learned that M. had entered into a civil union in Vermont before they wed, and that the civil union was never dissolved.

Uh-oh: did M. and F. have unfinished business in Massachusetts?

A Massachusetts appeals court said yes. To reach that decision, the Massachusetts court looked to Vermont law, which forbids a partner in a civil union from marrying. Since Vermont, as we've seen, intended civil unions to provide equal rights to marriage, M.'s civil union was the functional equivalent of a marriage, and that meant his marriage to F. had to be void.

FOR MORE INFORMATION

If you think you could benefit from a civil union or domestic partnership, the National Conference of State Legislatures (ncsl.org) keeps an updated list of state laws so you can identify what options are available to you and your partner. And the IRS offers an FAQ page about domestic partners and couples in civil unions at irs.gov.

If you have issues related to a civil union or domestic partnership that is same sex, it may be best to consult an attorney familiar with same-sex family law in your state. One source is Lambda Legal, a nationwide advocacy group that maintains a legal help desk to address individual situations at lambdalegal.org.

6

PRENUPTIAL (AND POSTNUPTIAL) AGREEMENTS

OPENING STATEMENT

Perhaps you are marrying later in life. Perhaps you are younger than springtime but engaged to wed someone with a few years on you. Your families may have wildly different asset levels, or one (or both) of you may be a self-made financial success. Perhaps you or your beloved has been down this road, or aisle, before.

For all these reasons, you and your partner may come to your wedding day with savings, property, and sometimes even children and grandchildren to consider and protect.

If that is your situation, you should be thinking about a prenuptial or postnuptial agreement.

You would hardly be alone: in a 2013 survey, the American Academy of Matrimonial Lawyers found that most of its members reported an increase in prenup work. More to the point, these lawyers said that almost half of the discussions were initiated by women.

The main reason their clients contemplated a premarriage contract? Overwhelmingly, it was to protect separate property.

EAT, PRAY . . . SIGN A PRENUP

Elizabeth Gilbert, the author of *Eat, Pray, Love*, signed a prenup before remarrying and had this to say: "Marriage is not just a private love story but also a social and economical contract of the strictest order. If it weren't, there wouldn't be thousands of municipal, state and federal laws pertaining to our matrimonial union."

I find it reassuring that a woman with a big heart and admirably robust emotional ambition would urge other women to enter a marriage—which, let's face it, is a contract—with a binding plan B in case it fails.

Despite their recent spike in popularity, prenups remain relatively rare: a 2010 survey found that only 3 percent of engaged or married couples had one.

Should you be a member of that 3 percent? Let's walk through what a prenup or postnup can do for you, and identify potential pitfalls.

IT'S THE LAW

Decades ago, state courts (marriage, after all, is governed by state law) were just as reluctant to enforce prenups as couples were to consider them. The idea of a prenup was burdened with the sense that merely making the agreement would somehow encourage couples to seek a divorce, which is sort of like thinking that buying health insurance will prompt you to get sick.

Times have changed, and today all states enforce prenuptial agreements, though their standards for enforcement vary. (So-called postnups, or agreements made after marriage, are newer, and courts' approaches are less consistent for now.)

What's in a prenup?

Typically, a prenuptial agreement focuses on assets and how they will be shared if you divorce. One of the great advantages of a prenup negotiation is its enforced candor. Couples find it difficult, if not impossible, to talk about finances. The prenup requires a full, fair exchange of information about your financial situation, your assets, debts, and attitudes about money. This is challenging, I know, but an early exchange of information can reduce the risk of awful surprises later.

WHAT CAN YOU PUT IN A PRENUP?

- *Premarital income, assets, and debts.* How much do you make? How much will you spend on shared expenses? Will you commingle your assets or keep them separate? If your spouse pays off your debt with premarital money, will you have to pay that back if you split?
- *Managing assets.* How will you make financial decisions? Do you need each other's permission to buy big-ticket items? Will you set up a joint bank account? How will you save for retirement?
- *Working.* Will either of you stay home, or switch to a less

stressful, less remunerative job, if you have children? What if one of you gets a dream job offer that is out of state?

- *Spousal support and alimony.* Do you want to waive or limit the right to seek support payments if you split?
- *Family gifts.* If you receive a family gift, do you want to confirm in writing that it's not a loan so that disgruntled family members won't demand repayment if you divorce?
- *Taxes.* Will you file separate or joint returns?
- *Duration.* Do you want the agreement to change or disappear after a set number of years, or a family event, such as having children?

Finally, a word about estate planning: If you are drafting a prenup so that you and your spouse can keep separate property separate, then make sure to synchronize your plans with your wills and, if you have them, trusts.

Spouses can use a prenup to renounce inheritance claims. (Without a prenup, spouses cannot be disinherited; most states allow spouses to demand one-third to one-half of an estate if they are not named in a will.)

Given the particularities of state law, it's best to work with a lawyer on your prenup. Actually—and this is important—you and your partner should have two lawyers. Why? If either of you decides to challenge the agreement later, a court will examine whether one spouse was coerced by the other to sign, and individual representation provides evidence that each spouse approved the deal.

While a prenup can cover a lot of ground, certain topics are technically beyond its scope, even if you and your spouse would be willing to agree on those matters in writing.

- Child custody can't be set in a prenup (though it can be helpful if you've thought through the topic together, in writing, as a template for an agreement that a court can approve).
- You cannot agree in a prenup to pay (or accept) child support payments that are lower than the amounts set by your state's guidelines.
- You cannot agree that each spouse is responsible for his or her nursing home care to try to shield marital assets from those high costs.

FINANCIAL DISCLOSURE WITHOUT A PRENUP

You may be reading all of this warily, and with good reason. If you are young and about to marry for the first time (and neither you nor your fiancé comes from a family with wealth to protect), perhaps a prenup is premature. After all, your lives together are bound to change through children, career fortune or misfortune, or abrupt changes in health or other circumstances.

If you forgo a prenup, then at the very least aim for a candid and disciplined premarital discussion about finances. Everyone knows money disagreements are a common cause of couples' problems. If you join together in financial candor, as well as for better, for worse, in sickness and in health, you improve your odds of reducing strife.

Here are five sensible topics for young couples to discuss, as suggested by the *Wall Street Journal:*

1. *Student loans.* The average graduate of the Class of 2013 carries $35,200 in college-related debt. Chances are, you or your be-

loved does, too. Talk about what you owe and how you plan to pay. Experts also suggest exchanging your credit scores, which sounds skin-crawlingly unpleasant but is an excellent idea: it is a crucial, and difficult-to-improve, measure of financial vitality that will affect your ability to buy a home or other property or big-ticket items together.

2. *Budgets.* You are young, and therefore perfectly situated to use online tools to plan a joint budget, like those available through websites such as Mint and LearnVest.

3. *Children.* College looms over any sensible would-be parent's plans. Let's cue the scary tuition stats: according to Mass-Mutual, the cost of four years of college for a student entering in 2022 will reach approximately $305,000. Perhaps your savings plan (and you should have one) can include monthly deposits in a college savings account; you can start one and name your child as a beneficiary later.

4. *Combining finances.* Many experts think it best to open a joint account while keeping separate accounts for individual expenses. This also affords you a legal advantage: keeping savings you bring to the marriage separate, which can reduce the prospect of confusion if you split. (Sorry to raise that prospect so soon! This is a legal guidebook, and we must prepare for all contingencies.) Also consider securing health insurance coverage through the partner with the superior plan, and even combining cell phone coverage.

5. *Retirement.* The sooner you both start to save, the more you will have (barring investment catastrophe), because compound interest helps savings grow large over time. Employer matches can turbocharge your efforts.

EXHIBIT 6: ENFORCING (OR RETHINKING) YOUR PRENUP

Okay, you listened to me. You were diligent. You and your fiancé or spouse had the challenging conversations, shared deeply personal, sometimes unflattering financial information, and carefully considered what you would do if your romance fades. You hired lawyers to review your agreement and you even signed it and had it notarized.

Are you set if you split?

Not necessarily.

Prenuptial agreements are intended to lessen the odds of postmarriage battles, but they can't eliminate them. Sometimes for legitimate reasons, and sometimes just for spite, spouses may go to court to argue that the prenup they signed should be tossed.

When judges hear these cases, they struggle between the presumed finality of a signed contract and the possibility that a deal is so deeply unfair that it should not be enforced.

Typically in these disputes, a wealthy spouse squares off against a furious one who seeks a bigger settlement. Assuming the prenup was crafted with some care, the furious spouse faces a difficult task: persuading a judge (who can be expected to favor upholding deals) that the agreement cannot be enforced because (a) it is unconscionable or (b) it was signed under duress. The latter argument has particular traction when a prenuptial agreement is signed mere days before the wedding. (Look, we've all put off difficult decisions, but this is one you need to make early on.) Another argument: the opposing spouse can claim she didn't really know how much the other spouse had; courts may sympathize if there's evidence that a spouse withheld information.

When you read about failed prenuptial agreements, sometimes you have to marvel at how the couple ever thought they reached a fair deal that would stick.

Let's examine, for example, the agreement struck by a couple we'll call K.C. and M.C., as detailed by a California court. After they met in California in 1990, K., a saleswoman at a department store, stopped working and M., a partner at a law firm, helped her with expenses for her and her two children from a prior marriage. When they planned to wed, M. insisted on a prenup and advised his bride-to-be to have a lawyer explain it to her, but told her certain provisions were nonnegotiable. K. said her lawyer failed to explain one of those nonnegotiable deal points, which allowed M. to keep everything he earned after marriage—money that is usually shared—as his own. The agreement also denied K. spousal support payments and limited the child support she could expect to receive.

When the couple split and she challenged the prenup, the trial court decided, and an appeals court confirmed, that M. would have to support K., since their financial circumstances—and bargaining skills—were so different as to make it unfair to enforce a no-support clause. The wife "devoted her efforts to child-rearing and maintaining the family home" while her husband made money, and the court felt she deserved support despite the punitive prenup. (M. gave up trying to enforce the child support limits, which the court correctly noted could not supersede state law.) But the court also upheld the portion of the agreement that allowed M. to keep everything he earned after marriage, rather than share it as community property.

Notice the nearly Solomonic delicacy with which the court dismantled and recast the terms of the prenup. The guiding principle: fairness. What did each spouse bring, in assets and experience, to their intimate bargaining table? What did each spouse give up in the event of a split? If your spouse seems parsimonious in your prenup discussions, you (or your lawyer) should point out that an imbalanced deal stands the chance of being rewritten by a sympathetic judge. And that holds for you, too—remember that if your spouse challenges your prenup, you may have to defend its fairness, and make it clear that you both understood what you were doing.

EXHIBIT 7: NEW YORK PRENUP PERILS

As I was writing this chapter, interesting things were happening to prenups and postnups in New York state courts. Unhappy soon-to-be-ex-wives were challenging their prenups, and in a surprise development for New York, a state with courts that generally support marital agreements, courts were ruling for the rebelling wives.

The city's local tabloids paid the most attention to pretty Elizabeth Petrakis of Long Island, who posed for the *New York Post* in tight jeans, high boots, and a beaming smile for an article describing what the *Post* labeled as her "pre-nope" victory.

No doubt, the conditions under which Elizabeth reportedly signed her prenup were unreasonable. Make that incredibly unreasonable. Merely four days before their wedding, Elizabeth's husband-to-be, Peter, gave her a prenup to sign and threatened to cancel their wedding if she refused. The terms: if they split, Elizabeth would receive up to $25,000 for each year they were married and one-third of the husband's business interest. In court, Elizabeth argued, successfully, that Peter's verbal promise to tear up the prenup if they had a child, and her reliance on that promise, meant the agreement could not be enforced. The decision surprised some lawyers, since verbal agreements typically do not trump written contracts, but the court noted that matrimonial deals deserve special scrutiny.

After the decision, Empire State matrimonial lawyers were aghast. Dire predictions abounded about the end of reliability in prenup negotiations. (Peter Petrakis's bid to appeal was denied.)

Not long after, another case in New York seemed to validate the lawyers' concerns.

A.C. and E.C. (as we'll call them here) lived separately when they first started courting, with A. paying for vacations, car repairs, and even summer camp for E.'s two kids. Marriage talk ensued.

E. yearned to remarry; A. was less enthusiastic, in part because of his painful divorce. So when A. told E. he would need a prenup to marry again, E. told A. she would "sign any piece of paper you put in front of me and I won't even read it."

Reader: do not ever utter those words.

A. called his lawyer, who prepared a prenup that would provide E. exactly nothing in the event of a split: no home, no bank accounts or other assets, no financial help. Then A. asked his own lawyer to find a lawyer for E.; his lawyer went no farther than the next desk at his office and asked his office suite mate to represent her. Did I mention that E. earned $5,000 a year as a part-time teacher's assistant and A. was a multimillionaire businessman?

In a rare, and therefore touching, display of attorney emotion, the lawyer who represented the pressured bride-to-be remembered their signing day eleven years later in court, so vivid was his memory of presenting her with the document and telling the bride-to-be that it was nonnegotiable. E.'s response to this legal advice was to burst into tears—and then sign.

Not entirely surprisingly, the couple eventually split. More surprisingly, when the marriage dissolved, E. finally had the gumption to challenge A.'s unilateral worldview in court.

Her courage was rewarded when the judge declared the prenup unenforceable. And to reassure matrimonial lawyers who by now must have wondered if they had wandered into a Lifetime movie instead of a take-no-prisoners New York courtroom, the judge took pains to note that courts would continue to uphold prenups—just not ones that "scream inequity or . . . leave one party practically destitute."

The victory was hard fought and the result surely correct. But perhaps the victorious ex-wife would have spared herself a lot of grief, and time in court, had she thought more carefully about whether to marry a man so clearly bent on sharing nothing. This is why it's absolutely critical to have the prenup discussion well before the wedding . . . and pay close attention to your position and that of your would-be spouse. If either of you feels that stingy, should you truly be together?

FOR MORE INFORMATION

As we've discussed, you will ultimately want two lawyers to review your prenup and make sure each of you understands what rights you may be giving up. Before that step, you can work together to outline your preferences. A simple guide to getting started is available on the Bankrate website: bankrate.com.

7

FOUR-PRONG PROBLEMS: WHO KEEPS THE ENGAGEMENT RING?

OPENING STATEMENT

Ah, the engagement ring. Whatever year finds you reading this book, let's agree that we have found ourselves a timeless topic: the allure of the solitaire. For some women, the ring is a fairy-tale dream fulfilled; for others it's a point of pride: the ultimate symbol of acquisitive victory, not unlike the pelt of a successfully hunted animal, or the not-particularly-luxurious towels my mother used to steal from the Raleigh Hotel in the heart of New York's Catskill Mountains. (Look! Towels from the Raleigh! They're embellished! With the name of the resort! Robert Klein killed at the late show!)

That said, I was beyond excited about my own engagement ring. Not only did it sport a beautiful solitaire, but the sufficiently substantial stone was flanked by charming rectangular baguette diamonds. My fiancé and I nicknamed them "nag-ettes" because I had nagged him into proposing to me. Given what transpired, I have to laugh-cry as I type this.

You probably know that the diamond solitaire ring became a primary symbol of the intention to wed thanks to an astonishingly clever ad campaign by the diamond manufacturer DeBeers. Traditionally, the ring also served as collateral against a fiancé's change of heart. States used to have laws on the books that allowed brides to sue for breach of promise to marry. But when those laws faded in the 1930s, a costly ring became the at-risk-for-jilting woman's next-best bet for keeping her boyfriend's wandering eye fixed on the altar.

Sure, the engagement ring is an anachronism. But marriage is a traditional venture, and the ring remains the traditional way to mark your assent to the lifetime of happy heavy lifting known as marital bliss. Is it any surprise that when engagements falter, couples focus on the symbol of their mistake, which often happens to be worth some serious coin?

IT'S THE LAW

In general, an engagement ring goes back to the giver if the wedding is called off. Often the ring giver wants a return with good reason: a study of engagement rings recently published by a wedding website found the average cost of a ring in 2011 was $5,200. That's particularly striking because in 2011, recession's smoke still hung heavily in the air, especially over young people who might be getting hitched.

(Does the continued popularity of engagement rings in modern times seem outdated to you? Then consider this: the same study also found that 77 percent of grooms proposed on bended knee. What century is this again?)

So how does the law deal with feuding former fiancés who can't resolve their ring disputes? It's time to meet R.G.

EXHIBIT 8: AN ENGAGEMENT RING IS A CONDITIONAL GIFT

R.G. was angry. A man of "inconstant affections," according to one of the judges who heard his case, this suitor proposed to T.H. not once, but twice. She accepted the first time, then he called it off. They made up, R. proposed again, T. accepted again . . . and R. changed his mind, again. This time, when his feet grew cold, so did T.'s heart, and she refused to return the ring.

Conceding that his powers of persuasion over T. were now limited, R. filed an arbitration complaint in Pennsylvania, and the panel awarded the ring to his former fiancée. Next stop: the quaintly named Court of Common Pleas: advantage, his. The Pennsylvania Superior Court confirmed his victory. But the single-minded—and newly single—T. persevered, and the case was heard by the judges of the Pennsylvania Supreme Court. Five years and four tribunals after R. changed his mind, he won his case in a close 4–3 decision. A less-than-happy T. had no choice but to relinquish the ring.

Why? The court applied what is now the general rule: an engagement ring is a "conditional" gift that you can keep only if the marriage goes through. Otherwise, it doesn't matter who is at fault: if the wedding is called off, the ring must be returned.

If the premarital battle over an engagement ring isn't sad enough, consider the ring's fate after a divorce. Generally speaking, it's the wife's property to keep (since the condition of marriage was met), so she can decide whether to store this sad memento away or recycle it for future use. One California jeweler identified a trend among her divorced clients: repurposing an engagement ring into the "F-you ring," redesigned to be worn on the middle finger of the right hand.

PART TWO

SEPARATION AND DIVORCE

8

SEPARATION WITHOUT ANXIETY

OPENING STATEMENT

I recently heard from a longtime acquaintance who had a problem and wanted to meet over drinks to talk about it.

We'd met through our sons, who played together when they were about three years old (or, more accurately, alongside each other, as is the preference in that demographic). This friend knew that my marriage had ended, and that my life was proceeding happily, and she wanted some advice.

Her plight? She was bored with her hardworking husband, the father of her children, and had reconnected with an old classmate on Facebook.

At this point in the narrative, you'll be relieved to learn I signaled the bartender for a big refill of his value-priced sauvignon blanc and steeled myself for the inevitable.

The inevitable wasn't long in coming.

Predictably, they had texted each other, leaving an easily discoverable trail of attraction. Predictably, their feelings crested and they smooched in a car, or was it a hotel lobby? Predictably, he "made her feel alive." Predictably, she was contemplating a divorce.

Separation was invented for situations like this. How on earth can anyone make a permanent, life-altering decision on so little evidence? If you think you want a new life—emphasis on *think*—then separation can provide a legal baby step. And if you ultimately decide to divorce, the decisions you make when you separate can provide the legal blueprint for your future.

IT'S THE LAW

Most of the time, law is soothingly concrete. Bright lines, as lawyers love to say, exist between what is legal and what is against the law. Words have distinct meanings—often translated from the Latin. *Separation* is not one of those words.

For one thing, couples who are separated are still married. This is a useful point for mature daters to remember: no matter what the seemingly promising guy you met online describes as the situation with his wife, she remains his wife until a divorce is finalized.

Not that I'm speaking from personal experience in any way.

For another thing, couples who are legally separated may continue to live together. Conversely, a couple can split up, and even sign a separation agreement, without obtaining a legal separation from a court.

Confused? Let's sort it out.

A *physical separation* is not necessarily legally recognized, serious though it may be when one spouse moves out. As a result, along with the wrenching emotional issues you will face about whether to try to reconcile, if you live separately you may have to face some immediate practical problems:

- Whose name is on the lease of your home? If it's both of your names, will you both continue to pay rent? (Same question applies for a mortgage, of course.)
- Can the spouse who moved out stop by unannounced?
- Can the spouse who moved out afford her own place? If not, how will that work?
- If you have children, where will they live and who will look after them?
- What if either of you rings up debt?
- Will you be dating, and if so, does your spouse need to know?

No matter how you structure your lives during this time, if you are thinking of moving out during a separation, it makes sense to consult with a lawyer first. Some states may consider the move itself grounds for a divorce (as "abandonment"); if you have children, the move could leave you vulnerable to a custody argument, fair or not, that the parent who remained at home with the kids deserves to be recognized as the primary caregiver.

In any event, separation-related questions are thorny, and when you are trying to answer them, relations with your spouse are likely at an all-time low. That's why they may be best answered in writing. And that's why couples who choose a physical separation may decide to sign a separation agreement.

A *separation agreement* is a contract. In it, a couple can agree to divide property, assets, and debts, create a child custody schedule, and provide spousal and child support. The agreement can also ensure that both spouses and children remain covered by one spouse's insurance plan.

The scope of these agreements can vary. Some couples can work from a single sheet of paper that contains terse instructions about paying bills, living arrangements, and custody. Other couples, sensing the end is near, can take years to work out the details, in part because courts can incorporate the terms of a separation agreement into a divorce judgment. This is why it's crucial that you don't agree to terms of a separation agreement in haste, or assume they will be temporary. If you are thinking of separating, you may want to consult a lawyer sooner than later, depending on the course you think your separation will take.

For a more specific look at the contents of a separation agreement, let's visit findlaw.com, home of wide-ranging legal advice. Their sample separation agreement is only that; you will have specific needs, and, since marriage is governed by state law, your state may have unique requirements. Nonetheless, as a starting point, here's the site's summary of what an agreement can cover:

- Preliminary matters: you agree about where and when you were wed, that you have made a complete, fair, and mutual disclosure of financial matters, and that you've each been advised by your own lawyers
- Custody and visitation
- Child support
- Spousal support
- Homestead, or who will live at the family home and how it will be paid for
- Other debt and expense payments (Remember: the agreement is between the two of you. Your creditors can chase both of you for jointly held debt.)
- Personal property—how it will be divided
- Insurance

Some agreements include a provision that directs each spouse to treat the other as if she is single and unmarried, and allows each spouse to visit the other only if invited. (This is not tantamount to permission from your spouse to commit adultery, in case you were wondering.)

Again: whether your situation is acrimonious or hearts-and-flowers amicable, don't sign a separation agreement without careful review by a lawyer. These agreements are very often the foundation for the terms of a divorce, and while they could be set aside if you can claim you were defrauded or misled, you are better off considering the agreement as the blueprint for your future. Burdened by the pain of a deteriorating marriage, it can be tempting at times to give in and avoid conflict. The signing of a separation agreement is not one of those times.

A separation agreement is enforceable as a private contract, but it is not a court order. Some states allow couples to seek a *legal separation*, which is enforceable through family court. A legal separation, which is not a divorce, allows couples to stay together for child-rearing reasons or for insurance (though you will want to be absolutely sure that any insurer will extend coverage once you're separated). This agreement also can be incorporated into a final divorce agreement; again, this is why you should take care to set terms you can live with over the long haul.

One more thought about separating: if you are nearing your tenth wedding anniversary, you may want to wait. If your marriage lasts ten years, you may qualify for Social Security retirement benefits based on your spouse's earnings, even if you divorce thereafter. (To qualify, you have to reach the age of sixty-two, you can't remarry, and the benefits have to be larger than those you would collect on your own.) That alone might be reason enough to grit your teeth and stick it out together. Timing also matters because the date of the separation agreement may mark the moment when marital assets and debts are counted and valued for division in the event you divorce.

TEMPORARY SUPPORT

As divorcing couples and their lawyers know, it can be hard to persuade quarreling couples to pay support. If you are separated and need support, and your spouse isn't paying, you can file for temporary support, also known as pendente lite support (which means "pending the litigation"). You can file for immediate help yourself or hire a lawyer; your state likely has information on its website about how to file, and what you can expect.

EXHIBIT 9: DON'T SIGN ANYTHING UNLESS YOU ARE SURE

If you feel pressured or rushed into signing a separation agreement, resist! Judges may say they're more willing to set aside an agreement between a couple than a standard business contract because of the fraught nature of negotiating with a loved one, but the truth is that courts love finality and loathe do-overs.

Case in point: the tale of New Yorkers we'll call E.M. and O.M., which seems like what would happen if a first-year law school contracts exam collided with an episode of *Lifestyles of the Rich and Famous*.

After a twenty-seven-year marriage, the couple signed a separation agreement, then divorced. O., the wife, kept an Upper East Side town house, property contained in the couple's London flat, and millions of dollars. One year later, she claimed in court papers that "chance or divine guidance" led her to financial records kept in the trunk of a car. Lo and behold, the records revealed that E., her secretive ex, also owned a multimillion-dollar home in California, an interest in a racehorse, a cache of luxury cars, and offshore accounts and foreign business assets.

O. was not pleased, and sued to undo the separation agreement while also demanding $10 million for each claim against her husband.

Are you sympathetic? Then step down from the bench, because a New York court ruled for E. Why? Because the once-trusting O. neither sought a net worth statement nor investigated E.'s holdings before she signed the deal, and the agreement made it clear that neither party was relying on the other for a full accounting of their stuff. Since she never demanded more information from E., the trunk treasures, so to speak, were his to keep.

EXHIBIT 10: WHAT IF YOU MAKE UP?

If your separation morphs into a divorce, you won't be alone. An Ohio State University study found that about 79 percent of married couples who separated ended up divorced. In an interesting wrinkle, the researchers found that most reuniting couples separate for two years or less; once they hit three years, either divorce or ongoing separation was much more likely.

What about the couples who remain separated, in a form of marital suspended animation? Those couples may be perfectly comfortable, and may see no reason to rush to any conclusions, but sometimes dramatic life changes intervene and courts are forced to rule on whether a couple was firmly on their way to divorce court or one romantic dinner away from reuniting.

An example: the story of R.C. and S.C. of North Carolina. Married since 1954, they separated in 2004, and R., the husband, moved out of state. In retrospect, their behavior seems like a master class in marital ambivalence. The couple drafted a separation agreement but never signed it. The wife, S., filed for divorce, but R. kept her as the beneficiary for his retirement account (though she wasn't named in his will).

In 2006, R. was hospitalized with untreatable cancer. S. rushed to his side, sleeping alongside him, then with him, and cared for him until he died.

So what became of the divorce proceedings?

The executor of R.'s estate, his nephew, wanted to make S. divide up their property as if the couple planned to finalize their divorce. A court refused to help, finding that they had reconciled, rendering the divorce action moot.

That result sounds correct. But it would have been easier and far less messy had the couple made their new intentions clear. A legal battle—which had to be sensitive, since it was among family members—could have been avoided had they formally withdrawn their divorce suit. The stalwart wife was able to prove that in this case, separation turned out to be no more than a tentative step.

FOR MORE INFORMATION

In addition to the issues we just reviewed, a separation has tax implications too complicated to explain thoroughly here. The IRS comes to the rescue with its Publication 504, Divorced or Separated Individuals. It's thorough and clear, and can be found at irs.gov.

9

ALL ABOUT ANNULMENT

OPENING STATEMENT

As we explore the options available to anyone who wants out of her marriage, I'd be remiss not to include that age-old favorite of royal families and impulsive celebrities: annulment.

Annulment doesn't just end the marriage, it erases it, with a ruling that the marriage never existed because of a later-discovered problem.

Can an annulment solve your marital problem, if you have one?

It's unlikely.

IT'S THE LAW

Religion is the most likely reason a couple will seek an annulment rather than a divorce. Civil annulments are available, typically in cases where a spouse was defrauded about something important (like whether her spouse was single), the marriage was not consummated, the couple is related, or one spouse lacked the ability to consent to marriage. These criteria are rarely met, unless you are a celebrity.

CELEBRITY LAW LESSON

A Very Brief, and Highly Selective, History of Annulment

Chapter One: The year: 1533. Braving the wrath of the Catholic Church, Henry VIII of England secures the annulment of his marriage to Catherine of Aragon from newly appointed Archbishop of Canterbury William Cranmer.

Actual Reason for the Annulment: A swooning Henry has fallen in love with Anne Boleyn.

Convenient Excuse: Henry raises a sticking point he already knew: Catherine had been married to his brother before they wed.

Annulment Consequences: Henry, breaking from the Roman Catholic Church, establishes the Church of England; before her beheading, Anne, who was expected to produce a male heir, gives birth to Elizabeth I of England.

Chapter Two: The year: 2004. Braving the wrath of TMZ, Britney Spears secures the annulment of her marriage to Jason Allan Alexander from Clark County (Nevada) District Court judge Lisa Brown.

Actual Reason for the Annulment: A remorseful Britney awakens from a wild Vegas weekend.

Convenient Excuse: Once married, Britney discovers that despite a nearly lifelong friendship, she and Jason "did not know each other's likes and dislikes."

> *Annulment Consequences:* Did Britney shave her head as a result of her annulment? She never said, and we'll never know.

EXHIBIT 11: CIVIL ANNULMENT IN ACTION

Let's say you are neither a Catholic seeking a religious annulment (granted by the church, not by a court) nor a pop star having second thoughts. What would motivate you to ask a court to declare that your marriage didn't exist?

Have you ever heard of myelodysplastic syndrome?

G.C. and A.C. had divorced after a thirty-year marriage. Three years later, in 2003, G., the former husband, told his ex-wife he had a terminal illness—specifically, myelodysplastic syndrome—and she agreed to remarry him so he wouldn't live alone.

Myelodysplastic syndrome, it turns out, is an ailment so unnerving that I would have volunteered to marry G. to keep him company, too. A severe, life-shortening, and essentially untreatable disease of the blood and bone marrow, it typically strikes men over the age of sixty.

The only problem was, G. wasn't terminally ill at all. When his duped wife sued, saying she had been tricked into remarriage by the lie, the Colorado court agreed and granted her an annulment.

10

DIVORCE: GETTING STARTED

OPENING STATEMENT

Whether you've been following along from the beginning of this book, or are joining me because you immediately flipped to this page, I suspect we are gathered together, at the start of the divorce chapter, because of urgent necessity. Almost certainly, your sense of urgency is mixed with sadness, grief, and anxiety. If that's the case, I am very sorry, and we should get to work. Divorce is a sad event, but even sad events can be tempered if they are approached with focus, steady nerves, and, most of all, a plan.

Let's begin by stating the obvious. Divorce is hard, in part because the process has a way of magnifying everyone's flaws. So prepare for problems, even if you have a soon-to-be-ex who insists you can settle your differences amicably. Even "amicable" divorces, which are rare beyond the dismantling of a short-lived starter marriage, can hit some rocks along the way.

Before we dig in, let me share a personal divorce mishap story. It concerns the excruciating conversation in which divorcing parents break the news to their unsuspecting children.

When my ex and I decided to untie the knot, we knew we owed our kids a thoughtful explanation that accounted for their tender age, the powerful emotions the news would surely stir, and their questions about what the future might hold.

How did we do it?

We approached our children, who were seated, the pictures of school-age innocence, in front of the family television, watching a rebroadcast of *Star Wars*. During a commercial break, we launched our plan. We hit the mute button on the remote, which caught their attention, and one of us announced that Mom and Dad had decided we were splitting up, that it certainly wasn't their fault, that we loved them and always would, and that we were available to answer their questions. (Back then the approved terminology was to tell your kids "Your father and I don't love each other in the married way." So that's what we said. In retrospect, what on earth does that mean?)

After we spoke, our children were silent, surely because what we announced made no sense to them. Fortunately, soon enough their eyes darted back to the set when the movie resumed. Our impromptu briefing was over, so we restored the TV volume to normal and left the room.

This was not a high-water mark in the annals of sensitive parenting. So why do I bring it up? To reassure you that despite that false move, and some very tough going in the early rounds, my ex and I managed to salvage our children's well-being—and our relationship, now friendly—after the divorce was final. Barring an especially acrimonious split, so can you.

Over the years, I've advised many friends, acquaintances, and colleagues who are contemplating divorce. No matter what circumstances they face, I tell every woman the same thing. Divorce is almost always a marathon, not a sprint, trendy chirping about "conscious uncouplings" aside. Prepare for a long process and one that you can't fully control. Most of us are gifted organizers who prefer to take charge of everything. Divorce (like pregnancy) is a life event that doesn't allow us to exert our usual absolute authority over how it will turn out.

If you are unsure about whether to proceed, consider this: the American Academy of Matrimonial Lawyers, which should maintain a vested interest in widespread divorce, sells a handbook called *Making Marriage Last*. Barring an emergency, as in a case of domestic violence, lawyers should be the last professionals you consult, after friends, therapists, and ministers who might help you keep your union intact.

After that, if you are prepared to obtain a divorce, or need to participate in one against your will, it's time to get acquainted with its legal framework. Fundamentally, when we talk about divorce, we are talking about undoing a contract and following state law.

IT'S THE LAW

To launch a divorce proceeding in your state, the first place to look is your calendar. Almost all states require that you've been a resident for a minimum amount of time before you can ask its courts for a divorce. If you meet the residency requirements, you will have to file (or, if this is your spouse's choice, you will receive) a document called a petition or complaint. It will state the reason for the divorce and what the petitioner wants the court to do. If you are conducting a DIY divorce, which we'll discuss in detail in chapter 15, you should be able to pull a form complaint from your state court's website. Even if you aren't doing it yourself, I recommend a look at that website before you consult a lawyer. You'll get an overview of your state's specifics without running up a tab as your lawyer explains them to you.

Court petitions require formal answers from the other side (once known as the love of your life, now known as "the respondent"). After that, you could both, in a perfect world, agree about the terms of your divorce and craft an agreement that a judge would sign to grant your split. That order would detail how money, property, and children's issues would be resolved. If the two of you are less trusting, you will probably conduct information exchanges known as discovery; you will query each other, probably through your lawyers, about assets and, less often, behavior that might affect what you think you deserve.

A word about grounds for divorce: once upon a time, in an attempt to protect and preserve marriage contracts, traditional state law made divorce possible only for specific and serious reasons: abandonment, adultery, desertion, mental or physical cruelty, or drug or alcohol addiction. What if a wife wanted a divorce but couldn't find evidence to accuse her husband of the requisite wrongdoing? A robust business in private investigating (and a heck of a lot of lying under oath) resulted. It reached its colorful pinnacle in the early twentieth century, when women were hired as "correspondents" who lured a lecherous husband into a hotel room so that detectives, cameras poised, could capture courtroom-ready evidence of wrongdoing.

Ironically, just as the Internet made it laughably easy for everyone, including married adults who should know better, to memorialize evidence of their bad behavior, changes in divorce law rendered that information much less useful. Once New York (finally!) allowed no-fault divorce in 2010, it became possible in all fifty states for spouses to split without detailed accusations. In some cases, you may be able to simply file for a no-fault divorce. In other states, you may need to give a reason like "incompatibility," "irreconcilable differences," or, my personal favorite, "general indignities." (Thank you, Arkansas. That's adorable.) You may need to back up your claim by living apart for a set period of time.

Some spouses still channel their inner Inspector Javert, pursuing each other with surreptitious taping, private investigators, and other spy methods. That may feel satisfying, but except for serious malfeasance, garden-variety bad marital behavior (such as cheating) won't affect your ability to file for divorce, though it may affect custody and support, depending on your state and even your judge. It's an issue to discuss with your lawyer. In a few holdout states, adulterers can find themselves writing a huge check to the spouse they wronged.

PAY UP, PARAMOUR: SUING OVER ADULTERY

As we just learned, evidence of adultery doesn't have the same lethal power in divorce court as it did before no-fault laws took hold. Nonetheless, a handful of states allow a court to award a betrayed spouse damages for an affair. In these states, a spouse who is the victim of adultery can sue her rival for criminal conversation (a legal name for extra-marital sex) and alienation of affection (a legal name for the emotional destruction extramarital sex can cause).

Inexplicably, North Carolina seems to be the epicenter of modern-day adultery lawsuits. In recent years, a wrestling coach won a $1.4 million verdict against a Florida physician who became involved with the coach's wife, while a woman who sued her husband's paramour won a $9 million verdict and the questionable privilege of seeing her story turned into a Lifetime movie, *The Price of a Broken Heart*.

Family court lawyers and judges have tried, without

success, to repeal North Carolina's adultery recovery laws, but the closest reformers got were changes in 2009 that imposed stricter time limits on these lawsuits and protected employers who were being sued when coworkers started a dalliance.

Does the law help preserve marriage in North Carolina? Judge for yourself. In a recent study, the state ranked seventeenth in number of divorces per capita in the United States.

BOSSES OF THE BAR:
EMILY PENTZ WOOD

When New York became the last of the fifty states to allow no-fault divorce, it ended a long era of misery for unhappy spouses who wanted to split but needed to offer a specific reason for booting their former partner. Thanks to enlightened West Coast thinking, some couples were able to avoid that painful and time-consuming step long before no-fault divorce took hold nationwide.

Famously, those impatient couples traveled to Nevada. In 1931, eager to improve a Depression-hobbled economy, Nevada lawmakers made it possible for an unhappy spouse to obtain a divorce after spending only six weeks in the state. (The soon-to-be-ex could stay home while this transpired.) The ploy for divorce tourism dollars worked: unhappy spouses, largely from the East, flocked to ranches to wait out the residency requirement while enjoying spectacular scenery, and Nevada divorces rose from a thousand a year in the 1920s to more than nineteen thousand in 1946.

The ranches upgraded their facilities to cater to their

well-heeled, soon-to-be-unwed patrons. Notable among them: the colorful Flying M E Ranch, run for decades by its owner, Emily Pentz Wood.

Emily and her husband, Theodore, were New Yorkers who traveled to Reno to visit Theodore's brother and fell for the dude ranch life. They remodeled a historic hotel, tailoring it to their East Coast preferences; guests (including Eleanor Roosevelt, though not for a divorce, of course) soon followed. After the couple divorced in 1946, Emily operated the ranch herself for fifteen years, catering to a chic clientele that included celebrities and other elites. She kept the press away and made sure guests had fresh air, exercise, and the proper witnesses for their divorces; some even struck up romances with strapping wranglers. The Flying M E Ranch met a dramatic end in 1963, when it burned to the ground; Emily died in 1966. A few years later, other destinations, including Mexico and then the Dominican Republic, competed with Reno as quick-divorce getaways.

EXHIBIT 12: A WORD ABOUT THE MATRIMONIAL BAR

Even if you and your ex-in-waiting can hash out the terms of your divorce together, and even if you pursue a DIY divorce to try to save money, you will want a matrimonial lawyer to review your settlement. Of course, if you can't work together—and in my experience, most couples cannot—a lawyer will be an early partner in your split.

I explain how to hire a lawyer in chapter 29, but before you turn there for guidance, I want to share a few thoughts about the matrimonial bar.

What do I think of divorce lawyers?

To answer that question fairly, let us begin by pondering the life of the divorce lawyer, or more specifically her clients: an endless conveyor belt of hysterical, often dishonest adults who argue over nonsense, can't or don't pay, and reliably make counterproductive decisions, before or even after asking for advice.

Can you blame these counselors for becoming a little cynical over the years?

Then again, given how sensitive clients can be, and how much is at stake, some of the behavior I observed when I hired my own divorce lawyer still gives me pause.

In fairness, my circumstances were unusual. I was both a wife going through the agony of a divorce and a lawyer watching the process, and the lawyering, with a trained gaze.

So the lawyer part of me was appalled at the condescension shoveled out by Famous Manhattan Divorce Lawyer, who sat me down in a vast office festooned with plaques and grip-and-grin photos and gave me a "there, there, little lady" talk about how I could leave all the heavy lawyering to him.

No retainer for you, big guy.

Then there was the lawyer I hired, who often, and incorrectly, warned that I would never, ever be able to trust my ex to live up to the terms of our agreement. When we met, I began to notice a pattern: he would share names and details about other clients' cases, an apparent violation of attorney-client privilege, which is supposed to keep your conversations with counsel secret. What, I agonized, was he telling other clients about me?

Obviously, most divorce lawyers are ethical, hardworking, and client-focused. Then again, the matrimonial bar is not exactly populated with tweed-jacketed constitutional scholars. Divorce lawyers are a breed apart: salty, cynical, sometimes profane, and often charging more than you feel good about spending.

But they are also indispensable in almost all cases. That's because no matter how friction-free a divorce you hope to achieve, it's just as important (more important, I would argue) that your final result be fair and protect your interests. Even if you are ordinarily levelheaded, the divorce process will likely leave you second-guessing your judgment. If you are initiating the divorce, you may feel guilty and ready to give up money, property, and even custody to make the process easier on your spouse. If you are asked for a divorce, you may have a hard time trusting the partner who wants to dump you.

Your lawyer will act as your backstop, offering advice (which you are free to take or leave) about the contours of your deal. She can tell you when she thinks you are being too generous, or too stubborn. And given her experience, you should be inclined to listen to her advice.

Finally, a thought about professional camaraderie. When I was divorcing, I was alarmed whenever my lawyer exchanged pleasantries, or even smiled, at my husband's attorney. Whose side was he on, anyway? This concern was misguided. Even matrimonial lawyers have colleagues. Colleagues they train with, work with, and see at seminars, continuing legal education programs, and events at their very own professional organizations. It's a good thing when lawyers (even those in adversarial situations like yours) can work together.

EXHIBIT 13: PREPARING FOR YOUR LAWYER MEETING

The American Academy of Matrimonial Lawyers publishes a useful guide called *Divorce Manual: A Client Handbook,* which you can retrieve from their website (aaml.org). I highly recommend you follow its advice about the information you should gather before you meet with a matrimonial lawyer; including:

- A summary of the assets you and your spouse own
- Rough estimates of how much your assets are worth
- The addresses of property you own and who holds the title
- Estimates of your debt
- Sources of income—ideally a few past years' tax returns
- A timetable of the important milestones in your relationship (including the date you separated)
- Written agreements between you and your spouse, including wills and estate plans
- An estimated budget once you live apart (warning: it will be higher than you expect)
- A list of the assets you feel are important for you to keep

What should you ask your lawyer when you meet? The AAML has an answer to that question, too. Here are some of its suggestions, along with my thoughts:

- *What are your qualifications?* Ideally, your divorce lawyer focuses on family law and has practiced long enough to have seen situations like yours before, so she can offer a time-tested strategy for how you should proceed.
- *How will your office handle my case?* Some clients want reassurance that their lawyer will handle every aspect of their case. But to save money and time, it's absolutely fine to let your principal attorney share the work with junior lawyers, paralegals, or even assistants. That said, while it's okay if your lawyer doesn't watch her smartphone every minute in case you text, it's not okay if your calls go unanswered for days. Ask your lawyer how she wants to communicate with you.
- *How much do you charge?* Your lawyer likely will charge by the hour; you can check that rate against other attorneys who practice the same type of law in your area. (If a paralegal or junior

lawyer does some of your work, they will cost less.) Some lawyers charge for initial visits, some don't. Many ask for a retainer (essentially a deposit). If the retainer seems high, ask if it can be negotiated, and make sure to ask what would happen if you ran out of money, or if you found your assets were tied up in a house or savings; would your lawyer be willing to wait for payment? See if there's work you can do to keep costs down; when I divorced, I became obsessed with copying documents myself to save a little money (since law offices charge for copying and other tasks, or "disbursements" in legal speak).

◆ *Where will you file my case?* Your lawyer may prefer one county over another because it's quicker or because the judges are better regarded; find out why. And ask if there's any advantage to being the first to file for divorce, if you have that option.

◆ *How will this end?* Your lawyer should be able to summarize the law of your state and offer guidance, if not a prediction, about your outcome. State law will offer clues about these key issues: How is property divided? How can you collect support payments, or will you be expected to make them? Will you and your spouse be jointly responsible for paying each other's lawyers? (Yes, I know that can seem outrageous.) Also, feel free to ask for a time frame, then treat it the way you do the predictions you hear from a general contractor about your renovation: well meant, certainly possible, but probably unlikely.

One more thing. It's true for any lawyer-client relationship, and it's especially relevant here. Tell your lawyer the truth. Tell your lawyer the truth about money. Tell your lawyer the truth about whether you are seeing someone. Tell your lawyer if you've misbehaved and your spouse knows, or if you are spying on your spouse because you are convinced it's worth capturing a misstep. It's unfair to expect a lawyer to offer good advice without all the background information you can provide, especially if your lawyer is unaware of a situation your spouse and his lawyer know about. Your discussions about your case will have some privacy protection under what's called the attorney-client privilege (though some of the information you give your lawyer will be shared with your spouse, especially if you need to settle finances).

NAME CHANGE

When you wed, did you agonize over whether to take your spouse's name or keep your own? I did not. I couldn't wait to rid myself of my last name. For one thing, when I married I was a budding journalist, and as a byline "Lisa Green" barely took up enough space to justify the effort I put into the article it accompanied.

So like a Scrabble player with a hot hand, I was thrilled at the opportunity to pick up bonus letters. Plus, as was fashionable at the time of my marriage and still popular today, I wanted to adopt the triple name, nonhyphenated version. Behold, a new and improved byline. At which point I celebrated by giving up journalism and becoming a lawyer.

After the split, I thought it only fair to return my spouse's last name to its source. Lisa Green, the name I once disdained, suddenly seemed like a clean, sleek reversion to my younger form, the punctuation on the final sentence in a chapter of my life.

If you want to accomplish the same goal, it's fairly easy to do. Just make sure your name change is on your divorce order. Then you'll use a copy of that order to notify state and federal agencies to update your driver's license and insurance and other records.

You are not obligated to change your name back if you prefer the continuity (or have a recognized byline).

EXHIBIT 14: ENDING A SAME-SEX MARRIAGE

Same-sex marriage is the civil rights issue of our day, and the ability of couples to marry in the United States has expanded in just the months it took for me to write this book. As the number of same-sex marriages increases, inevitably some couples will break up.

Unless and until the right to marry is established throughout the land, the issue of a same-sex divorce can be complicated by geography. Specifically, if a couple legally weds in one state, then moves to a state that doesn't recognize same-sex marriage, where can they divorce?

At least one state allows same-sex couples to undo their marriage even though they couldn't wed there in the first place. Other states don't: the marriage is not legally recognized, so a divorce can't be granted. What about returning to the state where you wed? Some states permit a quick return home for a divorce, but others impose residency requirements before a couple can legally split. To get a better sense of how your own situation will play out, consult a state-by-state guide, such as the one published by the National Center for Lesbian Rights, at nclrights.org.

FOR MORE INFORMATION

The American Academy of Matrimonial Lawyers (aaml.org) has a wealth of information about divorce, including the guide we discussed earlier, *Divorce Manual: A Client Handbook,* as well as an online directory of members who meet its admissions standards. It's not a requirement that your divorce lawyer be a member, but similarly to board certification for a physician, membership is evidence of your lawyer's dedication to a divorce practice.

Nolo, the publisher devoted to making law accessible through self-help books and forms, offers divorcenet.com, a site with comprehensive information about divorce law and links to their offerings. Their clear, thorough, and reassuring book, *Nolo's Essential Guide to Divorce,* is updated regularly in print and online.

Nebraska-based publisher Addicus Books is developing a useful series on divorce law by state, written by local lawyers. You can learn more at addicusbooks.com.

DIVORCE: PROPERTY AND SUPPORT

OPENING STATEMENT

A quick history lesson: in England, the land that bequeathed Americans the template for law as we know it, marriage made a husband the owner of his wife's property. Faithful watchers of *Downton Abbey* will remember how well this rule worked for the Earl of Grantham, who was able to retain his magnificent family home by conveniently annexing the fortune of his new bride, Cora, the wealthy American.

English law gave women short shrift for centuries, and no wonder. Until a few hundred years ago, the deaths of women in England weren't considered important enough to record in public registries. The law also denied a wife the right to contract with anyone independently—that was exclusively a husband's privilege. These presumptions—and many others—carried into early American life as well, and the few pioneering women who dared fight the status quo on either side of the pond found an army of smug, self-righteous, precedent-preferring men who condescendingly insisted that nothing had changed since the Middle Ages as regards women, and nothing ever would.

To see why women fought for reform against those considerable odds, let's meet one of my feminist legal heroines.

BOSSES OF THE BAR: CAROLINE NORTON

Caroline Norton was the granddaughter of playwright Richard Brinsley Sheridan (who famously wrote *The School for Scandal*, and yes, that is a portent of her fate). Born to an artistic family that was left penniless when her father died, Caroline married badly out of necessity. To make matters much worse, her husband, George—who also beat her—accused Caroline of conducting an adulterous affair with the prime minister. George sued the prime minister for adultery and lost, but was still legally able to deny Caroline access to their three small children, sending them all to Scotland.

All this was enough to transform Caroline from long-suffering wife to crusader for women's rights. First, she wrote a pamphlet with the unwieldy but comprehensive title *The Natural Claim of a Mother to the Custody of Her Children as Affected by the Common Law Rights of the Father*. Pamphlets were the cable news shows of that era, and this one helped Caroline persuade an initially reluctant Parliament to pass a law that would allow mothers to petition the court for custody of children up to age seven, and grant them access to older children. Caroline then helped pass legislation that eased the way for Englishwomen seeking divorce. Despite these successes, Caroline still couldn't reunite with her children: they were, after all, in Scotland. Only after their eldest son, William, was gravely injured in a riding accident at age eight did George relent and permit Caroline to visit. She arrived too late to see her little boy before he died.

Two more points about this pioneering feminist. Under English law, her unspeakable husband, George, had the right to collect the money Caroline earned as a prolific novelist and poet. And when George finally died, Caroline was able to remarry, at age sixty-nine, to Sir William Stirling-Maxwell. They enjoyed about three months of married life together before Caroline passed away.

IT'S THE LAW

Fast-forwarding to today, the law regarding marital property has improved considerably for us. Let's review the basics.

Broadly speaking, you and your spouse have two types of property.

The assets and debts you collected while married—the paychecks you each earned, the home you bought together—are *marital property*.

The assets and debts you collected before you got married are *separate property*, as are gifts and inherited property you received while married. Generally, this property remains each of yours after the divorce, though some state laws make it possible to include separate property as part of a divorce settlement, too. (Some of these states are nicknamed "kitchen sink" states.)

What if you mix separate property and marital property, such as taking money you brought to the marriage and depositing it in a joint account? Generally, individual property, once mixed with marital property, becomes marital.

As you may have sensed, this division is seldom as clean as you might wish. Take a parental gift. We did when my husband and I purchased an apartment and his parents offered us some money to help with the costs. Was that a gift to him (separate property), a gift to us (marital), or a loan we needed to repay? It wasn't as if we called in lawyers and documented their intent when they gave us the money; they simply wanted to help out. These murky issues arise all the time.

In any event, if you are readying for divorce (and frankly, even if you're not) you should have a current picture of your personal and shared financial status at the ready. Get a worksheet from your lawyer, or pull one of many useful lists from the web, and make a list (with current statements to back it up) of the assets you and your spouse own, and how much they are worth. The Institute for Divorce Financial Analysts has a good starter list:

Retirement assets
Liquid assets
Real estate
Personal property
Cash-value life insurance
Business interests

Now that we've defined property, at least generally, let's turn to how it will be divided if you need a court's help. For many splitting couples this situation can get a lot messier than the *Downton* problem of coping with a son-in-law who was once your chauffeur.

Again, speaking generally, division of property is state-specific and states apply one of two philosophies:

1. Equitable Distribution. Most states employ this approach, which assumes at the start that the spouse whose name is attached to the property owns it, and allows a judge to divide property in a way she considers fair, based on a set of state-specific factors. For example, in Ohio, courts look at ten representative factors, summarized here:

1. The length of the marriage
2. The assets and liabilities of the spouses
3. Whether the family home should go to the spouse with physical custody of the children
4. Whether the property to be shared is liquid
5. Whether it makes economic sense to keep an asset intact
6. Tax consequences
7. The costs of selling an asset in order to divide it
8. Whether and how property was divided in a separation agreement
9. Retirement benefits
10. Any other relevant factors

2: Community Property. As I write, nine states (Arizona, California, Idaho, Louisiana, Nevada, New Mexico, Texas, Washington, and Wisconsin) start from the proposition that the property a couple acquires during a marriage generally is property they own equally and should split equally after a divorce, no matter whose name is on the title or is listed as the owner.

Some states are more orthodox about this principle than others. California famously starts from the proposition that this property must be divided fifty-fifty. Other community property states aim for giving each spouse a fair share of community property, so the division might be more flexible. Do community property principles yield easier, cut-and-dried outcomes? Hardly. For one thing, couples can still argue about whether property they have should be labeled community or separate.

While plenty of divorcing couples direct their anger at each other into a campaign to retain a particular personal item (more than a decade later, I am still nursing mild resentment over my failure to keep our wedding flatware, for heaven's sake), the tougher division-of-property issues tend to arise about where you live and what you've saved. (Family businesses can be another major issue; that's a complicated matter beyond the scope of this book.) Let's take a closer look.

EXHIBIT 15: CAN YOU KEEP YOUR HOME?

As crushed as I was about the dissolution of my marriage, my heart also broke over the possible loss of the first apartment we purchased together, aka the "marital residence." That starter home so often looms large in the hopes of young marrieds. I still remember the day our real estate broker took us for a visit and we asked her, with poignant optimism, if the place would be large enough for us to raise our children to maturity. She thought so, and we were relieved, since we loved the apartment and its particulars. The charming, treetop-level view of a little park and the river. The kitchen we renovated with carefully chosen appliances. The reassuring solidity of a nice home with a good address in a reliable neighborhood with solid schools and a playground so close I could watch our children play from the window.

With divorce, my real estate fortunes changed faster than the fate of a bachelorette who seeks a rose but comes up short. I contemplated making a bid for the place, but the carrying costs were simply too high. So off the children and I moved, to a smaller place on a busier street. It was wrenching. One day I ran into two of the fancy matrons who were my former neighbors. They gazed up with undisguised distaste at the dingy white brick of my new home, and then, appropriately, down at me. In an attempt at reassurance, they murmured that this . . . situation . . . would be temporary, and predicted I would be trading up, eventually. They may literally have said, "There, there, dear." Then they made a beeline for the fresher air of their zip code.

They were correct, but it took patience, thrift, and a well-timed downturn in mortgage rates to be able to relocate to a new place near my ex. Had I kept our beloved, expensive marital residence, I would have been struggling to make my monthly payments and unlikely to have been able to save for retirement or college tuition. By moving—and really downsizing—for a while, my children and I eventually were able to afford a home that may lack the grandeur of our original apartment but is wholly ours and a symbol of the new, hopeful life we built.

Personal story aside, you will make a decision about your marital home based on circumstances too varied to summarize here. Ideally, you'll get advice from your lawyer and also an accountant or someone who knows your financial situation.

What are your options? To summarize, you'll either sell your home and divide the proceeds, one of you will buy out the other, or you'll both hold on to it.

If you sell, you'll have to decide a fair way to split the price (and one or both of you will have to keep paying your mortgage, taxes, and other maintenance costs while you are in the process of your split).

If you decide on a buyout, the purchasing spouse can refinance the mortgage and pay the selling spouse (who will want to be removed from that mortgage, as well as the deed); the spouse who keeps the house will give up other assets (typically, retirement savings) in the property settlement. To be sure this plan will work, it's a sensible idea to have the spouse who will keep the home prequalify for a mortgage before the divorce is final.

Short of these options, spouses can agree to keep the home for their children and take turns living there (sometimes called "birdnesting"), or rent the house either as an investment property or to one spouse who pays the other.

If you are thinking of owning your marital home alone, make sure you've carefully considered whether you can afford its upkeep—

mortgage payments, taxes, insurance, and the everyday costs that go with home ownership. After all, while a home can be valuable (financially, and emotionally) it's not a liquid asset, like money in the bank. And if you are selling, be mindful of tax considerations.

EXHIBIT 16: RETIREMENT SAVINGS

If you and your spouse have been diligent savers, you likely have retirement savings accounts and pensions. You may think each spouse keeps everything he or she earned and saved at his or her own job. Think again. The assets that were accrued during your marriage are likely subject to division when you divorce.

Since moving retirement money around can trigger tax obligations, the spouse who will receive a chunk of retirement money likely will need a court-approved document called a QDRO: a qualified domestic relations order.

This acronym sounds a little daunting, but I can assure you that it's a routine part of divorce proceedings. To demystify the QDRO, I'm going to quote the Department of Labor's definition, then explain it in English. Save your applause until the end of this chapter, please.

> *A "qualified domestic relations order" (QDRO) is a domestic relations order that creates or recognizes the existence of an alternate payee's right to receive, or assigns to an alternate payee the right to receive, all or a portion of the benefits payable with respect to a participant under a retirement plan, and that includes certain information and meets certain other requirements.*

In other words: under a QRDO, a spouse who receives a portion of a retirement plan as part of a divorce settlement can place that money, tax-free, into a retirement account. With that move, the money maintains its status as retirement savings that are protected from taxes. Also, the paying spouse doesn't get socked with early withdrawal penalties. Without the rollover, taxes and penalties would apply.

These are highly technical documents with strict and specific requirements. Make sure a lawyer drafts a QDRO for you.

SOCIAL SECURITY: A BENEFIT THAT SURVIVES A SPLIT

Even after a divorce, you can collect Social Security benefits based on your ex-spouse's record, if you were married for at least ten years, are sixty-two years old or older, have not remarried, and, significantly, do not earn a higher Social Security benefit on your own.

The beauty of this benefit: you don't have to negotiate over it, or even include it in your agreement. You can check directly with Social Security for an estimate of the benefits you can collect.

My ex and I finalized our divorce after nine years of marriage. Had we known about this potential benefit, perhaps we would have stayed together for a few more months.

EXHIBIT 17: JOINT DEBT

Remember that couples also accrue debt while married. How do you divide up those obligations? Courts can look at who incurred the debt, whether it was before or after you wed, and perhaps who is better able to repay.

Remember that creditors pay no mind to your marital status. In other words, if you have an outstanding balance on a joint credit card, you are jointly responsible for paying off the balance. If you and your spouse agree that he will pay off that debt, and he fails, you are on the hook.

Citigroup offers some sensible tips on managing debt while divorcing:

- Make a list of all your credit accounts and loans, and note your balances and which are owned individually or jointly.
- Keep making required payments. Even if your spouse is solely responsible for a debt, late payments can become part of your credit history, which could hobble you later should you want to take on new debt, like a mortgage for a new home.
- Contact your creditors. They may not be obligated to change their approach to you, but some may be willing to work with you so they can keep your business.
- Untangle your marital credit. Creditors won't close accounts independently if you are divorced. Contact them and ask to close joint accounts or remove users from your individual ones. (They may not be willing to convert joint accounts to individual accounts.)
- Establish your own credit. If you haven't built your own credit history already, or if you did in your single days, but didn't bother to maintain it while married, this is the time. Make an application and talk to your lender. Maybe your credit limit alone will be lower than that you enjoyed as a couple, but it will be an important step toward your fresh start.

CELEBRITY LAW LESSON:
THE DODGER DIVORCE

The rich and famous engage in the same disputes over property and possessions that all divorcing couples endure. Most of the time, the only real differences between them and us are decimal points and size of the legal teams they employ. But even among the wealthy, some divorce dustups stand out. Take the epic Frank and Jamie McCourt divorce saga. Yes, at heart it involved a fight over assets, but in this case, those assets included the fate of a storied Major League Baseball franchise, which meant the battle provided months of heartache for long-suffering fans of the Los Angeles Dodgers. Along the way, the McCourt divorce also provided a harrowing cautionary tale for lawyers who are expected to keep track of revisions to legal documents. Finally, it offered a practical lesson in why community property law still matters, even as courts edge toward dividing property equitably rather than equally.

Frank and Jamie met as undergraduates at Georgetown University, married, and worked together to build a formidable real estate development business, with Jamie, who earned a law degree and an MBA, serving as general counsel. They moved to Massachusetts and together amassed a real estate fortune. Along the way they decided to hold nonbusiness assets (such as their multiple, lavish homes) in Jamie's name, with Frank holding business assets in his. The idea was to keep their business holdings protected from creditors while allowing Jamie and Frank to share their marital assets equitably under Massachusetts law.

When the McCourts bought the Dodgers in 2004 and contemplated their move to Los Angeles, it was time to draw up a postnuptial agreement. California is a community property state, and the McCourts wanted to be sure that once they moved, the homes would remain Jamie's property, and other assets would be Frank's, just as they were when they lived in Massachusetts.

Cue the lawyers. Hordes of lawyers. Court papers describe how the McCourts first signed a postnup in Massachusetts, then re-signed papers in California, just to be sure their agreement would be enforceable in that state. (The California court noted that no one ever explained why that would be legally necessary.)

Despite all that bicoastal lawyering, or more likely because of it, something slipped, and every lawyer's worst nightmare became a reality. The McCourt divorce had a contract problem. The Massachusetts version of the postnup described Frank's business property—including the Dodgers—as separate. The California version excluded those assets from Frank's separate property.

When the McCourts decided to split, the difference between the two versions of the postnup emerged, along with a critical question: which one was correct? Was this glaring omission simply an innocent mistake, or what lawyers charmingly call a "scrivener's error," which in our century would mean the fault of an overworked word processor? That was Frank's argument, but the court wasn't buying. Instead the judge held that the postnup could not be enforced, and that meant Jamie was free to demand more than it allocated to her—significantly, a share of the Dodgers.

At this point, you might ask: why do we have access to the juicy details of the McCourt family feud? Because in most states, divorce proceedings are public, open, and accessible to the curious citizen and the press. So as the McCourts fought over their split, reports flowed about their free-spending ways. Private jets at $12,500 an hour. A salary of $400,000 to a son who already held a job at Goldman Sachs. A hairstylist on retainer for $10,000 a month.

Eventually, the McCourts settled, with Jamie receiving $131 million and Frank retaining, and then selling, the team.

Did I say settled? Not so fast. In 2013 Jamie went back to court to argue for more than the $131 million settlement she and Frank had reached. Why? Because Frank had made a net profit of $1.278 billion on his sale of the Dodgers the year before, and Jamie argued that he had misled her about the team's value. Judge Scott Gordon, the same judge who ruled on the postnup, threw out her case. Predictably, Jamie's lawyer vowed to appeal.

EXHIBIT 18: ALL ABOUT ALIMONY

Not so long ago, the term *alimony* got its own euphemisms: "spousal maintenance" and "spousal support." I suppose they are more precise, but they also drain the term of the disdain it accrued after decades of serving as a punch line for lazy comedians and frustrated husbands.

Despite the rise of dual-career households, alimony still exists, and can now be collected by husbands as well as wives, thanks to a 1979 U.S. Supreme Court decision.

To summarize, very broadly, the state of play:

Who pays alimony? Generally, the spouse in a long marriage who earned more and has the work experience and earnings potential to help the other spouse maintain his or her marital standard of living. (Note the word *potential*—judges take note when a spouse abruptly abandons a lucrative career right around the time of an alimony or child support award.)

Who collects alimony? The spouse who would face a drop in his or her standard of living as a result of a split (the issue of children, who will care for them, and whether child care might limit earning potential, can come into play).

When does it end? Alimony is typically a temporary award, meant to tide a spouse over for a set period of months or years, until a youngest child leaves home or the ex receiving checks remarries. But occasionally an alimony award is permanent. In recent years, tales of "ali-moneyed" spouses who refused to return to work, or who chose to live with their boyfriends to keep those alimony checks flowing, rather than marry and lose the monthly payments, have earned sympathetic attention for the long-paying spouse. Take, for example, the story of Michael Morgan, a retired physician battling Alzheimer's disease in Florida who could no longer walk or talk but still had to make $25,200 in annual alimony payments to a spouse he had divorced fifteen years earlier, or Bob Beal, remarried and living in South Carolina at age ninety-two—but still sending monthly checks to his ex-wife in Florida. As one observer put it: even Powerball payments end after twenty years.

In response, some states are contemplating alimony caps like those passed in Massachusetts, where long-term awards are now limited, with payments ending when the check-writing spouse reaches retirement age.

What about taxes? Unlike child support, alimony is considered taxable income to the recipient, and tax-deductible for the spouse who pays.

Alimony payments can make ex-spouses livid, and understandably so. There's just something about writing a check to support a grown adult whom you grew to loathe that would rub even the Buddha the wrong way. One alimony-paying wife, Rhonda Friedman, told the *Wall Street Journal* that she so disliked writing $9,000 monthly checks to her ex, actor John David Castellanos, that she used to spit on them after filling them out. That's why some couples forgo alimony altogether and simply divide their assets in a way that substitutes for alimony for the less wealthy spouse. The obvious advantage is to remove the element of a change of heart, and the need to fight for monthly payments.

BOSSES OF THE BAR: MYRA STROBER

Back in 1995, a Connecticut housewife named Lorna Wendt had an audacious legal demand.

Her husband, Gary Wendt, was a star executive in General Electric's hypercompetitive upper ranks. Lorna worked as a "mother, homemaker, and corporate wife," in the words of a judge reviewing her case.

Corporate wife? The term sounds Betty Crocker–quaint now, but not long ago it was the proud job description of the woman who kept the family calm, the home well appointed, the clients entertained, and her spouse unburdened so he could turn his full attention to the office.

When Gary asked for a divorce after more than thirty years of marriage, he reportedly offered Lorna $8 million plus alimony.

Lorna had another idea. She wanted half of the $100 million she estimated as Gary's net worth. Their marriage, she argued, had been a partnership, and her contributions to team Wendt had made it possible for Gary to amass that fortune.

In the end, Lorna won a $20 million settlement and used her fame to launch an organization devoted to helping other wives win their fair share of divorce settlements. Lorna also encouraged other women in similar circumstances to speak up for bigger settlements, and surely unnerved high-earning men, and their lawyers, who were accustomed to (mostly male) judges approving what were (surely dismissively) called "enough is enough" divorce offers to their discarded wives. She undoubtedly drove a spike in prenups among high-earning husbands eager to avoid Gary's fate.

Lorna's battle became famous. And to make her famous case, Lorna and her lawyer had the good sense to call on pioneering Stanford business professor Myra Strober, who testified on Lorna's behalf.

Here's how Myra explained her economic theory of the case to a Stanford alumni magazine in 1998:

Mrs. Wendt made a human capital investment in Mr. Wendt's career; just look at all the different kinds of labor she performed. When you make an investment, you expect a return. Had the marriage not ended, Mrs. Wendt would have received a very handsome payoff on her investment for her whole life. Enter divorce. This was a divorce that Mrs. Wendt did not want, and from an economic point of view, the divorce interferes with the return on her original investment.

Myra's observations about marriage and work are spot-on. She described being a stay-at-home wife as "an exceedingly risky job," and while she insisted her view of marriage did not preclude strong, even spiritual, emotional attachment, she encouraged husbands and wives to form prenups for "simply good protection."

The Lorna Wendt/Myra Strober legacy is important, but will it last? Some lawyers see a shift away from giving credit to the non-wage-earning spouse, which may be the result of an even newer trend: the number of women who leave a marriage with the larger career and bigger business assets, and who may find it easier to argue against a fifty-fifty split with a nonworking husband.

EXHIBIT 19: INSURANCE ISSUES

As you divide property and look ahead to your separate financial futures, don't forget to sort out insurance as part of your overall settlement.

If you were insured through your spouse's plan at work, a federal law called COBRA (which we'll also review in chapter 22) likely allows you (as the nonemployed spouse) to stay on the plan for thirty-six months after your divorce; the Department of Labor offers guidance about the intricacies of COBRA at dol.gov/ebsa.

If you expect support payments from your ex for you or your children, consider buying life and disability policies to cover your spouse; some experts advise that the spouse receiving support own the policy and pay the premiums, just to be sure. (You'll want to review homeowners and auto insurance, depending on where those assets land, as well.)

EXHIBIT 20: CHANGED CIRCUMSTANCES

With any luck, the agreement you and your spouse reach about property and maintenance will last, undisturbed. But what if the spouse responsible for support payments loses a job? Remarries? Or simply stops writing checks?

In those situations, you may be back before a judge.

If circumstances change—for example, the paying spouse loses her job—the judge can grant a modification that changes the amount owed for maintenance (or child support).

If you or your spouse do not pay support, a court has powerful options, including diverting (or, as lawyers say, garnishing) wages or bank funds for support payments, calling in a sheriff to take away property of the nonpaying spouse, or even, if the nonpaying ex is in contempt of court, a jail sentence.

These are legitimate avenues to pursue if you think your return on investment (in time and lawyer fees) will make it worth the effort. That said, I know several women who, faced with deadbeat spouses, simply gave up and made do. For these women, it was the better of two unpalatable choices. They were realists and refused to chase their ex simply for psychic satisfaction: they knew additional funds were nonexistent and in any event, not forthcoming. Whatever you do in this bad situation, use common sense and consult a lawyer about the cost of a money chase. We'll learn more about child support in chapter 13.

FOR MORE INFORMATION

The Institute for Divorce Financial Analysts offers a series of practical articles on financial planning during and after divorce: institutedfa.com.

For tax planning: IRS Publication 504, Divorced or Separated Individuals, Internal Revenue Service, irs.gov.

The Insurance Information Institute's "Life Stages" pages include helpful tips about adjusting insurance for divorce: iii.org.

The Women's Institute for Financial Education (wife.org) was founded by two women who offer financial planning advice to other women; their site has accessible advice and lively message boards.

12

CHILD CUSTODY

OPENING STATEMENT

If you read the introduction to the divorce section of this book in chapter 10, you already know about my limits as a soon-to-be divorcing parent. I shared my story of incompetent communications with my children not to make you think twice about whether to trust me, but to reassure you that this is perhaps our toughest legal assignment: helping kids, who are faultless, absorb what may be the biggest blow they will face as they grow up.

We lawyers are not therapists, although I've met therapists-turned-lawyers, which can be an invaluable combination. But we are human, and that's why I want to cushion our discussion of child custody with empathy and awareness of the special nature of this dispute. You care deeply about your kids, and so, in almost every instance, does your spouse. The legal options we'll explore are yours to consider; if you can, try to make decisions that best ensure your kids get the nutritive parenting they deserve. No matter what you decide, they will need every ounce of your parenting skills to weather the storm.

IT'S THE LAW

Before we dive in, an important distinction between two types of custody: *physical custody*, which determines where your children will live or spend time; and *legal custody*, which identifies which parent will make key decisions about their education, health care, and religious instruction, if any, and other important child-centric matters. You can share legal custody, or joint decision-making authority, even if the children live primarily, or exclusively, with one parent.

The days of assuming mothers make better custodial parents are essentially over, unless you end up in court before a very old-fashioned judge. As is so often the case in legal matters, California led the pack and launched the joint custody trend in 1980, and today state law does not favor one parent over another. (There can be a residual assumption that mothers are better custodians for younger children, but many dads would contest that proposition.) Instead, the central question when it comes to custody is: what's in the best interest of the child?

It's seldom an easy question to answer, but most divorcing parents seem to figure it out on their own. According to the American Bar Association, more than 95 percent of custody plans are made outside of court.

What goes into a plan? You can find useful templates on the web, where many states post their own plan forms for parents to fill out. As a representative sample, let's take a parenting agreement worksheet published in Minnesota. It asks parents to decide, among other issues:

- Education, including who will attend parent-teacher conferences and select extracurricular activities
- Medical care, including scheduling doctor's appointments
- Religious upbringing
- A residential calendar, and an agreement to be flexible if necessary
- A schedule for holidays, vacations, school breaks, and birthdays
- How the noncustodial parent can stay in touch
- Child care
- Maintaining family relationships
- Whether either parent can move
- How to settle disputes

As children age, their custody schedules probably should change (assuming they spend time with both parents). As one eminent family psychologist put it, younger children generally benefit from a steady home base; school-age kids can manage more intricate schedules, and teens will have their own plans to compete with yours. In the heat of my own divorce fights, which centered exclusively on this issue, my husband half joked that when the kids were teens, we would fight over who had to take them, rather than who could.

All of this means that if you are sharing physical custody, you will likely engage in all sorts of calendar math to set up as predictable a schedule as you can. One website that offers automated scheduling (a godsend, trust me) suggests some of the following options:

- The 2/2/5/5 schedule: the children live with parent one for two days, parent two for two, parent one for five, parent two for five.
- The 3/3/4/4 schedule: you can do the math.
- The children spend weekends and several evenings with parent one; parent two gets the other days.

- The children live with parent one during the school year; parent two during the summer and school breaks.

I can almost hear you thinking: Forget these sample calendars. These are my precious children. Just tell me: which plan is best? The answer is as unique as your own family's dynamics. The wisdom I received from a trusted friend, a child psychiatrist at Yale, will illustrate my point. During my divorce, I turned to him and asked that exact question. He said, simply: the best custody plan is the one you and your spouse can agree to implement. If you agree to a plan, it is more likely to be kept. That's the "best" approach to child custody, because it limits postdivorce arguments that often implicate the kids.

If you and your spouse disagree about custody, a judge will have to weigh in and will likely appoint a guardian ad litem—specifically, a guardian to look after the legal rights of your kids in court. That person is charged with advocating for the best interest of the children, which, by the way, is not necessarily what you believe, nor what the children say they want. The guardian will likely want to meet your children, together with parents and then separately, before reporting to the court.

Do your kids get a vote in custody disputes? Generally, no, but they may be able to inform the court of their preference. The older the child, the more weight her opinion will have. Two states—Georgia and West Virginia—give children age fourteen or older an absolute right to choose which of their parents to live with.

EXHIBIT 21: CUSTODY PITFALLS

Can you harm your own chances for the child custody award you seek?

This question often arises if a parent has been having an affair. It's certainly something that can tear a family apart, but in most states a romantic liaison will not affect how custody is allocated, unless the affair has led to behavior that has harmed the children.

What if a parent is gay? If the parent was part of a same-sex marriage, of course it's not an issue. If a parent comes out after a separation, the impact will depend on the state. Some states do not hold sexual orientation against parents, but courts in other states have denied custody based on a reluctance to allow children to stay with the parent's new partner. In our era of rapidly expanding gay rights, those decisions should be disappearing.

EXHIBIT 22: BAD-MOUTHING

You may hate your ex, but chances are your ex will do a good job (or, at least, a good enough job) helping you to raise your children. No matter your differences, you almost certainly both love your kids.

Parents can be objectively bad, of course: insensitive, withholding, negligent, violent—perhaps the type of person who should be denied significant time with his or her children. Then there's the perfectly capable parent who gets a terrible reputation with his or her own child, thanks to a targeted campaign by the other parent to undermine the relationship. Psychiatrist Richard Gardner labeled this behavior "parental alienation syndrome" in the early 1980s. The idea of an alienation "syndrome" was controversial from the start (some feuding fathers deployed the claim to retaliate against mothers in custody fights), and it's not been embraced by courts or doctors. Syndrome or no syndrome, a judge can listen to evidence that one parent is trying to persuade a child that the other parent is unfit, and can respond to that evidence by awarding a more robust custody schedule to the targeted parent.

It's undoubtedly tempting, in the heat of a custody war, to want to win your child's affections away from your spouse. In pursuit of your goal, you may resort to carrots, like elaborate gifts and other inducements, or sticks, like monopolizing parenting time or outright trash talk.

When we were divorcing and trying to settle our custody agreement, my soon-to-be-ex and I sought to demonstrate our parenting superiority and win our kids' hearts and minds . . . through a cook-off. The kitchen we still shared became our custody battlefield as we took turns preparing increasingly elaborate meals—even baking—surely to the astonishment of our bewildered offspring, who were more accustomed to the after-work, make-do meal. In retrospect, although our culinary duels provided robust sustenance and set the stage for the delicious family dinners we now all enjoy together from time to time, our competition was, finally, a waste of time for custody purposes. No judge should care about which spouse is the more skillful chef. That said, we were always careful to keep whatever adverse thoughts we might have had about the other to ourselves, and more important, away from our children, and it made all the difference in achieving the comfortable relationship the four of us have today.

To keep your custody options open, and to pave the way for the possibility of a healed relationship over time, it's critically important to keep your anger in check. If you loathe your ex, call your mom or a friend to vent. Don't tell your kids.

HOW TO BEHAVE AROUND YOUR KIDS

The American Academy of Matrimonial Lawyers—a group that has seen every variation on vicious divorcing-parent behavior—offers sensible advice about how to comport yourself during this stressful time. If you and your spouse can follow even a few of these suggestions, your children will suffer less through this ordeal.

- Be sure your children have ample time with the other parent. They need it.
- Don't introduce your children to your new romantic interest until the children have adjusted to your separation and your new relationship is stable.
- Don't bring your children to court or to your lawyer's office.
- Keep to the schedule. Give the other parent, and the children, as much notice as you can when you will not be able to keep to the schedule. Be considerate.
- Be flexible. You may both need to adjust the schedule from time to time.
- Giving of yourself is more important than giving material things. Feverish rounds of holiday-type activities during every visitation period, or lavish gifts, may be viewed as a crude effort to purchase affection, which is not good for the children.
- Do not use your children as spies to report to you about the other parent.
- Do not use the children as couriers to deliver messages, money, or information.
- Try to agree on decisions about the children, especially matters of discipline, so that one parent is not undermining the other parent's efforts.
- Avoid arguments or confrontations while dropping off or picking up the children, and at other times when your children are present.
- Don't listen in on your children's phone calls with the other parent.
- Maintain your composure. Try to keep a sense of humor. Remember that your children's behavior is affected by your attitude and conduct.

- Assure your children they are not to blame for the breakup, and are not being rejected or abandoned by either parent.
- Don't criticize the other parent in front of your children. Your children need to respect both parents.
- Do not let guilt you may feel about the marriage breakdown interfere with discipline of your children. Parents must be ready to say "no" when necessary.
- You are only human. You cannot be a perfect parent. When you make a mistake, acknowledge it and try to do better next time.

One more thought. We're often encouraged to live in the moment. When you are a divorcing mom, do the opposite. Think about the future. What relationship would you like to have with your children and their other parent in five, ten, or twenty years, at graduations, weddings, and births? If you want those events to be happy, then reverse-engineer a plan to behave well now, even if it's difficult. You will increase your odds of a satisfying family future.

In an appalling and contemporary twist on how bad parental behavior can influence a custody case, a New York court upheld a decision granting a father sole custody of his three children after their mother, among other concerns, called her eldest son (who was ten at the time) an "asshole" on Facebook. The oversharing mom testified that she wrote the post about her son because, she said, that is what "[he] is" and she thought it was important for her Facebook friends to know. In addition to taking away custody, the judges in the case also upheld an order prohibiting the mother from posting anything to or about her children on social media.

A more common form of aggression (or irresponsibility) during custody battles is one parent's failure to make child support payments. But parents who don't make child support payments do not necessarily lose visitation and custody rights. If you are not receiving support, and want to retaliate by restricting custodial time, don't: not only is it counterproductive, but in some instances a judge could hold you in contempt, or take your behavior into consideration and reduce your time with your children. We'll examine child support in greater detail in chapter 13.

EXHIBIT 23: WHEN PARENTS UNDERMINE THE PLAN

The biggest problem with custody plans may be that they have to be carried out by adults who already have trouble getting along, and who may have wildly different ideas about appropriate parenting regimes for the children they share.

Consider, for example, the case of a couple we'll refer to as W.S. and B.K. The two met in 1989; they fell in love and had a daughter. (The court decision in their case suggests they never married.) When they separated, the couple agreed to an informal custody arrangement. Then B., the mother, got restless. First, she moved out of state with their daughter without telling W. He secured a court ruling granting them joint legal and physical custody, which brought B. back to his home state. A few years later, B. again wanted to move, this time to relocate with her new husband, a U.S. Army officer. But could she bring along the daughter she had with W.? A magistrate judge said no, and the Supreme Court of Idaho agreed. B. insisted, among other arguments, that she had a constitutional right to the relocation, but the court said that right was trumped by the government's authority to look after the daughter's best interests.

Bottom line: you generally cannot make unilateral decisions about where you and your children can live. If you have a custody plan that requires you to stay in one place, or within a certain area, then stay there you must, absent powerful arguments to upend the plan. It's also worth noting that if you or your ex has moved to another state and the two of you disagree about child custody, your dispute (if it gets to court) likely will be heard in the court of the state where your children live most of the time.

What if one of you moves to another country? International custody cases are governed by the Hague Convention on the Civil Aspects of International Child Abduction, which aims to return children to their country of "habitual residence." More than eighty nations, including ours, have signed on, but decisions made in accord with the Hague Convention do not necessarily lead to international harmony.

For one thing, the Hague Convention drafters didn't want to define "habitual residence," a phrase that cries out for some context. Instead they wanted courts to make case-by-case decisions about where to place children caught in a global custody tug-of-war. Over time, courts have relied on factors that include whether the parent seeking custody has a job, owns a home, has bank accounts, has a driver's license, or holds citizenship in the country she wants to live in with her child. Courts also look at whether the child is acclimated in the country. Is she enrolled in a local school? Old enough to feel established in her home? In essence, the same determinations that a domestic court might make, but the added uncertainty of distance, and the possibility that other courts might get involved, make these fights particularly high-stakes affairs.

BOSSES OF THE BAR:
CHARLIE AND BARBARA ASHER

Charlie Asher is a former trial lawyer in Indianapolis who, along with his wife, Barb, a social worker, has turned to advising divorcing adults (and never-married parents who have split) about cooperative approaches to parenting. Some of the Ashers' insight is professional, but other ideas surely come from personal experience: they have a blended family with five children.

Along with in-person counseling and mediation at their home office, where they can spirit clients outdoors for mind-clearing walks in "scenic local areas," the Ashers post videos and other content on websites that include uptoparents.org, proudtoparent.org, and whileweheal.org. They are anti-litigation and pro–alternative dispute resolution (I discuss some of those alternatives, including mediation and collaborative divorce, in chapter 15).

Even if your custody battle is heated, it's worth perusing the Ashers' web offerings. A less combative approach is almost always in your child's best interest, though as a local Indianapolis judge, reflecting on new family court rules in his circuit that are based on Charlie's approach, points out, "cooperative rules are only as good as the people who are party to them."

EXHIBIT 24: GRANDPARENT RIGHTS

Grandparents have the right in every state to ask a court for permission to visit their grandchildren, though the extent of that right varies. The court's decision will depend, in part, on how the state defines the rights of all three generations. Take the grandchildren. Some states want to see proof that grandparent visits are necessary to prevent harm to the child. Other states want proof that grandparent time is in the child's best interest.

In Alabama, one particular visitation war between parents and grandparents was so furiously contested it almost reached the U.S. Supreme Court. Along the way, the desperate grandparents, barred from contact with their granddaughters, were spotted waving signs describing their love for the girls along their bus route to school and attending extracurricular activities just to be able to see them. Nonetheless, the grandparents could not prevail in court, where a panel of judges agreed that the parents had the right to make decisions about their children, including whether their grandparents could visit.

FOR MORE INFORMATION

It's helpful to have a template to create your parenting plan. You'll find a wide variety on the web, and you will want to tailor your plan to fit your particulars, which will change over time as your children mature (and, with luck, your relationship with your ex thaws). One thoughtful set of suggestions can be found at emeryondivorce.com, the website of Robert Emery, a psychologist and professor and director of the Center for Children, Families, and the Law at the University of Virginia.

The Association of Family and Conciliation Courts (afccnet.org) is made up of judges, lawyers, psychologists, and other professionals who work on family court issues. Its website contains a series of brochures with answers to common questions about custody, parenting agreements, mediation, and related topics.

Back when my ex and I shared custody, he was the conscientious keeper of the calendar, which he wrote out by hand and photocopied for us to share. Quaint, no? Today you and your coparent can go online and register on sites like ourfamilywizard.com or jointparents.com to keep track of your schedule and shared expenses.

13

CHILD SUPPORT

OPENING STATEMENT

Deadbeat dad. I doubt there's a more disparaging term in all of marriage and family relations. At least when moms don't fulfill their support obligations, they are spared catchy, critical labels. Men? No such luck.

Perhaps you know women who are struggling because their exes fail to make legally required payments to support their kids. Perhaps you are one of those women. If so, I salute your perseverance under challenging, unfair circumstances. Two women I love (a relative and a close friend) have suffered from the deprivations of a deadbeat ex. They both developed strong self-sufficiency muscles and do an admirable job of financing their families solo, but it pains me that they don't have the help they deserve.

How widespread is this problem? A 2011 U.S. Census Bureau report found only 43 percent of the 6.3 million custodial parents entitled to child support received payment in full. About 30 percent collected partial child support payments, and about 25 percent of those expectant parents, so to speak, got nothing at all.

Perhaps these statistics shouldn't surprise us, because setting child support is nearly always an inherently unstable—and emotionally fraught—enterprise. In part, that's because of its duration (it might be owed for much longer than alimony or spousal maintenance, if those are part of the deal), and also because support checks go not to the kids, but to an ex-spouse, two factors that easily create hostility. Throw in the intricacies of determining finances for shared custody, the likelihood of income swings, and the possibility of remarriage, and you find that fixing a "fair" amount for support can be like trying to plant a flag on an ocean wave.

But if you have children and are divorcing, chances are that child support will be a part of your overall settlement, whether you pay it or receive it. Let's see how it's determined.

IT'S THE LAW

Simply put, child support is the money one parent pays to another (usually, to the parent with physical custody) to underwrite a child's basic needs: food, shelter, clothing, education, health insurance.

If you are divorcing and asking for child support, the amount you'll receive will be based on a mathematical formula set by your state. The formula generally focuses on both of your incomes (or, in a few states, just the income of the parent without primary custody, who is generally the parent paying support) and how many children you have. If you share physical custody, the formula will consider how much time your children will spend with each parent. States post these formulas online, and it's worth plugging in your own data early in your divorce to see where you stand.

Does that mean you and your spouse simply plug some numbers into an app, hit "calculate," and expect a check? Not exactly: there are some situations that lead to a support number above or below the formula (and, of course, different states have different approaches). But in general, if you and your spouse agree to a support plan that varies from what the guidelines would suggest, you'll have to explain your thinking to reassure a judge that you believe the number is fair and reasonable for your children.

Of course, this being divorce, nothing is easy—not even data-driven determinations of a monthly check. For example, support is usually based on income. But what is income?

It's easy enough to calculate income if your spouse trudges to an office job and receives a W-2 form featuring those magic numbers at the end of each year. If your spouse is self-employed, though, you will need to review the numbers more carefully, especially if your spouse reports a suspicious decline in income, either when you are negotiating or after you reach an agreement.

Need an example to encourage your vigilance about this issue? Look no farther than the efforts of a New York mom whose attention to detail paid off when a judge ruled she could collect more than $282,000 in child support and maintenance owed by her ex. He had tried to wriggle out of his obligations by starting a company out of his studio apartment, sharply reducing his earned income (the basis for calculating his support payments), and then claiming trips as business expenses, including a trek to Mount Everest and one to Israel coincident with his son's bar mitzvah.

When you work out a support agreement with your spouse, you'll want to think beyond the basics and consider how to pay for other predictable expenses—summer camp, extracurricular activities, religious rite-of-passage celebrations, and other bills—and perhaps agree on how those costs can be shared. My ex and I applied a percentage formula to split child and teen rearing costs; other couples divide up the bills.

When does child support end? In most states, it stops when a child reaches age eighteen, though some states expect parents to pay support for children in college. As for taxes, child support is neither deductible by the check-writing parent nor considered income for the parent who cashes the check. (You and your ex generally can decide who gets to declare which child as a dependent on your tax returns, but you cannot split a child's exemption.)

As we've discussed, if you are in immediate need of child support, your lawyer can ask the court for immediate help, formally known as pendente lite support, before your divorce is final.

EXHIBIT 25: ADJUSTING SUPPORT

In a perfect world, the child support agreement you reach holds up until your children reach maturity. In our real world, situations change, and the paying parent may need to return to court for an adjustment.

Whether a child-support-paying parent cannot make required payments or a parent receiving support wants an increase, the road to a change starts in court with a motion for modification of the support award.

Most state judges will want proof of a significant change in the paying parent's income to justify raising—or dropping—the support obligation. Life changes, such as a parent's or child's illness or special needs, can also prompt a court-ordered change in child support. And while some states will allow a working mother who remarries, has more children, and decides to stay home to cut back on payments, courts will not allow paying parents to deliberately depress their income to avoid paying support.

All of this means a parent seeking a support adjustment should collect documents that back up her claims of changes in income and expenses. The more evidence you can deploy, the better. You can apply for a support change without a lawyer, and even try to renegotiate directly with your ex; if you do that, get your new plan in writing and approved by a judge, to make sure it supersedes the (enforceable) earlier agreement.

EXHIBIT 26: BACK TO THE DEADBEATS

What if your ex doesn't pay?

Governments have been concocting novel ways to solve this vexing problem for a long time, and their efforts echo the battle between exterminators and pests: as soon as a solution is invented, the targets find new ways to survive. In Broward County, Florida, seven deadbeat parents were falsely told that they won five hundred dollars; when they arrived at a local recreation center to collect, they were sent to jail for failure to pay support. Clever idea, but it's unlikely to have done much to improve overall child support collection in the Sunshine State.

Every state has an agency dedicated to enforcing child support agreements. These agencies have a range of less flamboyant options to deploy, including collecting a deadbeat's salary, vacuuming up tax refunds, suspending driver's licenses, and placing liens on property, including real estate and cars, to secure those assets for repayment. (A lien is a notice that pegs the owner of property as someone in debt who might have to hand over the property to repay. Would you buy a used car from a deadbeat? Exactly.) In extreme cases, your ex can be held in contempt of court, which could result in a fine or jail time. And the federal government also can fine, or in some cases imprison, deadbeats who live in a different state than their kids.

If you need to collect support from a nonpaying parent, the financial planning website learnvest.com offers some sound advice, including the following:

- Make sure your child support agreement is in writing so you have something to enforce.
- Try talking to your ex before you take action. If that works, and you agree, get your agreement in writing. This is also good advice, by the way, if you are paying support and ask your ex for a temporary reduction; if your ex changes his mind, you won't have recourse unless you can prove you agreed on a change.
- Use the written child support order to collect. Take your paperwork to an employer to garnish wages or to the government to collect that tax refund. To get a lien, you record the judgment in your case in the county where your ex owns property.
- Every state has a child support enforcement agency. The agency can perform all the collection actions we just reviewed at a low cost, but it may not work as quickly as you'd like.
- If you want private help, you can hire a lawyer, which would be especially helpful if you want your ex held in contempt. Or you can check out private collection agencies that will take a percentage of the debt they collect.

Some of these options may yield money; others, such as seeking a contempt charge, may provide more retribution satisfaction than dollars. But before you pursue any of these avenues, ask yourself: will their yield justify the time and expense you'll invest? Some mothers think about chasing a deadbeat ex, then give up and devote themselves to attaining self-sufficiency instead of continuing a losing battle. The more you know about your ex's resources, the better you will be able to decide how to proceed.

BEAST OF THE BAR: ROBERT SAND

As I mentioned earlier, some states post photos of deadbeats on websites to help identify those who are missing, or shame those who are not. The Child Support Enforcement branch of the Office of Inspector General of the U.S. Department of Health and Human Services runs one of those sites, which features a collection of the nation's worst deadbeat dads, shared in an "America's Most Wanted" style.

Of all the serial evaders, debt beaters, and irresponsibility junkies crowding the site over the years, one man takes pride of place.

Ladies, meet Mr. Robert Sand.

Sand, who was arrested in 2012 while trying to enter the Philippines without the correct travel documents, owed $1.2 million in child support payments to three children by two former wives. He admitted leaving New York, first for Florida, then to depart the United States altogether after authorities issued arrest warrants in 2000 and 2002. Once caught, Sand was sentenced to two and a half years in prison and ordered to pay more than $900,000 in support.

Sand set the bar high, but just as with athletic achievement, his incredible record surely will be eclipsed one day. Meanwhile, though Sand surely deserved prison time, opinion is divided about whether prison truly deters deadbeats. About fifty thousand people reportedly are incarcerated in the United States for failure to pay child support, but it's a controversial punishment, prompting arguments about whether it's effective (it's hard to imagine a parent writing support checks from his or her cell) and whether it unfairly penalizes low-income parents.

14

FIGHTING OVER FIDO: THE PAIN OF PET CUSTODY DISPUTES

Come here, Spot.

No, come here, Spot!

When couples split, even when they don't have kids or significant financial assets to divide, their furry, barking reminder of happier times may present an intractable issue. How do you partition a beloved pet? It's a problem faced by married couples, of course, but also by unmarried ones, since so many couples bring home an animal as a sort of gateway drug, or practice round, before having children.

I am sorry to admit that I'm not a pet person. We never kept pets growing up, in part because my mother, who maintained an unreasonably immaculate home, would not have been able to cope with any pet-provided grime, and in part because she would have been unable to coerce the pet into participating in the weekend cleaning tasks assigned to me and my siblings (my job, no joke, was Pledge-ing the radiators). So, sadly for my kids, the no-pet rule survived as a legacy of that squeaky-clean upbringing.

But when I was divorcing, I had a brief encounter with pet joy, through the rewarding company of a small, beady-eyed, chunky hunk of love called Fluffy. Fluffy was the hamster my kids were allowed to bring home from preschool for a short stay. Residing in her metal cage atop our tiled kitchen floor during her brief study-abroad program, Fluffy impassively greeted me each night when I returned from work to our tense, divorcing family home.

Never judgmental, always low-maintenance, Fluffy was undemanding, reliable, perhaps even wise. Within the first day or so of her arrival, I started talking to Fluffy. After just a few banal recaps of my workday or mission statements about my culinary ambitions for the evening meal, we established a comfortable interspecies complicity. Fluffy was the only family member I was neither angry at nor worried about traumatizing. We shared a love of iceberg lettuce and occasional bursts of frenzied exercise. As laughable as it may sound, my acquaintance with this dear fur ball gave me a sense of what might be at stake for a couple who share a cat or dog.

IT'S THE LAW

It was once derided as a ridiculous topic, beyond the scope of judges, who to this day largely treat pets as property rather than cherished family members. But efforts are currently under way to rethink pet custody in order to create better solutions for this emotionally charged problem.

If you look around, you can find lawyers and, yes, even law professors who specialize in practicing law on a pet's behalf. Since your pet is unlikely to hire counsel and pay her own bills, I absolutely recommend doing whatever you can to settle this issue with your ex. If you have kids, factor in their feelings and consider the logistics of your new arrangement. Where will your pet live more comfortably, if that's relevant?

If you have any concern about a fight over the pet you think should be yours, take steps to build a record of your ownership and care of your animal. *Pets Weekly* magazine suggests you secure the following paperwork:

- A sales contract or adoption application
- Veterinary records, and anything that proves you pay for your pet's care
- Licensing forms
- Microchip documentation, if your pet has a chip for identification

Of course, not every couple can settle on a solution for a problem with this much emotional weight. And, as always, when splitting couples disagree, extreme behavior can't be far behind. Linda Goldstein spent thirty days in jail when she refused court orders to relinquish Beanie and Kacey, the cats a judge awarded to her ex, even though Linda got to keep the couple's three dogs. Linda committed this act of legal disobedience because, she claimed, her ex-husband would be a "bad parent" to the pets. He ended up looking after Beanie and Kacey while Linda served her time, but there's no word on whether the cats minded the custody plan.

Short of prison martyrdom, affluent pet owners can use money to express their hostility about sharing. A popular example in the colorful annals of pet custody is that of Stanley and Linda Perkins, who in 2002 subjected their pointer-greyhound, Gigi, to a battery of "bonding" tests to determine Gigi's level of attachment to each human. An animal behaviorist observed and then opined about Gigi's performance on these tests, which makes me wonder why we haven't seen an *American Idol* for puppies. (And long before YouTube made pet videos ubiquitous, Linda underwrote the production of a short film, "A Day in the Life," which showed the pup playing, exercising, and relaxing, presumably feeling happy, fit, and Zen in Linda's presence.) Six figures in legal fees (and production costs) later, Linda won custody.

Do you want to spend that much money to resolve a residential custody fight over Fido?

Even if your answer is "yes," remember that if you, your ex, and your pup end up in court, you are rolling the legal dice: some judges, possibly softened up by their own animal attachments, express sympathy for the issue, while others are irritated that it's before them at all.

CELEBRITY LAW LESSONS: PET CUSTODY

The *Hollywood Reporter* compiled a list of five famous celebrity pet custody battles. (I assume the fame attaches to the celebrity, not the pet or the court proceedings.)

1. *Hugh Hefner v. Chrissy Harris.* They broke off their engagement in June 2011. Hef obviously kept the mansion, but who retained Charlie, their dog? Victory: Hefner.
2. *Britney Spears v. Kevin Federline.* Thank you, Britney. Without your legal exploits, this book might be a pamphlet. When Brit and Kevin split, the pet advocacy group People for the Ethical Treatment of Animals urged Kevin to seek custody of the couple's pets, not just the couple's children. To persuade Kevin to act, PETA cited Britney's standing as "the overwhelming choice" for worst celebrity

dog owner by readers of *New York Dog* and *Hollywood Dog* magazines. Victory: unreported.

3. *Drew Barrymore v. Tom Green*. Remember them? They were married for less than six months, but the relationship continued as they battled over Flossie, a yellow Lab. Victory: Drew.

4. *Jon Gosselin v. Kate Gosselin*. Jon and Kate: It wasn't enough to subject your kids to the glare of reality show cameras and torture us all with your cavalier behavior? Apparently not, because you acquired two dogs, Shoka and Nala, during an episode of your quick-fading reality series. Victory: Shoka and Nala. Jon returned the dogs to their breeder.

5. *Tiger Woods v. Elin Nordegren*. The *Hollywood Reporter* says that Tiger, responsible for the most unforgettable instance of a golfer striking a tree in the history of the sport, and his wife had to work out custody of their three dogs. Victory: unclear, but apparently Tiger has been seen walking the dogs.

While courts attempt to sort out these disputes for pet owners both famous and private, advocacy groups like the Animal Legal Defense Fund sometimes submit court papers to support the pet at the center of the battle. They've extolled decisions like the one made by a Virginia judge who granted custody of Grady the cat to the ex who didn't originally own him, reasoning that property rights aside, "Grady's happiness took priority." These advocates have made some fairly creative arguments, including the notion that if other nonhumans have rights—like the now-infamous free speech rights of corporations—then nonhuman pets should have rights, too. Or they might make the case that our beloved animals are more like humans than they've let on, a position that seems to have support from scans of canine brain activity that indicate dogs can feel love and attachment, just like us.

These advocates suggest that pet owners call themselves "guardians" rather than "owners"—a sensible semantic approach to make it clear that pets are different from property.

Meanwhile, while well-meaning animal rights attorneys think earnest thoughts about how best to serve their clients, matrimonial attorneys cluck with disingenuous concern over the lengths to which their clients will go to keep their pets. Surely they swap stories about Rocky the Dog (reportedly stolen on behalf of a disgruntled noncustodial ex while being walked), Lucy the Lamb (a rare fleecy custody battle ultimately won by a rescue center), and Jakob the Horse (the ex-husband, a local politician, moved the horse to a new field without telling his ex-wife, who staged a silent protest at a local council meeting, then two days later allegedly threw a punch—at the ex, not the horse).

All of this makes me wonder: Do our beloved pets realize that when it comes to them, we are nuts? Does that bark really mean: hey, humans, cut it out, already?

15

DIY, MEDIATION, AND COLLABORATIVE DIVORCE

OPENING STATEMENT

So you've decided you want a divorce (or that decision has been made for you), but you don't want to "involve the lawyers." You are pronouncing the word *lawyers* the same way my mother and her friends used to utter the word *cancer* a generation ago.

Don't worry. I'm not insulted by your disdain. Even my father, a prototypically striving immigrant, was disappointed when I opted out of journalism for law school.

But professional animus aside, do DIY divorces ever make sense?

If I were writing this chapter one year ago, it would have been one paragraph long, and would have read something like this: A DIY divorce? Are you nuts? With all the anger, rancor, and shared property you've accrued, not to mention children, do you really think you two angry ex-lovebirds can agree on anything without professional help? And by the way, when was the last time you were able to draft a binding legal document all by yourself, much less deal with fiendishly arbitrary court rules and deadlines?

But to my astonishment, in the past year two of the most important people in my life—my hairdresser and my boyfriend—were both able to secure divorces without lawyers. I'm envious. And my bank account is wistful. If you think you can reach a fair agreement with your spouse, and you pull off a do-it-yourself divorce, I will envy you, too. The rewards can be great. Let's take a closer look.

IT'S THE LAW

Websites abound that will sell you forms that you can fill out, pronto, for a quick and cheap DIY divorce. Have you checked them out? Perhaps you were especially drawn to the cheesy stock photos of a formerly happy couple frowning and gazing past each other. (The swankier sites Photoshop a jagged tear in the middle of the photo to denote—get it?—a split.)

At worst, these sites may be inaccurate, but at best, they are superfluous, because you can gather DIY papers on your own from your state court's website. Slogging through those forms and instructions may be tedious and not always intuitive. But if you and your spouse agree on a deal, and on the backup information you must disclose about your assets and other financial issues, you can get it done. Believe me, your judge wants a smooth path to an agreed-upon result.

One possible obstacle to this arrangement is that real mental toughness is often required to make it work. Here's what I mean. A wife tells her husband she wants a divorce. Her husband insists that lawyers are not necessary. Even as their marriage collapses, taking along with it the last remnants of mutual trust, the wife heeds that advice, either out of a residual belief that her soon-to-be-ex still has her best interests at heart, or because she feels intimidated about pressuring him into a more robust settlement, or because she feels guilty and simply wants it over with. Next thing you know, the husband has either engineered terms that are favorable—to him—or has decided that he is in no rush whatsoever to finalize the divorce. And the wife, with her instincts possibly clouded by that guilt, either gives up benefits she will need or feels powerless to push the situation to a conclusion.

That's a questionable set of circumstances for DIY divorce. It's a better path if you and your spouse agree on terms (generally easier the fewer assets you have) and you are confident you fully understand your collective finances (you don't want to, for example, lose out on a portion of your spouse's pension, or retirement savings, because you were unaware you had a right to a chunk of that change).

If you and your spouse have some unresolved issues that make a full DIY divorce impossible, but still want to avoid a full-lawyer press, one of several options may work: collaborative divorce, mediation, or arbitration. Let's take a closer look.

EXHIBIT 27: WHAT IS COLLABORATIVE DIVORCE?

Sounds like the Merriam-Webster definition of an oxymoron, I know. But in a collaborative divorce, the couple agrees to negotiate their split with the help of lawyers. This makes it a different approach than mediation, which we'll discuss next.

Collaborative divorce was born in 1990 when Minnesota lawyer Stuart Webb became fed up with the ceaselessly combative nature of his family law practice. He began working with other lawyers to develop an alternative, and hit upon a collaborative process. Lawyers and their clients would agree to work together, and the lawyers would be free to withdraw from the case if it turned adversarial.

Today, tens of thousands of lawyers worldwide are said to be trained as collaborative lawyers and the process has resolved thousands of cases. It's also been adapted for use outside of family law.

How does it work? Unlike traditional litigation, where each side is discouraged from communicating directly with the other, collaborative law requires both spouses and their attorneys to sign a "participation agreement" up front, in which they agree to settle without going to court. If they can't, or if one spouse decides to litigate, collaborative lawyers for both sides depart and traditional lawyers move in. The notion is that an initial agreement to invest in the collaborative process makes it less likely that either side will pull a fast one and switch to an adversarial posture.

Collaborative divorce can be cheaper and less stressful, and lead to a more successful outcome, than old-fashioned fighting. And it allows a divorcing couple to negotiate sensitive issues, like finances, in private, without the depositions or expert reports that are public in a typical divorce case. Collaborative divorce won't necessarily be an obvious choice at the onset of a split, when emotions and anger run high. And it won't necessarily protect a spouse who is faced with a severe imbalance of power. But it's touted as a new, if not new-age, solution to the cost and pain of traditional divorce, and if you think it might work for you, it's certainly worth a look.

EXHIBIT 28: MEDIATION AND ARBITRATION

Unlike collaborative divorce, couples in a mediation don't have to hire counsel (though they can employ attorneys to coach them and review any agreement). Instead, a neutral third party, the mediator, hears both sides out and then helps both sides find a solution on their own, with a bit of nudging. Theoretically, anyway, a mediation could work either to solve big disagreements or smaller, intractable issues.

You may decide together that you want to mediate; or a judge, who is probably fed up with you and every other divorcing couple who has approached her bench, may direct you to mediation.

How should you choose a mediator? No differently than you would a lawyer. Check a prospect's credentials and experience; ask about fees (after all, mediation should be cheaper than litigation) and, if your state makes it possible, whether your mediator is certified.

We know that law school turns humans into lawyers, but how are mediators created? Through training courses, and sometimes apprenticeships with more experienced mediators. Mediators who belong to professional associations have to meet certain requirements. The Association for Conflict Resolution, for example, requires that its approved member mediators complete at least sixty hours of family mediation training and two hours of domestic violence training. These ACR-approved mediators also have completed at least 250 hours of mediating in at least twenty-five cases.

The mediator will start the process with a meeting to set the ground rules, then either speak with you together or travel between two rooms if you can't get along, like a French bedroom farce without the humor or bedrooms. Sometimes two mediators will take on the case. Both you and your spouse should have lawyers review any agreement you reach.

Mediation advocates say that because divorcing spouses are more deeply involved in the process than they are when lawyers fight on their behalf, they are more likely to be satisfied with the results. Also, unlike a court fight, a couple can keep the details of their mediation private (though if the mediation agreement is filed in court to obtain a divorce, that deal may be public; check with your mediator and lawyer if that's a concern).

Can mediation resolve parenting issues? An intriguing study by Robert Emery, a professor and mediation expert at the University of Virginia, followed divorcing families over twelve years. Following a coin flip to determine which direction their cases would go, half of the families tried a few hours of mediation to settle their differences and the other half litigated. The results? Even when the mediation didn't work, the families who tried to mediate reported much better collaboration. A parent who tried mediation, then didn't live with his or her kids, still was much more likely to speak with them by phone every week than a parent who went to court. After mediation, the parent with custody reported much better cooperation with his or her ex on all the key issues, from discipline and dress to holidays and the ability to discuss problems together.

Emery concludes that even brief exposure to mediation sets a consensual tone that allows families to work together while splitting up. He extols the process for encouraging feuding spouses to:

- have a voice;
- take the long view;
- work as a team;
- learn about children's needs and coparenting; and
- recognize their own grief and how it causes anger.

Some mediators are beginning to consider something called "child-inclusive" mediation, which gives children a more participatory role in the process. This approach, more common in countries like Australia, Canada, and New Zealand, includes safeguards so that children don't misunderstand the process and wrongly believe, as kids understandably might, that their preferences will carry the day.

But what if you tried mediation, or even simple negotiation, and hit a wall? Or if you can't agree on anything other than wanting to avoid court? In these instances, you may be a candidate for arbitration, which is akin to a personal courtroom with a judge you choose and logistics you set. (Check to make sure your state allows matrimonial arbitration before you choose this option.)

Unlike a mediator, an arbitrator has the authority to make a final, binding decision for the parties, and can also call witnesses and conduct a more formal proceeding. You and your spouse will schedule the date, time, and place for your hearing. Compared to a traditional trial, the process is faster and more streamlined, and you and your spouse will pay the arbitrator for her time. Unlike court, however, the proceedings are private.

When couples arbitrate, they typically agree not to appeal the decision, which can be a good thing, as it promotes one of lawyers' favorite terms: finality. It can be a bad thing if you want another shot at a more favorable result. If so, you can agree in advance that the arbitrator's decision can be appealed to another arbitrator, a group of arbitrators, or to a court. And issues related to children are always open to reconsideration.

Who can argue, if you'll excuse the term in this context, with alternatives to costly, contentious divorce court? But the same caution I raised with other nonlitigation alternatives applies here. Mediation or arbitration may not be your best bet if:

- You and your spouse have complicated finances.
- You are not absolutely sure you know everything about your spouse's assets.
- You are in an abusive relationship.

FOR MORE INFORMATION

If you'd like to do your divorce on your own, check the web for your state's divorce guide; some states even post videos to walk you through the process.

Websites mediate.com and arbitrate.com, which are related sites, offer lists of contacts, searchable by state and topic. The Association of Family and Conciliation Courts (afccnet.org) is another detailed resource; academyfamilymediators.com is another for mediators who have met its criteria. And sometimes state-specific sites offer general information; the Massachusetts Council on Family Mediation (mcfm .com) is one.

For collaborative divorce, try the International Academy of Collaborative Professionals, collaborativepractice.com, for a list of practitioners, searchable by state and subject. A pioneer in collaborative divorce, Ron Ousky, offers details about the approach on his website, ousky.com.

PART THREE

BABIES, CHILDREN, AND TEENS

16

MAKING BABIES

OPENING STATEMENT

According to the Centers for Disease Control and Prevention, data from 2006 to 2010 shows that 10.9 percent of women between the ages of fifteen and forty-four had problems either getting pregnant or carrying a baby to term, and 7.4 million women in that age group had used infertility services.

Demand for these services has developed hand in hand with our unprecedented ability to time our pregnancies, overcome fertility roadblocks, and influence our child's genetic makeup. These delicate, emotionally wrought opportunities bring with them complicated legal consequences that are only beginning to coalesce into established law. Once again, the law is like our adorable, elderly uncle who pulls us aside at a holiday dinner to seek guidance about the latest pop-culture craze: charming, but clueless about how to digest recent developments.

So as we look at the legal landscape for assisted pregnancy, whether it's artificial insemination or assisted reproductive technology (ART) that combines sperm and egg in a lab, we should pause to marvel at modern medicine's ability to outpace the law (much less societal norms about how new lives can be created).

IT'S THE LAW

ART has awarded women unprecedented flexibility to create a family, with or without a partner. Lawmakers began to contemplate how non-traditional families should be treated back in 1973, which, given how radically our notions of family have changed in just the past few years, might as well have been 14 B.C. Back then, an unmarried mother had no right to seek support from her baby's father, and an unmarried father no power to assert custody rights over his child. As a first step out of that Dark Age, state legislatures began to embrace the notion that parents could have equal rights over their child without being married, which helped relocate the awful term *illegitimate* to its well-deserved resting place in the dustbin of history.

As the twenty-first century dawned, lawmakers had still more catching up to do. A law was proposed to help states address the medical miracles that allow the cheerful intermingling of people, married or not, for hire or for love, contributing egg, sperm, or uterus to the creation of a baby. Only a few states have fully embraced that model law, and unlike other countries, the United States has no federal law or policies governing ART. As a result, we live in an era of deconstructed parenting in which a woman who gives birth might not be a legal mother, and a so-called genetic father might not be a legal father. Under certain circumstances, up to six different adults can lay claim to a newborn: two people who intend to be parents, two people who donate egg and sperm, and a woman acting as a gestational carrier and her spouse. In other words, these days Father's Day also can be celebrated as Happy "Adjudicated Father in a Proceeding Confirming a Gestational Agreement" Day.

To navigate this legal labyrinth of reproductive rights, let's try to scatter some trail-worthy bread crumbs. For one thing, the donor of an egg, sperm, or embryo that yields a baby might not legally be considered that baby's parent. At least, that is the result urged by the lawmakers who drafted that model law about parents; they want states to agree that "[a] donor is not a parent of a child conceived by means of assisted reproduction." But actual laws, as opposed to model legislation, are still in flux when it comes to donors' obligations, so we can brace for more fraught court cases about parental rights. For now, and especially with potential children in the mix, the best approach if you are considering ART is to consult a lawyer in your state so you can learn and follow current laws—if any—and make any necessary agreements in advance, and in writing. A written agreement between donor and would-be parent carries different authority in different states: some legally recognize these agreements; others don't but will consider them as useful evidence if a custody battle breaks out. Either way, it's important to remember that you should not rely on verbal agreements, or hope, if a dispute erupts over parental rights.

Are there real-world examples of that unstable intersection where law, love, and assisted reproduction converge? Of course.

EXHIBIT 29: SPERM DONORS

You could say that William Marotta, Angela Bauer, and Jennifer Schreiner met cute, by way of Craigslist, in 2009. Angela and Jennifer, a couple living in Topeka, Kansas, had advertised for a sperm donor and William, a local resident, was willing to help. All three reportedly signed an agreement that shielded William from any financial responsibility for a baby, and the couple gave birth to a girl.

When Angela and Jennifer broke up and Jennifer began to rely on public assistance to raise the girl, the Kansas Department for Children and Families, looking to recoup some of the state's costs, sued William, the sperm donor, for child support.

Remember, Angela, Jennifer, and William signed an agreement that absolved him of any responsibility, fiscal or otherwise. Why wouldn't that agreement hold up? Because Kansas, like several other states, has a law that allows a sperm donor to deny paternity only if the donation is made with the help of a licensed doctor. Since William reportedly handed over his sperm directly to the couple, a Kansas judge found him the presumptive father, liable for child support. It's worth noting that courts are seldom enthusiastic about parents who try to contract away their responsibilities.

Six hundred miles away from the hapless William, a state court in Muncie, Indiana, tried to allocate the parenting responsibilities of a couple we'll call S.P. and C.P. The couple decided to use the sperm of one of C.'s friends to have a baby when S.'s vasectomy could not be reversed. Their DIY insemination produced a son in 2004, and another round created a daughter two years later. When the couple separated in 2009, S. paid child support at first, but then fought a court order to continue payments, asserting that the children were not "products of the marriage."

Weren't they? The state appeals court ruled that because S. consented to the insemination and raised the children as his own, he couldn't disavow paternity. But let's peer in a bit closer. Just as in the Kansas case, the insemination took place without the aid of a doctor. So shouldn't the sperm donor be responsible for the children? After considering that argument, the court decided that since C. and S. were married when C. used the sperm donor to become pregnant, that line of reasoning wouldn't apply to their case.

Is your head spinning faster than a fertility lab centrifuge? Then lie down for a minute, because sperm donor law is much more established than egg donor law. We are about to wade into some truly uncharted territory. But first: a celebrity law lesson.

CELEBRITY LAW LESSON: CONTROVERSIAL CUSTODY BATTLE

Actor Jason Patric, semifamous for his broody, cleft-chinned good looks, wanted to be recognized as the legal father of Gus, who was conceived with his sperm in fertility treatments for his former girlfriend, Danielle Schreiber. In California, since Jason and Danielle were not married when she received the treatment, Jason would not have parental rights as a sperm donor unless the couple agreed in writing before conception that the donor—Jason—would also be a legal dad. (Jason argued in court that he deserved those rights anyway.)

Jason deployed his celebrity (cultivated through films like *The Lost Boys, Speed 2: Cruise Control,* and *Narc*) to secure television interviews and lobby for a law that would grant parental rights under more relaxed conditions. (For example, a donor could gain parenting rights if he openly acknowledged the child as his own and received the child into his home.)

The proposal is controversial, however, with some gay rights groups supporting the bill, and other groups dissenting. Notable among the naysayers is the state's National Organization for Women, which claimed the proposed law would "reinstitute male dominance over women by privileging the male sperm donor's right to exercise ownership in the child over the reproductive liberty of the mother." In other words: Jason's demand demonstrated a lot of chutzpah.

Nonetheless, what is clear is that the proposed law would upend a simpler test—is there an agreement in writing about paternity, or not?—and therefore open the issue to more paternity claims in a state with the most fertility clinics in the country.

EXHIBIT 30: EGG DONORS

You could argue that rules that apply to sperm donors logically ought to apply to egg donors as well. The problem with this argument is that unlike sperm, which is much, much easier to harvest, retrieving a viable egg requires careful excavation and a lot of prior planning. (This difference offers a window into the essential distinction between men and women, does it not? Discuss amongst yourselves.) An egg donor has to take drugs for several weeks, first to stop her menstrual cycle and then to stimulate her ovaries. Extracting eggs, at least at the time of this writing, requires a minor surgical procedure. Along the way, a donor needs to submit to ultrasounds and blood tests to keep track of her egg's development. It's time consuming, potentially problematic—and irregularly regulated. Some states ban egg sales. Others allow them, but insist that a would-be parent's payments to an egg donor can cover her time and expenses, but not the actual egg. The American Society for Reproductive Medicine, noting that compensating women for egg donation can lead to some murky ethical issues, recommends payment to an egg donor be limited to $10,000.

If you use an egg donor, have a lawyer help you with a contract that defines your rights and obligations.

Some would-be parents want no relationship with their donor. Others might want their donor to promise to meet her child later in life. You can include that promise in a contract, but it will not be easy to enforce if the donor changes her mind. Similarly, an effort to penalize a donor for backing out of the procedure before she donates an egg may be doomed to failure.

If you are an egg donor, review your consent form carefully. If you know the would-be parent, consider having a lawyer look at a written agreement that ensures that the parent bears financial responsibility with respect to the donated egg. You can expect the parents (or clinic) to purchase insurance to protect you in case of complications related to the egg retrieval.

What if you listen to me, sign a clear contract about rights related to a donated egg, and then one party changes her mind? A couple of real-world examples show how judges are trying to wade through this exceptionally complicated terrain.

EGG WARS

Two cases in two different states illustrate what happens when happy parenting relationships go awry.

In the first, would-be parents J.F. and E.D. hired a private surrogate agency in Indiana, which identified an egg donor in Texas and a surrogate mother in Pennsylvania to carry the couple's embryo to term. (J.F. provided the sperm.)

Even though everyone signed a contract that gave J.F. and E.D. parental rights, the surrogate, who carried triplets, changed her mind, and took the newborns to her home. Custody battles broke out. And while the surrogate, despite the agreement, secured an early victory in a Pennsylvania court, on appeal J.F., the father, eventually won custody of the triplets. (Remember that while E.D. was the intended mother, she hadn't physically participated in the conception or birth.)

While the surrogate lost in Pennsylvania, in California an egg donor with a close relationship to the surrogate was able to win. K.M. (apologies for the initials, but we can all appreciate a woman's preference for privacy in these matters) donated eggs to her partner, E.G., and signed a standard consent form, including a provision that she would not claim parental rights. (K.M. later said that even though she signed, her intent was to raise any children together.) E.G. gave birth to twins, and E.G., K.M., and the babies lived together for five years. When K.M. and E.G. broke up, K.M. wanted to maintain a relationship with the babies. Had she signed away that right?

The California Supreme Court said no. Despite the agreement, the couple had raised the twins together, and that was enough to grant K.M. parenting rights.

As courts ponder these complicated relationships, science once again provides a new wrinkle: women are freezing their own eggs in the hope of making babies later, and the law will surely need to adapt as these would-be moms set up college savings plans for their unborn children and attempt to conduct estate planning for beneficiaries who may or may not exist in the future. One thirty-eight-year-old woman asked her soon-to-be-ex-husband to underwrite the cost of egg freezing and storage as part of their divorce settlement, so she could start a family without him.

But long before this newest wave of parenting technology took hold, parents who couldn't get pregnant put their faith in a woman willing to carry their child and then hand the child over. The legal history of surrogacy includes an awful, unforgettable showdown.

EXHIBIT 31: THE STATE OF SURROGACY

Diane Hinson, a Maryland lawyer, maintains an online map of surrogacy laws across the United States. She needs ten different colors to keep track of the variations. Some states flat-out ban surrogacy contracts. Others allow and regulate them. Some states permit the intended parents to be named the baby's legal parents before birth, eliminating the need for an adoption. Other states don't. It may go without saying at this point in the book, but all of this is subject to change.

In short, potential parties to a surrogacy agreement—the carrier of the baby, and the would-be parents—need lawyers to work through issues that can include identifying who is responsible for finances, details about how the surrogate parent should care for herself during the pregnancy, and specifics about prenatal testing and even possible fetal reduction or abortion in the event of multiple pregnancies or abnormal fetal development.

A HISTORY OF SURROGACY IN TWO ACTS

Surrogacy in the United States can be divided into two periods: pre–Baby M. and post–Baby M., and it's worth a brief detour to review that story and its consequences for a nation newly alerted to both the promise of surrogacy and the emotional pain it could wreak on the parties involved. (It surely had a huge influence on the baby herself, Melissa Elizabeth Stern, who eventually grew up, married, and moved to London after writing a master's thesis on the impact of surrogacy.)

Baby M. was born on March 27, 1986, to Mary Beth Whitehead, a housewife married to a sanitation worker, who was paid $10,000 to carry a baby for New Jerseyans William and Elizabeth Stern. The baby would be the product of Mary Beth's egg and William's sperm. The couple—William a biochemist and Elizabeth a pediatrician—had contracted for Mary Beth to surrender the baby at birth and terminate her rights. But after giving birth, Mary Beth, who already had two children, had second thoughts. She persuaded the Sterns to let her keep the baby, whom she named Sara, for a week, then fled south with her husband and the baby to Florida.

The dispute that followed was unprecedented, and the thirty-two-day trial was replete with specific (and, in retrospect, specious) testimony meant to help determine which two adults would make the best parents to the baby girl. When you read about the case decades later, you are jolted back a generation or two, to a time when experts could attack the competence of a mother (Mary Beth) because she was found to be "narcissistic, impulsive, immature, and of below-average intelligence." (Let's be honest: many moms we know exhibit at least one of those attributes.) The case unfolded in an uneasy blend of apprehension about new reproductive technology coupled with unease about burgeoning feminist and class issues.

The trial judge terminated Mary Beth's parental rights and awarded custody to the Sterns. Undaunted, Mary Beth appealed, and New Jersey's highest court awarded William custody, but reinstated Mary Beth's parental rights because it found the surrogacy contract invalid. Not just invalid, but what courts describe as contrary to public policy, which is one way judges indicate their special abhorrence toward a particular result. Here's what they said:

"The surrogacy contract is based on principles that are

directly contrary to the objectives of our laws. It guarantees the separation of a child from its mother; it looks to adoption regardless of suitability; it totally ignores the child; it takes the child from the mother regardless of her wishes and her maternal fitness; and it does all this, it accomplishes all of its goals, through the use of money."

Following the decision, Mary Beth was awarded visitation rights with the daughter she carried for the Sterns.

In the aftermath of the Baby M. battle, infertile couples seeking surrogates got the memo: to avoid the same potential outcome, do not create a baby with a surrogate's egg. And New Jersey law changed to bar payments to surrogates.

Did that clear up the confusion? Not exactly. A quarter century after the Baby M. case, another New Jersey couple selected a surrogate, took every conceivable precaution to avoid problems, and still ended up in court; this time it was to try to enforce their judge-approved agreement that the intended mother could put her name, and not the surrogate mother's name, on the baby's birth certificate, rather than having to adopt the newborn. The state (not the surrogate) challenged the agreement, and faced with another surrogacy case, the New Jersey Supreme Court deadlocked, and the would-be mom prepared to launch adoption proceedings.

EXHIBIT 32: WHOSE STORED GENETIC MATERIAL IS IT, ANYWAY?

But wait: what about the materia prima, the actual stuff of life? Infertile couples who store their sperm, embryos, and, more recently, eggs are probably at least as likely to separate or divorce as those able to conceive. Since we know that splitting couples will often turn bitter about a shared membership to a health club, imagine how nasty a fight can become over shared genetic material.

In general, if one member of a separating couple who created and stored embryos wants to conceive a baby with them, and the other does not, courts will decide in favor of the would-be parent who no longer wants to have a baby. That's true, in some cases, even if the couple signed an agreement that allowed each would-be parent more leeway.

In a macabre wrinkle to this problem, fights also erupt when the person who donated the genetic material dies, and the widowed spouse wants to create a child. The results lead to new questions. Here's one: are children born of their dead father's frozen sperm entitled to collect Social Security survivor benefits?

Karen Capato gave birth to twins eighteen months after her husband, Robert, died. Karen applied for survivor benefits for the twins, and when they were denied, she took her fight up to the U.S. Supreme Court.

A sympathetic Justice Ruth Bader Ginsburg wrote for the unanimous Court, finding that the federal law determining Social Security benefits looked to state inheritance laws. In Florida, where the Capatos lived, children could inherit property from their parent only if they were conceived while that parent was alive. While their claim might have been successful in other states, it was a loser in the Sunshine State.

FOR MORE INFORMATION

The American Academy of Assisted Reproductive Technology Attorneys, aaarta.org, provides attorney referrals for women undergoing ART.

Creative Family Connections is a Washington, D.C.–based law firm and surrogacy matching agency; its website offers a fifty-state survey of surrogacy laws and a host of other information: creativefamilyconnections.com.

For same-sex couples who are planning a family, the Human Rights Campaign, hrc.org, offers resources that include a state-by-state analysis of relevant parenting laws.

17

ADOPTION

OPENING STATEMENT

If you are considering adoption, good for you. Adoption is a beautiful, generous gesture—like a multigenerational wedding ceremony that brings people together to create a new family, but with much better odds than a conventional marriage.

Once shrouded in secrecy and permitted only for straight married couples and children born within our national borders, adoptions have changed dramatically in recent years, and for the better. Today, single parents and gay couples can adopt. And adoptions are often open, either by design or because details have been uncovered by children with curiosity about their roots and access to the Internet. Impressively, given our stubbornly sclerotic legislative branch, Congress has passed a host of laws, including the Adoption Assistance and Child

Welfare Act of 1980, the Multiethnic Placement Act of 1994, and the Fostering Connections to Success and Increasing Adoptions Act of 2008, to encourage adoption and help at-risk children find permanent homes.

Despite all this evolutionary growth, the act of adoption still raises important legal and emotional issues. When birth (or adoptive) parents change their minds, for example, the results can be wrenching. And abrupt changes in international relations have slammed the brakes on some would-be adoptive parents on the verge of bringing their children home.

So let's see how you might take advantage of the law and welcome a new member of your family with maximum joy and minimum stress.

IT'S THE LAW

Adoption law has complicated, state-specific elements, and you will almost certainly need a locally savvy lawyer to help with the process.

For starters, states may regulate who can adopt. Some states set a minimum age of eighteen (sometimes even older); a handful require a ten-year age gap between the adoptive parent and the adoptee. A private adoption agency may impose other restrictions.

If you are considering an adoption, you essentially have four options. In a public adoption, you'll work with a government agency placing a child who is in state custody because of abuse, neglect, or dependency issues. A private adoption is conducted by a state-licensed agency that represents children whose birth parents turned over custody to the agency. In an independent adoption, a lawyer brokers the adoption between the birth parents and the adoptive parents while the birth parents maintain custody, and in an intercountry adoption, prospective parents work with a private agency or attorney. Of course, sometimes adoptions take place within a family, if the death of parents prompts aunts, uncles, or even grandparents to adopt younger relatives; stepparents may adopt if a birth parent is absent or deceased.

However you choose to adopt, would-be adoptive parents participate in a home study, which can take three to six months. The study is meant to make sure the adopting family is both appropriate and prepared to welcome a new member of the family. The agency conducting the study will seek information that can include the following:

- Health records
- Financial statements
- Personal statement
- Character references
- Criminal background checks (this has been known to unearth information spouses didn't know about each other before the adoption)

The goal isn't to find a "perfect" family or to make sure adopting parents are superhuman millionaires, but to ensure that a child will enter a stable home.

No matter which method you choose, your journey to parenthood will end up in court, where your adoption will be finalized and made legal through an adoption decree. A judge will hold a hearing, speaking to the would-be parents, the child (if he or she is old enough to understand), the family's lawyer, and a social worker. If all goes well, the court will issue an adoption decree (or certificate) and the child will receive an amended birth certificate.

A financial note: Obviously, it's costly to raise a child, and adoption requires additional spending even before you bring your child home. To encourage adoption, the federal government offers a tax credit that offsets some of its cost (up to $12,970 in 2013) including court costs, attorney fees, and travel. Parents who adopt a special needs child can qualify for the full tax benefit even if their adoption costs less.

SINGLE-PARENT AND LGBT COUPLE ADOPTIONS

As we just learned, state law controls who can adopt, and in general those regulations have become more permissive. Just look at single-parent adoptions. They've exploded, with one study showing that they made up 12 to 25 percent of adoptions nationwide by 1995, compared to only 2.5 to 5 percent of adoptions until 1990. Just fifty years ago—a split second if you follow legal time, which moves in slo-mo—singletons couldn't adopt; the Child Welfare League of America harrumphed, back in 1958, that adoptive families should include a mother and a father. The League revised its standards a decade later, concluding that single parents could adopt in "exceptional circumstances" when a child might not otherwise find a home.

For lesbian, gay, bisexual, and transgender families who are would-be parents, the law is changing, too. At this writing, almost half the states make it possible for same-sex couples to petition to adopt a child together. Other states don't have specific laws addressing LGBT couples, so a successful adoption will depend on approval from the individual child welfare officials and judge involved.

Adoption can be important to married same-sex couples too. For example, the woman in a lesbian couple who gives birth to their baby has rights as a biological parent. Many lawyers recommend that the other parent pursue a second-parent adoption, similar to a stepparent adopting a partner's child, to gain full legal rights as a parent. (This is allowed in many states; a few have laws barring the practice.)

Even as same-sex marriage laws continue to shift, however, couples can't always count on consistent adoption results. For example, in a surprising ruling in liberal New York, a judge would not allow a married lesbian couple, Amalia and Melissa (their last names were withheld for privacy), to pursue a second-parent adoption after they had a son through artificial insemination. Even though both women's names were on the baby's birth certificate, the couple wanted the adoption because they worried about whether Amalia, the nonbiological mother, could assert her parental rights if the family traveled to states, or countries, that do not recognize same-sex marriage. The judge was unmoved. Even though she had approved similar adoptions before, the judge said she didn't want to grant the adoption and somehow suggest that same-sex marriages were not sufficient to create a parent-child relationship. The couple pondered whether to appeal.

EXHIBIT 33: OPEN ADOPTIONS AND OPEN RECORDS

How much should birth and adoptive families know about each other?

Open adoptions, where birth and adoptive families remain connected, and adoptive children know their origins, may seem modern. But the current trend toward openness actually represents a return to that approach, following an era in which the prevailing wisdom held that less information was better. That trend began in the 1930s, when closed records were thought to provide adoptive parents a better foundation for establishing their new family ties and protected an adopted child from the reputation-scarring assumption that her birth was illegitimate.

Over time, adopted children and birth parents went public about the negative impact of secrecy, and experts began to listen to the demands of adopted children for any information about their roots. By 2012, according to one study, only 5 percent of infant adoptions were confidential. Another 55 percent were open, and 40 percent were mediated, meaning a mediator, who can be a social worker or a lawyer, helped each family communicate indirectly.

While adoptive parents generally have the right to decide who can spend time with their child, lawyers can help birth and adoptive parents agree on a plan together by drawing up a postadoption contract (for adoptions that are not closed) to determine the type and amount of contact a child will have with her birth parents. About half the states will enforce these deals, and specifics can vary: some states limit the agreements to children adopted from foster care, and others allow them only for children aged two and older. The court that approves the adoption also reviews and approves postadoption agreements.

But while open adoption is on the rise, many adoption records remain inaccessible, yet another example of the law dragging, slowly and with a side order of conservatism, behind social trends and powerful arguments for freeing up that family information. For example, for some adopted children, the quest for their original birth certificate could yield not only family ties, but useful genetic information about health issues that run in their birth family.

Perhaps the most radical remnant of a closed adoption era is this: when a child is adopted, she gets a new birth certificate, which lists her adoptive parents as birth parents.

BOSSES OF THE BAR: BASTARD NATION

The members of Bastard Nation want to close the door on closed adoptions. The group, which was launched in 1996 to wage a public battle against sealed adoption records, calls attention to the lingering stigma of adoption and tries to banish it through sunlight. While their goals are serious and remain controversial, the group fights its battles with caustic humor. The group's name, of course, pays sly homage to the concerns that led to closed adoptions. And their tongue-in-cheek Adoptee Products Catalogue features items like silver jewelry to "affirm your position as an adoptee with the metal long known for being second best."

Despite their efforts, only a handful of states allow adult adopted children unrestricted access to their birth records. Other states have created mutual consent registries that unlock birth records only with the permission of a birth parent and the adopted child (plus an adoptive parent if the child is a minor). That is a complicated process that probably yields very few insights for adopted children about their origins.

But in states that have opened the closed door of adoption records even a crack, adoptees have a chance to satisfy their craving for information about their origins. In Illinois, for example, adoption records had been sealed since 1946, until a local legislator (and adoptee), Sara Feigenholtz, sponsored legislation to make birth records available to adult adoptees unless a birth parent asked for anonymity. When birth certificates were unsealed in 2010, thousands of adoptees (8,800 as of August 2013) claimed their unsealed birth certificates.

EXHIBIT 34: TURMOIL ABROAD: THE STATE OF OVERSEAS ADOPTION

Adoption in America suffers from a supply-demand imbalance. Ready access to contraception and a sea change in attitudes about unwed mothers have reduced the number of available infants. Meanwhile, as we've seen, relaxed laws have made more adults qualified to adopt. Factor in the accelerating pace of globalization and it's little wonder that Americans faced with adoptable child shortages have moved their search overseas.

If you adopt a child from another country, you will have to turn the legal equivalent of a triple play: follow your state's law, federal law, and the law of your child's homeland. More than seventy countries, including the United States, have signed on to the Hague Convention on Protection of Children and Cooperation in Respect of Intercountry Adoption, which requires the use of accredited adoption agencies and special parent training, aimed at protecting children and parents.

But the Hague Convention can't force countries to work together. And in recent years, the transfer of children to new American homes has grown increasingly erratic. According to the State Department, the number of foreign adoptions plummeted to 8,688 in 2012 from a high of 22,991 in 2004, a 62 percent drop.

Why? Mostly because of internal politics in some of the countries Americans have considered for adoptions. Countries like China, South Korea, and, most notably, Russia have restricted the once-easy availability of children to potential parents here. Korea, for example, seeks parents who are married and have a body mass index (BMI) of 30 or lower.

On our side of the pond, the State Department halted adoptions from popular countries including Guatemala, Vietnam, and Cambodia, hoping those governments would institute stricter standards.

These changes have had harrowing consequences for parents and children in the middle of the process. A Virginia couple, Joe and Peggy Femenella, met their son, Andrew, in Guatemala in 2007 when he was four months old. Weeks later, the Guatemalan government stopped adoptions. By then, the Femenellas were determined to bring Andrew home, and their commitment led to a five-year ordeal that included multiple court hearings, tens of thousands of dollars in legal fees, and agonizing bureaucratic setbacks, including an incorrectly stapled document that stalled the case for six months.

Their story ended happily with Andrew's successful relocation to Virginia. But when he left Guatemala, another 112 incomplete adoption cases remained open.

Once home, a child adopted from abroad can benefit from a federal law that automatically confers U.S. citizenship when the child is under eighteen, at least one parent is a citizen, and the adoption is final.

FOR MORE INFORMATION

The American Society for Reproductive Medicine offers a thoughtful guide for would-be adoptive parents who are looking for alternatives to infertility therapy: "Adoption: A Guide for Patients," American Society for Reproductive Medicine, asrm.org.

For an attorney: the American Academy of Adoption Attorneys (adoptionattorneys.org) provides a list of members who have been in practice for at least five years and have advised on at least fifty adoptions, as well as a list of adoption agencies.

Human Rights Campaign offers information and guidance about adoptions; its All Children, All Families project encourages child welfare organizations to improve their work with LGBT youth and families: hrc.org.

The Child Welfare Information Gateway (childwelfare.gov) provides state-specific resources and other information about foster care and adoption; it's run by the U.S. Department of Health and Human Services.

Adoption.state.gov is the U.S. Department of State website for information on overseas (or what State calls "intercountry") adoptions.

18

SCHOOL SUPPORT

OPENING STATEMENT

My suburban childhood, while perfectly happy and comfortable, was not what you would call carefree. I was an anxious child with an unhealthy attachment to school. Most kids I knew, even the conscientious ones, welcomed the occasional sick day break from the elementary school grind. I was not one of those kids. When I took ill and my mom, wielding the family thermometer like a magic wand that with a precise number of shakes could make me disappear for several hours, reluctantly concluded that I had to stay home, I would throw a tantrum. When that failed, I would retreat, sick, sullen, and disappointed, to the room I shared with my sister (who was away at school; the injustice!) and endure the unspeakable punishment of Lipton tea, margarine-dabbed toast, and pre-cable TV.

A generation later, my worldly, wised-up New York City offspring would glide through grade and high school and off to college with a sophistication and social poise that far outstripped my own. But, differently from in my mother's day, that all transpired while my sister moms and I adopted a far more engaged role in our children's schooling. The reasons are obvious: in this age of highest-stakes testing, ever-earlier competition for college, and fiercely contested scholastic sports, no conscientious mother feels she can delegate education to her child. We all know parents (or can admit to being the type of parent) who leave nothing to chance when it comes to their kids. Can the law aid this quest, and also offer appropriate limits on a parent's influence in school?

Pull up that charming little chair with the bolted-on half table attachment and the permanent scars from generations of Bic pen gougers. It's time to learn about school-related law.

IT'S THE LAW

You don't need to have school-age children to be aware of the No Child Left Behind Act of 2001. The current version of a Great Society program enacted in 1965, No Child Left Behind has attained legislative near immortality as the federal law that requires public schools to administer annual standardized tests that measure whether students have achieved proficiency in math and reading. (Less famously, the law also addresses school safety, teacher standards, and school choice.) The fact that the U.S. Department of Education website offers a video called "Teacher's Guide to Fixing NCLB" shows that no matter how well intentioned, education policy is always a work in progress and subject to endless adjustments.

We could review a lot of statutes, notification requirements, guidelines, and booklets pertaining to education law. It's a growing field, and lawsuits are multiplying like blotches on a preteen's complexion. But numbers and results aside, the focus of this chapter is the well-being of your child. How can the law help you intervene when appropriate and make sure the system is working?

EXHIBIT 35: GRADES

Life is unfair. Grades shouldn't be. If your child puts in the time, raises her hand, submits appropriate homework, and otherwise makes the case that (as you already recognize and broadcast whenever possible) she is way above average, her grades should reflect that reality. If she fails to measure up to her teacher's expectations, her grades should reflect that setback, too.

But what if a student's grade reflects her professor's assessment, and the student disagrees? Can a court help?

C'mon. Or, as John McEnroe might say: you can't be serious.

Sure, if you search hard enough—or perhaps surf the web for a few idle minutes—you might find a lawyer who will agree to litigate a grade dispute. But here's a prediction: the judge will want nothing to do with your child's report card. Chances are, your judge was once a student, and since she was probably a really good student (or law school would not have been an option), she believes that teachers should have the prerogative to grade according to their own assessment of a student's performance.

If your child has grade or other school issues and you are tempted to race in, rhetorical guns (or hired guns) ablaze, stop. Breathe. Listen to this advice from the American Academy of Pediatrics. I know, they are not lawyers. But they have an even better vantage point than attorneys for advising on school issues. Start by remembering that you may lack full context about why your student received her grade. Seek details from the teacher. Did your student complete her assignments as directed? What is she doing in class?

If speaking to the teacher doesn't satisfy, move up the ladder and engage the principal. At every step, listen, and when you speak, push the conversation toward the fact-based and dispassionate as much as possible. Take notes. Follow up. Good lawyers know that so many disputes are best settled without recourse to formal legal proceedings.

EXHIBIT 36: STUDENT SPEECH

The teenage years are rich with rebellion and the first stirrings of maturity. So where better to assert your nascent independence than . . . inside your school?

It should be no surprise (actually, I'm pleased) that students are constantly testing the boundaries of school authority—after all, why should parents be the only adults subjected to their sarcasm and tentative attempts at wit?

As a result, sometimes courts are asked to try to balance the free expression rights of students against the need to keep order in our nation's fractious school hallways, within the pages of its student newspapers, and most particularly inside its ominous restrooms.

If your student is a shrinking violet, you may never need to worry about student free speech (unless she is quietly communicating online; we'll get to that shortly). But if your student seems destined for her own cable news shoutfest, you both should familiarize yourselves with robust information the American Civil Liberties Union (ACLU) provides in its role as champion of free speech. (As a side note, private schools may have more leeway to enforce speech restrictions than public schools.)

Here's a brief guide to whether your student can speak up or should pipe down:

- *Can students express unpopular opinions at school?* Yes, thanks to a Supreme Court decision that upheld the rights of students who wore black armbands to protest the Vietnam War. It's okay as long as the speech does not "materially and substantially disrupt the work and discipline of the school."

◆ *What about vulgarity?* Sorry, foul-mouthed freshmen: the Supreme Court has held that schools can ban vulgar or innuendo-laden speech.

◆ *Can students publish controversial information in the school paper?* Not necessarily. If the paper is school run, administrators can censor speech if they believe it is inappropriate or harmful, though several states have passed student free-expression laws that afford junior journalists more leeway than federal law provides.

◆ *What else is off-limits?* Threats, especially in this anxious era of school violence. For example, a student tried a First Amendment argument to fight his suspension after his school learned he posted online messages about staging a school shooting on the anniversary of the Columbine massacre. But an appeals court upheld the suspension and said the school did the right thing by intervening.

The social media revolution presents a fresh challenge for school administrators. Where should their supervision begin and end? Do students deserve privacy for their online musings, or should schools take an active role in monitoring posts?

Logically, a school can exercise authority over school equipment and email addresses, similar to the rights your employer has to check out your work-related technology use. That means schools can restrict Internet access and limit how school email accounts are used.

Once students leave school, their online freedom expands. That said, schools generally can intervene when students post threats or propose illegal activity. And if school authorities learn of off-campus cyberbullying, they may take action to make sure the bullying isn't taking place on school grounds.

BOSSES OF THE BAR: BRIANNA HAWK AND KAYLA MARTINEZ

We shouldn't expect too much of middle school students. Caught in that awful purgatory between childhood and adolescence, these kids deserve the option of homeschooling so they can quietly make peace with acne and avoid "frenemies"; instead, they get a mandatory three-year sentence inside America's least appealing educational institution. So when two middle school girls can pull themselves away from texting, take a stance in favor of the First Amendment, then power their position all the way up to a federal appeals court, they deserve our attention.

Brianna Hawk and Kayla Martinez were suspended from Easton Area Middle School in Pennsylvania (the name alone screams low-security penitentiary) in 2010 when they wore silicone wristbands they bought with their moms that said, adorably, "i ♥ boobies! (KEEP A BREAST)."

The bracelets were distributed by the Keep A Breast Foundation, which provides them to promote young girls' awareness of breast cancer. Unfortunately, some teachers thought the bracelets would promote a different sort of awareness, acting as a sort of circular permission slip for middle school boys to unleash lewd comments. Not that middle school boys need a rubber bracelet with the word *boobies* to encourage impolite conduct.

In case you are worried that the Easton Area School District was targeting cancer support, you will be reassured to know that their dress code policy also has banned clothing that promotes Hooters and Big Pecker's Bar & Grill.

In any event, the girls challenged their suspension and their case went to court. The first judge found the suspension a violation of the girls' First Amendment rights to free speech.

On appeal, lawyers for the Pennsylvania School Board Association made what lawyers call the "floodgates" argument. That is, if you allow "boobies" bracelets you are opening the proverbial floodgates for much more awful messages. Messages like "I ♥ balls" for testicular cancer, or "I ♥ va-jay-jays" to send a message about HPV.

The majority of the fourteen appeals judges who heard the case sided with the girls, ruling that the bracelets were "not plainly lewd" and conveyed a message about a social issue, so Brianna and Kayla had every right to wear them.

EXHIBIT 37: BULLYING AND CYBERBULLYING

Bullying has been an intrinsic part of school life for many years, if not centuries, and it has taken its place in the spotlight as an especially ugly phenomenon in the digital age.

The impact of traditional torture, like name-calling and physical brutality, is now force multiplied through social media. And every so often, a victim takes her own young life rather than wake up one more morning to another deluge of mean-spirited abuse.

The National Center for Education Statistics recently took on the grim task of totting up the prevalence of bullying among students ages twelve to eighteen. Here's some of what they found:

- 17 percent of students surveyed said they were made fun of by their peers.
- 18 percent were the subject of rumors.

- 8 percent were pushed, shoved, tripped, or spit upon.
- 5 percent were threatened with harm.

If those percentages fail to depress you, this fact might: the Department of Education reports that bullying seems to tail off in the later teenage years; it's the elementary school crowd that may pose the biggest threat. This report showed that 61 percent of elementary and middle school girls, and 60 percent of boys, were bullied once a month or more by being teased, with 22 percent of girls and 33 percent of boys threatened with physical harm.

You might say: there ought to be a law.

Legislators agree. From 1999 to 2010, states passed more than 120 bills to try to reduce bullying in schools. All states ban harassment, which can include bullying and cyberbullying.

All reassuring—but when you look at antibullying sites for advice, you may be surprised at how little they rely on legal action.

The federal government's comprehensive antibullying site, stopbullying.gov, suggests talking to the following people if your child is being bullied: teacher, school counselor, school principal, school superintendent, and state department of education. Lawyers? Not on the list.

If your child is being cyberbullied, MTV offers these tips for teens who want to draw the line against online cruelty:

- *Don't doubt your instinct.* If something posted online or texted/IM'd to you feels wrong or threatening, tell the service provider, site admin, and a friend, parent, or teacher.
- *Secure your info.* Privacy settings are there for a reason. Use them.
- *Protect your identity.* Don't post school/team names, or photos with landmarks, license plate numbers, or your address. People online don't need to know where you live.

- *Don't delete.* Messages, posts, and comments with threatening or hateful content are worth saving—not for nostalgia, but as evidence, should you need it.
- *Shed your skin.* If reporting harassment doesn't stop it, consider a fresh start with a new online ID/email address. What's in a username, anyway?
- *Be sincere.* If you wouldn't say it face-to-face, don't say it online.
- *Be Zen.* It's no fun harassing you online if you don't respond. So . . . don't respond. It will only make it worse.

You may be wondering: why isn't legal action more prominent in these tip lists? Because employing the law to stop bullying is more challenging than you might realize.

For starters, if your child is bullied and you want to take legal action, who is your target?

Is it the bullying students? A fourteen-year-old middle schooler tried suing two classmates for libel when they created a phony, malicious Facebook page about her.

The bully's parents? A Wisconsin town made national news when its local council passed a law holding parents responsible, with a $114 fine, if they failed to respond to law enforcement warnings about their child's bullying.

Or do you harness the law to go after the school? Not necessarily.

For one thing, in many states, schools and school officials may have special protection, as government actors, from litigation.

And even if law enforcement can help, you may still want to refrain. Emily Bazelon, an author whose examination of bullying is thorough, nuanced, and empathetic, points out that once you get law enforcement involved, authorities may respond with a harsher, more heavy-handed response than the behavior might warrant.

For a real-world example of law's limits, meet the parents who sued their Pennsylvania school district after bullying that had become so bad they'd had to pull their two daughters from school. Specifically, they told the court, a schoolmate of the girls had attacked one daughter through phone messages, via MySpace, in the lunchroom, and notably (after the bully was already charged by local authorities with simple assault, terroristic threats, and harassment) in a stairwell, when she lashed out with a string of nasty insults.

The bullying student was placed on probation and ordered not to contact her victim. She disregarded the court order and elbowed the girl in the throat at a school sporting event. Later, according to court documents, a friend of the bully hit the girl's sister—at which point the parents had had enough. When they met with school officials, the parents were told that the school could not guarantee their daughters' safety.

Did the suffering parents have a case when they claimed that the state had a constitutional duty (there is no federal antibullying law) to keep their daughters safe from their attacker?

No. The court expressed sympathy, but held that the U.S. Constitution doesn't protect students from bullies, and that states are better situated to respond.

What about state law? Pennsylvania law required schools to set up an antibullying policy, but on closer inspection it offered no legal remedies for the bullied.

So if your child is bullied, even if you want to sue, courts will not necessarily step in to help stop the suffering.

Here's a big exception: if your child is harassed because of her race, color, national origin, sex, disability, or religion, the bullying may be a violation of federal civil rights law and litigation might yield results.

In one prominent example, a Minneapolis school district reached a settlement with six students who sued after they were bullied about their real or perceived sexual orientation. One of the students, who said he was harassed because he has two fathers and is a gymnast, was stabbed in the neck with a pencil and choked in a school bathroom.

Another student, a middle school lesbian, said that after a friend committed suicide other students asked, "Why don't you kill yourself too?" In the space of just under two years, four students, either gay or perceived to be gay by classmates, had killed themselves; all four were reportedly bullied.

The school district agreed to training, monitoring, and a $270,000 payment to the students, and the U.S. Department of Justice planned to track compliance until 2017.

EXHIBIT 38: SPORTS AND TITLE IX

As a mother, you quickly learn the cardinal rule that you must love all your children equally. As a mother who is also a lawyer, I know I should adopt the same approach to law. After all, there are so many laws to embrace. Laws that prohibit violent crime. Laws that protect the civil rights of the underprivileged. Laws that dictate that your lip liner should never be two shades darker than your lipstick.

But of all the laws on all those books, one occupies a special place in my heart.

It is Title IX, and this is what it says:

> *No person in the United States shall, on the basis of sex, be excluded from participation in, be denied the benefits of, or be subjected to discrimination under any education program or activity receiving Federal financial assistance.*

Signed by President Nixon in 1972 (which alone should improve his reputation, just a little), Title IX is a pathbreaking civil rights law aimed directly at education. Though most people think its reach is limited to athletics, the law covers much broader territory. For example, Title IX bars discrimination against students who are pregnant, and requires schools to address sexual harassment, a topic we'll address later in chapter 21.

WHAT CAN TITLE IX DO FOR YOU?

The National Women's Law Center outlines some of the ways Title IX can step in and protect women and girls in education, whether they are students or staff, by requiring that schools:

- Offer male and female students equal opportunities to play sports
- Treat male and female athletes fairly
- Give male and female athletes their fair share of athletic scholarship money

Schools also must protect students from the following:

- Insults, name-calling, and offensive jokes based on sex
- Intimidation by words or actions
- Unwelcome or inappropriate sexual touching
- Pressure for sexual activity or dating
- Sexual assault and rape

While there's little question that Title IX has had its most visible impact on student athletes, advocates for women's equality (and if you are reading this book, I presume you are one of us) note that we have a way to go to live up to Title IX's promise. The law requires that athletic opportunities be available to girls in proportion to their numbers on campus, but the Women's Sports Foundation found that while women made up 56 percent of college students in 2012, they accounted for only 43 percent of student athletes.

Is the battle for Title IX–supported equality worth the effort? I can't resist sharing just one supporting statistic. A survey conducted by EY (formerly Ernst & Young) of more than eight hundred senior managers and executives found that 96 percent of the women in their sample who held board-level positions had played sports in school.

Here's a quick list to make sure your sporty daughter is benefiting from the full protection of Title IX:

- She should have practice facilities, equipment, coaching, and support similar to what boys enjoy.
- Boys' teams should not always receive better time slots for their games.
- Girls' teams should have cheerleaders. Again, treatment need not be identical, but it has to be similar.

If you suspect your daughter's school is violating Title IX, identify your school's designated Title IX officer—every school should have one. Tell her about the situation and see if you can address it with your school. If not, you could try to escalate the issue, first through your school's procedures, then through a complaint to the federal Office of Civil Rights. If all else fails, you can file a lawsuit. Courts can provide needed muscle to correct inequality. For example, under legal pressure, Quinnipiac University backed away from its plan to dismantle its women's volleyball team and replace it with competitive cheerleading (no snickering; it's a sport). In a settlement, the school agreed to keep the team, beef up women's sports scholarships, and improve facilities for women athletes.

EXHIBIT 39: THAT'S ALL WELL AND GOOD, BUT MY DAUGHTER WAS BENCHED

Title IX–backed battles against institutional bias are one thing, but trying to reverse individual athletic assessments is something else entirely. Just like court fights over grades, enlisting a judge to get your child on a team is a steep uphill battle. Sure, judges are sort of referees, but that doesn't mean a judge will be eager to settle your particular issue with school sports. If you are unhappy about a coach's selection, and it doesn't involve actionable harassment or bias, take it up with your school and save the money you would have spent on lawyers. Or encourage your child to take up another activity, and remind her that failing to achieve one goal can open up the road to another.

FOR MORE INFORMATION

The Student Press Law Center is a nonprofit that works to protect freedom of the press for student journalists, offering budding investigators the tools to obtain public records and fight back against impermissible censorship. Its reports on nationwide battles between school administrators and students are entertaining, and its FERPA Fact Tumblr blog at splc.org is enlightening.

For advice aimed at girls aged ten to sixteen, girlshealth.gov is run by the Office of Women's Health, a part of the U.S. Department of Health and Human Services.

The School Law blog on the Education Week website (blogs .edweek.org) is a comprehensive and readable guide to all things education-law related.

Emily Bazelon's book *Sticks and Stones* (Random House, 2013) is a thoroughly researched and readable guide to the issue, and the companion website, emilybazelon.com, offers updates and resources.

On Title IX, titleix.info is run by the National Women's Law Center and features profiles, history, and resources about this path-breaking law.

For general advice about raising kids and teens, the Nemours Center for Children's Heath Media offers kidshealth.org, which has sections aimed directly at parents, kids, and teens.

19

ADVOCATING FOR A
SPECIAL NEEDS CHILD

OPENING STATEMENT

As we just learned in chapter 18, there's no shortage of laws that can be unleashed to protect your student. But with any luck, you will sail through the school-age years without needing to lawyer up. (Adolescence will pose its own challenges, and we will talk about those in chapter 20.)

If you are the parent of a special needs child, however, you don't get a pass. No matter what path you pursue—using public resources to pay for your child's care, your own resources, or a mix of the two—you will need to develop a near mastery of the body of law designed to help you and your child.

When I spoke with one very dear friend, the mother of a beautiful special needs girl, about this topic, she offered to help with a show-and-tell session. What did I see? File cabinets brimming with folders, and folders filled, in turn, with tidy, labeled files. What did those files contain? Every scrap of paper relevant to her daughter's care. Every letter attached to the postmarked envelope that delivered the letter to her home. Every fax annotated with information to prove it had been received, and who received it. Every telephone conversation memorialized in an email, printed, and saved. Every receipt carefully curated to serve as evidence.

My friend amassed this paper arsenal to ensure that her daughter receives the full complement of support she is guaranteed under federal and state law. And the lesson my friend asked me to share with you is this: there's help out there, but you will have to advocate relentlessly for your child to receive the best of it, both because your child cannot help herself and because you need to be prepared when authorities challenge the scope of help you seek.

So, with a virtual hug to my amazing friend, and to any of you reading this while shouldering a similar responsibility, let's take a look at the particulars.

IT'S THE LAW

Soon after parents learn that their child has special needs, they learn about a hopeful four-letter acronym, IDEA, and a three-digit number, 504.

The Individuals with Disabilities Education Act requires public schools to provide eligible disabled children a free and appropriate public education, with an emphasis on keeping those children in regular classrooms when possible. (Four of those words, *free appropriate public education*, earned their own acronym, FAPE, and are the subject of considerable negotiation between parents and school authorities.)

Through IDEA, schools collect federal funds to provide services, including an IEP, or Individualized Education Program, for each qualifying student.

The three-digit number, 504, stands for Section 504 of the Rehabilitation Act, a civil rights bill that prohibits discrimination on the basis of disability by any program that receives federal aid. It has a wider reach than IDEA, including private schools and colleges that receive federal funds, and it defines disabilities more broadly than IDEA. For those reasons, it's worth a closer look at how Section 504 might help your student. The National Center for Learning Disabilities identifies five key points about the law:

1. The 504 plan protects students who have a disability that substantially limits one or more major life activity. Those activities can include learning, reading, thinking, writing, or concentrating.
2. The 504 plan outlines educational services to be provided to the student. The plan does not have to be an IEP but it does have to be documented.
3. There is no standard 504 plan—every student has different needs and should receive a specifically tailored plan. Accommodations can include computer technology, extended time or privacy for taking tests, verbal or nonverbal cues, and note takers.
4. A 504 plan may be a good option for your child if your child is ineligible for services under IDEA. Students with a learning disability or attention disorders may not meet requirements for IDEA intervention, but if their disability "substantially limits them in performing one or more major life activity," they may qualify for 504 aid.
5. A 504 plan is a good way to formalize accommodations if your child is already receiving them on an informal basis. Your stu-

dent may be receiving help, but 504 lets you more firmly secure the promise of help from your school.

If a student has physical or emotional challenges that make it hard for her to function in class, Section 504 requires that a school accommodate those issues. If a student has trouble seeing in class, she may be entitled to a better seat. If she can't concentrate, she may be able to get more time to finish homework.

In short, if your child has a disability, you can ask her school to set up a 504 plan whether or not she qualifies for an IEP. The school will convene a team to assess your child and decide if she qualifies for 504 assistance. (If you disagree with their conclusion or with the offer of help, you can appeal that decision to the school district, and then the federal Office of Civil Rights.)

EXHIBIT 40: INSIDE THE IEP

Individualized Education Programs are meant for children who are struggling in school for reasons that can include:

- Learning disabilities
- Attention deficit/hyperactivity disorder
- Emotional disorders
- Cognitive challenges
- Autism
- Hearing, visual, speech, or language impairment
- Developmental delay

The road to an IEP usually begins when a parent, teacher, or doctor observes that a student is struggling, and asks the school to investigate whether the child qualifies for help. If the answer is yes, a school team will make initial suggestions and then meet with the parents to create an IEP.

The content of an IEP is highly regulated, and its goal is ambitious: to draw a map that sets individual learning goals for the child for the school year, and lists resources the school district will provide to help the student achieve those goals. The specifics will vary by state, but will generally include the following:

- An evaluation of the child's current performance, based on tests and performance
- Annual academic, social, or behavioral goals
- Special education services the school will provide
- Whether the child will join nondisabled children in class or activities
- Whether the child will take mandated state and district tests
- How progress will be measured

The IEP team, the student (when appropriate), and the parents meet every year to review the plan, but if a parent sees a need for an immediate adjustment, the team can convene at any time.

Parents of a student with an IEP have rights throughout the process, including, significantly, the right to disagree with the plan a school offers. Speaking up is hard work but can yield results.

Sometimes parents advocate together, publicly, for change. Parents in Broward County, Florida, made news when they confronted members of their school board, calling its special needs methods "toxic" and likening the process to "being in a war zone for our children." (For its part, the school board said only a small group of the parents of nearly 33,000 special needs students in the district were complaining.)

More often, parents take a more private approach. That starts locally, with a hearing or mediation in which a parent challenges a plan. If local authorities won't budge, parents can ultimately challenge IEP issues in federal court. Parents also can go to court to sue a school for failing to identify their child's educational needs. Forceful parent advocacy (aided, if possible, by a lawyer with expertise in special education litigation) can make a big difference in prodding educators to provide a full range of services for a child.

EXHIBIT 41: PLANNING AHEAD

As the thoughtful expression goes, a parent's job is to give her child roots and wings: a foundation of loving support, and then the freedom to pursue a satisfying life as an independent adult.

For parents of special needs children, of course, the latter goal may be impossible. Their children may need a lifetime of support, long after they leave school and even after parents are gone. It's a deeply worrying prospect, but planning may alleviate understandable fears. Specifically, parents, working with a lawyer, can create a special needs estate plan to secure their child's future.

The nonprofit Nemours Foundation, through its thorough and accessible kidshealth.org website, offers these steps for parents who want to plan for their special needs child.

◆ *Create a special needs trust.* It's critically important that parents do not give money directly to their special needs children. That's because your child may not qualify for federal benefits like Medicaid and Supplemental Security Income if she owns more than $2,000 in assets. The trust legally protects money for your child's needs and allows her to benefit from government help.

◆ *Write a will.* A will allows you to direct assets to the special needs trust and not directly to your child. Without a will, your child may inadvertently become a beneficiary and that might disqualify her from receiving government help.

◆ *Name a guardian.* Careful parents choose guardians in case they die before their children become adults. For a special needs child, of course, that obligation may extend well beyond an eighteenth birthday. A guardian will do the important work of caring for your child; make sure your guardian is willing to serve and knows your child (and your preferences about her care).

◆ *Name a trustee.* The trustee, not the guardian, manages the special needs trust after you die, making sure the assets are exclusively spent to care for your child. Because the trustee can authorize spending that the guardian thinks is necessary, it makes sense to assign those tasks to two different people to avoid any conflicts of interest. A trustee can be a friend or relative, a lawyer, or a bank or financial institution; some experts suggest appointing cotrustees, and you also should consider successor trustees in case circumstances change.

◆ *Build your savings.* We looked at your child's rights under federal law, but we know that the government may not provide all the services you know are necessary. They cost money, and so does the help of lawyers or other special needs advocates. Any amount of savings will help—just be sure not to save money in your child's name.

◆ *Educate family members.* Make sure well-intentioned relatives do not put any assets in your child's name, either directly or through a will. Instead, they can name the special needs trust as a beneficiary.

◆ *Write a letter of intent.* This letter is really a detailed plan for your child, listing her daily routine, her caregivers and their contact information, and her medications, if any. Write it, review it regularly, and update it as needed, and share it with your family and the child's guardian.

◆ *Plan for your child's independence.* When your child becomes a teenager, if not earlier, you will be thinking about her life as an adult and will begin to explore what resources you'll need to keep her at home, enroll her in day programs, or help her move toward independent living.

◆ *Apply for guardianship or power of attorney.* Once your child turns eighteen, she is legally an adult. If she cannot make decisions on her own, you may want to become her guardian, which offers you near-complete control, or simply seek power of attorney and a health care proxy.

Need help? Find an adviser. Certified financial planners who specialize in special needs plans can help unpack this complicated process.

BOSSES OF THE BAR: PAMELA WRIGHT AND PETER W. D. WRIGHT

When I began to research this chapter, I wasn't surprised to find ample resources for parents who need the equivalent of an instant J.D. in special education law.

I never expected to find two champions of those laws in quiet Stingray Point, Virginia, along Chesapeake Bay.

That idyllic location, where most families go to unwind, is where Pete Wright and his wife, Pam, run Wrightslaw, their multimedia special education law enterprise (newsletters, DVDs, training programs, seminars, books, and an impressively comprehensive website).

Pete suffered learning disabilities as a child, and in an

inspiring example of how adversity can shape a life, went to law school and specialized in education law, ultimately reaching the U.S. Supreme Court for a victory on behalf of the parents of a special needs girl who enrolled their daughter in private school and were able, with Pete's help, to secure tuition reimbursement from their school district. (Pete picked up a license plate reading 510 US 7—the citation for the case—to mark the win.)

Pete didn't rest on his laurels; since then he and Pam have published and lectured constantly on special education law. As we have seen, while supportive laws are in place, execution is complex; the Wrights seek to help empower adults to provide students with all the aid the law offers.

FOR MORE INFORMATION

For even more detail about the differences between IDEA and Section 504, the National Center for Learning Disabilities (ncld.org) publishes a comprehensive comparison chart.

The Special Needs Alliance (specialneedsalliance.org) is a national nonprofit that focuses on people with disabilities and their families. Its website offers information about special needs planning and a state-specific guide to attorneys who practice in the area; many of them have family members with special needs.

Peter and Pam Wright, featured above, operate wrightslaw.com, an in-depth guide to special education law.

The Council of Parent Attorneys and Advocates (copaa.org) directs parents of special needs children to member lawyers in their state.

The National Parent Teacher Association (pta.org) publishes a

Special Education Toolkit with definitions and step-by-step advice for IEPs and Section 504 plans.

The National Alliance on Mental Illness (nami.org) publishes a Special Needs Estate Planning Guidance System with detailed advice about financial planning for special needs; the Special Needs Alliance maintains a directory of lawyers who can help with financial planning: specialneedsalliance.org.

Disability Scoop (disabilityscoop.com) is a compendium of developmental disability news, compiled by two journalists, one of whom has an adult sibling with autism.

20

YOUR MISBEHAVING TEENS

OPENING STATEMENT

Motherhood. If you're lucky, it's equal parts joy and burden.

Some days you feel like a modern-day Rose Kennedy, confident that you've provided a service to our nation merely by giving birth.

More often, you feel like a warden trying to quell a prison uprising launched in your own living room.

Teenagers play our heartstrings like violin prodigies, and are evolutionarily engineered to push us to the breaking point. How can the law help us manage these maddening people who are located directly on the fault line where innocence meets uneasy early adulthood?

You can find advice about school-related issues in chapter 18. In this chapter, I want to take a dip into a tougher topic: criminal behavior. Specifically, the type of behavior teens—even "good" teens—perpetrate, despite our best efforts to raise law-abiding citizens.

An organization called Global Youth Justice, which helps facilitate peer courts and other programs to address juvenile crime, compiled an eye-opening list of the top twenty-five offenses teens commit when they aren't finishing homework (forget chores) or even video-gaming:

1. Theft/larceny (shoplifting; stealing a bicycle; stealing from backpacks and lockers)
2. Vandalism (tagging and graffiti; drawing on public restroom walls; keying a car and cutting tires)
3. Alcohol offenses (underage purchase or possession of alcohol; underage consumption; providing alcohol to underage persons; possessing an open container in public or a car)
4. Disorderly conduct (fighting in public; cursing at a teacher; flashing, mooning, and indecent exposure)
5. Simple assault or battery (bullying that amounts to assault; child/parent physical disagreements; shoving or pushing)
6. Possession of marijuana (possessing small amounts of marijuana; smoking pot in a public place)
7. Tobacco offenses (illegal purchase of tobacco; chewing or smoking at school; providing or enabling youth to use tobacco)
8. Curfew violations (sneaking out of home after curfew; walking home after curfew; violating a park curfew)
9. School disciplinary offense (disrupting class; food fights and cheating; violating dress code)
10. Traffic violations (speeding or failing to yield; not wearing a seat belt; riding in the back of a pickup truck)
11. Truancy (cutting class; excessive lateness; violating a court order to attend school)
12. Criminal trespass (entering a vacant building; entering land or a home without permission; returning to a store after being banned)

13. Mischief/criminal nuisance (damaging a mailbox; egging or toilet-papering a house; picking flowers in a restricted or private area)

14. Possession of drug paraphernalia (having a pipe in pocket with resin; using drug paraphernalia to ingest a controlled substance; possessing paraphernalia to grow marijuana)

15. Harassment (bullying; making telephone calls without good reason; insulting or taunting another person to provoke a disorderly response)

16. Fraud (writing bad checks; impersonating another person; committing email fraud)

17. Burglary (entering a friend or relative's home to steal something; entering a school building to steal something; entering a home or school and causing damage)

18. False reporting (pulling a fire alarm; making false 911 calls; calling in a bomb threat)

19. Loitering (hanging out with a group in front of a building; smoking in groups on a street corner; being in a park or store after it closes)

20. Possession of stolen property (having a bicycle you know is stolen; receiving stolen goods from a friend; being in the company of someone who is stealing)

21. Possession of a weapon (unlawfully possessing pepper spray; possessing a BB or pellet gun while underage; carrying weapons like metal knuckles or nunchucks)

22. Reckless endangerment (throwing snowballs at cars; hanging on to a moving car; speeding out of a parking lot)

23. Resisting an officer without violence (lying to a police officer, including about one's age; running away from law enforcement; refusing to move when ordered by an officer)

24. Runaways (running away from a noncustodial parent's house; going to another city or state when forbidden by a parent; staying at a friend or family's house without parental permission)

25. Unauthorized use of a motor vehicle (driving without a license; unlawfully using all-terrain vehicles; taking a parent's or friend's car without parental permission)

Unnerving, no? The majority of school-age "perps" on the list were male, though the number of young women making appearances in juvenile courts is rising. (Females accounted for 28 percent of the delinquency caseload in courts with juvenile jurisdiction in 2009—up from 19 percent in 1985.) Nonetheless, the question for mothers is identical, regardless of your child's gender: what do I do if my child has a run-in with the law?

The short answer: call a lawyer. The longer answer: call a lawyer immediately.

Lawyers who specialize in juvenile court cases can make an immediate contribution when your teen is in trouble. If she has been arrested, the lawyer can meet your teen at the police station and make sure she doesn't make any incriminating statements. (Teens have a tendency to want to cooperate; authorities have a tendency to want to capitalize on that inclination.) A lawyer might even speak with a local probation department, a conversation that might persuade authorities to dismiss a case.

Ideally, your lawyer will have experience in defending juveniles. The court process is not the same as the one for adults, with different language (juveniles are charged with "offenses" rather than "crimes") and different outcomes (they receive a "disposition" rather than a "sentence"). Once a case is completed, a lawyer can push to see if a record can be sealed (kept, and available to a select group) or expunged (destroyed); those options will depend on your state's law. Some states do not expunge records for juvenile cases, and if your teen is not convicted you should have no record to expunge.

By the way, if you hire a lawyer, the client is your teen. Not you. The lawyer may ask you to stay out of conversations with your teen, to guarantee that your teen is honest (and to make sure that your teen does not waive the attorney-client privilege that protects the confidentiality of her conversation with counsel).

In light of the possibility that any teen can get in trouble, and the certainty that having a criminal lawyer at the ready can improve that dire situation, I'm going to make a suggestion. My suggestion astonished some of my friends, but others wished they had thought of it themselves.

Ready?

Here's my advice: when your children are preteens, ask around for the name of a good criminal defense lawyer in your neighborhood.

Why?

Because when you get the call, as one girlfriend did, that her (Ivy League college–attending) son had been busted for partying and the police wanted him to take a Breathalyzer test right then and there, she was fortunate enough to have a family friend and criminal defense lawyer who could offer on-the-spot advice. (His advice for that particular situation: decline.)

When teens get together, trouble lurks. And if it strikes, you won't want to be the lone parent scrambling for advice while your teen's friends are covered.

Find that lawyer. Save that number. Maybe you'll never call. But if you need to, you will improve the odds of a better outcome for you and your teen.

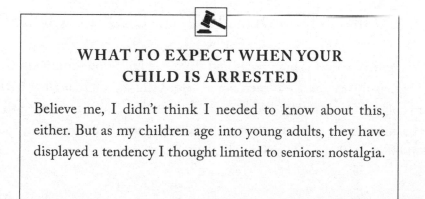

WHAT TO EXPECT WHEN YOUR CHILD IS ARRESTED

Believe me, I didn't think I needed to know about this, either. But as my children age into young adults, they have displayed a tendency I thought limited to seniors: nostalgia.

And their nostalgia has loosened their tongues, and now I hear about very close calls with the cops.

For our purposes, let's assume everyone involved in juvenile arrests is doing his job. The police are trying to keep order, and our kids are trying, but failing, to exercise rudimentary judgment. When the two parties intersect, trouble can ensue and good kids can find themselves under arrest.

Should you panic? Not necessarily. But you should follow the commonsense advice laid out by the Juvenile Law Center, a national public interest law firm headquartered in Philadelphia:

- Do not allow police to speak to your child without you.
- Try to see your child immediately, and when you do make sure she does not speak to police until a lawyer is present.
- If your child has a disability, bring documentation (such as your IEP) to the station.

Want to be even more realistic? Then tell your teen what to do in case she is stopped by police: never run away, lie, or argue; immediately ask for a parent and a lawyer; don't say anything until they arrive; and remain polite.

EXHIBIT 42: ADDICTED TO CLUELESSNESS

My willful naïveté about teens and drug use ended one summer evening, as my ex and I returned home after bringing our daughter back to college. As Amtrak took us south to New York and we enjoyed the passing scenery, an arena alive with pulsating blue light caught my ex's attention. What could that be, he asked?

Because I'm grimly determined to stay abreast of modern music trends, I knew it was Electric Zoo, a wildly popular multiday electronic dance music festival staged on an island just off Manhattan. Our daughter had attended similar events, and I was familiar with the concertgoing drill: skimpy neon clothes, bracelets galore, big sunglasses, water bottle at the ready, occasional texts from the venue to placate Mom.

Seemed safe to me at the time. Not for long. One day later, Electric Zoo made headlines. The festival ended a day early, canceled because two concertgoers had died after taking MDMA, aka ecstasy or "Molly," the drug widely known to be the stimulant of choice for dance music fans.

The concertgoers who died were only twenty-three and twenty years old, smiling in family photos and surely excited to catch up with their favorite DJs in a fun summer setting. Surely neither grieving family imagined their child would never make it home.

Do you know enough about drugs to be an effective parent and keep your teen out of legal (and medical) trouble? I didn't, but it's a simple matter to learn.

Our government and a host of advocacy groups publish incredibly useful information about warning signs, household dangers, and even secret decoders that help you understand the furtive texts teens use to hide information from you. (I imagine you've heard "MOS": Mom Over Shoulder? But what about "420" for marijuana?)

Where to begin? Let's start with your medicine cabinet. As many as one in five teenagers has taken a prescription drug that wasn't prescribed for her. You might be focused on the harm of illegal drugs, but these legal medications also pose serious risks for your teens, whether through overdosing or developing an addictive dependence. Think about it from a curious teen's perspective: these drugs are free, powerful, and immediately available, either from you or from their friends.

The Partnership for Drug-Free Kids (drugfree.org) offers a three-step plan for keeping teens from misusing prescription drugs. Here's a summary:

> *Step 1: Monitor.* If you have pills at home, would you know if any were missing? Count your pills, keep track of refills, and do the same for any medication your teen and other family members take.
>
> *Step 2: Secure.* A majority of kids ages twelve to seventeen who have abused pain relievers got them from usually unwitting friends or relatives. Remove your prescription drugs from your medicine cabinet and hide them. Ideally, lock them up.
>
> *Step 3: Dispose.* Take inventory and throw away any expired or unused prescription drugs when your teen is not home. Since some teens will retrieve drugs from the trash, mix them with something discouraging, like kitty litter or coffee grounds. Then dispose of the garbage (but do not flush meds down the drain or toilet).

TALKING TO TEENS ABOUT DRUGS

Everyone knows you should talk to your children about drugs. Easy to say, hard to do. The Drug Enforcement Administration's site, getsmartaboutdrugs.com, offers this advice about talking to your child or teen if you think she is using drugs:

- Be sure your child is sober or has not been using drugs before talking.
- Begin by voicing your suspicions without making accusations. "Susan, I suspect you may be smoking pot occa-

sionally. I love you and I'm concerned about you. Is there something going on that we need to talk about?"

- Be specific about what you have observed that made you concerned. For example, you found missing pills or an empty pill bottle. Or your child's appearance indicates a problem.
- Be prepared emotionally for possible reactions. Your child may accuse you of snooping or say you're crazy. Stay calm.
- If your child denies there is a problem, reinforce what you believe about drugs and how much you care for your child.
- If your child flatly refuses to talk to you about it, get help from the school counselor, school nurse, or family physician.

You surely don't need me to tell you that the legal consequences of drug use can be serious. But beyond the obvious (potential jail time, a criminal record that can make it hard to get a job, possible suspension of a driver's license), students who receive federal financial aid might find it suspended if they are convicted of a drug offense while receiving grants, loans, or work-study wages. And that's just federal law; states and localities also have laws to combat drugs.

Meanwhile, something new for mothers to contemplate: changes in marijuana law. As I write, Colorado and Washington State have legalized marijuana for recreational use, and the Denver City Council even voted to decriminalize possession of an ounce of marijuana or less for stoners between the ages of eighteen and twenty-one. Consequences in other states vary. But possession of pot is still a federal crime, and even the states that legalize marijuana for adults are expected to bar distribution to minors.

EXHIBIT 43: ON ALCOHOL: WHO'S RESPONSIBLE WHEN TEENS DRINK?

This is a book for women, so perhaps you've been wondering: where are the recipes? Fair enough. Here's one:

PARENT-TEEN PARTY DISASTER MIX

INGREDIENTS:

One (1) teen of your own making

Many additional teens: a blend of teens you know, teens you thought you knew to be models of sobriety, teens you vaguely remember from middle school, and teens you've never seen before

Your alcohol cabinet

INSTRUCTIONS:

Deliver from the top of the basement stairs in a reasonable voice: "People, this is the honor system, and I'm depending on you to behave. You heard me, right?"

Stir ingredients, retreat to your grown-up space, try—and fail—to overhear evidence of wrongdoing, then fall asleep.

Possible yield: A phone call with awful news; a lawsuit; maybe even criminal charges.

Your teen can be a football star or a star member of the debate team (which was the inexact substitute for the nonexistent football team at my children's geeky high school) and it won't change this fundamental truth: she will attend parties where the booze flows. And if the party is at your home, even if you forbid alcohol (and we'll discuss parent-permitted booze in a minute), some conniving guest will make sure it flows anyway, and perhaps (if he's really suave) without your knowing.

Does that absolve you of legal responsibility for what follows?

Uh, no.

First of all, a reminder: fake IDs notwithstanding—and every teen I know seems to have one—the legal drinking age in the United States is twenty-one. I am confident it won't change anytime soon.

Maybe that seems draconian to you, and you want to allow your teens the chance to drink in a safer setting than their usual impromptu watering holes. Can you get away with it?

According to the National Institutes of Health, more than half the states have social host laws that hold host parents responsible, sometimes criminally, when underage guests drink in their home, sometimes even if the parents didn't supply booze or know kids were guzzling it, and even if no one gets hurt.

Several other states have laws that hold host parents responsible only if someone is harmed as a result of underage drinking in their home. But if you know anything about teenagers, you know that no good can come of a drunken teen with the potential to cause harm, so these restrictions should do little to allay your concerns if you live in one of those states.

These laws are sound public policy. They recognize that teens are idiots who may not know enough—clearly do not know enough—to avoid getting dangerously drunk. So the law looks to adults, who know or should know that teen drinking is a mistake.

I deserve to be held accountable for what goes on in my home, and so do you. If you can't stop your teens from surreptitious drinking, for heaven's sake don't encourage them to drink with friends at your home.

Don't believe me? That's okay; here's a cautionary tale about Bill

Burnett, the Stanford University professor and dad who was arrested the night following Thanksgiving, after his seventeen-year-old son hosted a party at his home and teens drank—even though Bill and his wife forbade them to drink. Bill spent a night in jail. His potential crime? Contributing to the delinquency of a minor. After a six-month investigation (six months!), the local district attorney dropped all charges, unable to find evidence that the Burnetts supplied booze or that the partying teens misbehaved. But it was surely a difficult and highly unpleasant ordeal for this upstanding father.

You may ask why authorities would browbeat a professor at one of the country's most prestigious universities about a teen party. Because when it comes to teens and drinking, authorities want to send a powerful message to everyone in sight: teens are not legally allowed to drink, and when they do, bad things can happen.

The search for defendants when teens drink sometimes extends beyond parents and back into their cohorts. Authorities in Connecticut tried charging two teen boys with reckless endangerment when they didn't stop their seventeen-year-old friend from driving drunk; she plowed her car into a tree and later died. The charges were uniformly recognized by local lawyers as difficult to prove in court; no matter, the decision gave the police a platform to remind the community to take responsibility for teen drinking.

Meanwhile, back to you, the parent. Are you still wavering about whether you should allow teens to drink in your home?

The Partnership for Drug-Free Kids (formerly the Partnership for a Drug-Free America) and the Treatment Research Institute make a powerful case for forbidding alcohol through an interactive website, drugfree.org, which includes a state-by-state guide to your liability for hosting alcohol-fueled gatherings.

If you need one more reason to refrain from rolling out the bar cart, consider this: your homeowners' policy may not cover your liability if something happens after teens drink at your home. Even if your insurer finally decides to provide coverage, it's the definition of a Pyrrhic victory, as it must have seemed to a New Jersey mother whose daughter hosted a nineteenth-birthday party at their home. An eighteen-year-old guest left and had a car accident. The mom's insurance company balked at a payment, but a judge ordered the insurer to cover her $1.5 million settlement with the teen. Why Pyrrhic? Because the teen is paralyzed below the waist, has limited use of his arms, and needs a wheelchair. He left the house party with a blood-alcohol reading of .205, more than two and a half times the legal limit in the state. The legal case may be over, but repercussions from that party, and that teen drinking, will last for a very long time.

When teens drink in your home, nobody wins.

As an aside, it can be ill-advised to permit your teen to drink on a school trip, especially if you like her teacher. New York private high school teacher Daniele Benatouil collected permission slips from the parents of each of the seniors she took on a field trip to France in 2010, allowing the traveling teens a glass of wine during dinner. That Gallic plan, however civilized, galled the school, since it collided with its "zero tolerance" policy toward drug, alcohol, and cigarette use, and the teacher lost her job. A judge upheld the school's decision to let her go, and at last report Benatouil was considering an appeal.

CELEBRITY LAW LESSON: THE LEGAL LEGACY OF JUSTIN BIEBER

Justin who?

I fear you may be racking your brain to remember anything (certainly, anything positive) about this once-young, once-problem-free teen idol. The half-lives of most pop stars are fleeting, so in case you need a reminder, Justin Bieber is the YouTube-discovered, pompadour-rocking crooner who amassed millions of fans; perhaps the first social-media-spawned megastar.

While Justin's cultural legacy may wane, he surely deserves longevity in the annals of Young Adults Behaving Badly. Bieber's legal escapades could fill a law school class, if law school somehow became a fun and culturally relevant pursuit.

A brief review of the Biebs's Anthology of Appalling Behavior necessarily includes these head-shaking highlights:

- Acquiring Mally, a capuchin monkey, while in Germany, then leaving Mally behind. German authorities billed Justin more than 11,000 euros for Mally's care; Mally (presumably relieved) was relocated to a German zoo.
- Egging the home of his next-door neighbor, which prompted the Los Angeles district attorney's office to consider felony vandalism charges and led to a plea deal; Justin agreed to pay $80,900 in restitution and remain on probation for two years while attending anger management sessions.
- Driving his yellow Lamborghini in Florida, leading to his arrest for allegedly driving drunk and drag racing. At 4:19 A.M. Later, police documents indicated Justin was under the influence of pot, alcohol, and Xanax while driving.
- Perhaps to satisfy a growing curiosity about international law as it relates to unhinged celebrities, turning himself in to Toronto authorities, who charged him in the assault of a limousine driver after a hockey game. The charges were later dropped.

The pièce de résistance of Justin's legal history (at least at the time of this writing; he may yet top himself) is a widely circulated set of video clips culled from a 2014 deposition Justin gave in Miami in connection with a paparazzo's allegation that he was attacked by a Bieber bodyguard. While lawyers for Justin and the photographer spar in the slow-paced, obnoxious, and seemingly pointless manner all too familiar to anyone who has either taken or been subjected to a deposition, the star outdoes himself, slumping, responding with full-on hostility, rolling his eyes, and at one point winking at the camera (surprisingly adorable, but still). Under oath, Justin, perhaps misunderstanding a question about whether Usher was "instrumental" to his career, testifies, "I think I was detrimental to my own career." At least he wasn't perjuring himself.

EXHIBIT 44: TICKETED TEENS

Has your teen brought home a traffic ticket? Does the sun rise in the morning? Across the spectrum of potential legal catastrophes your teen might bring home and drop at your feet, like a guilty dog surrendering a dirty stick, a ticket can seem like the least of your problems. But before you pull out the checkbook and make a contribution to your municipality for indulging your new driver, stop and consider whether to retain counsel to fight the charge.

If your teen is ticketed, she can face adult consequences, including fines, a suspension of her driving privileges, and points, not to mention an increase in the insurance premiums you pay. Admitting guilt, no matter how minor it may seem, could yield problems down the road, should a victim emerge seeking damages for that forgettable fender bender.

There's no guarantee a lawyer can reverse the damage, but traffic lawyers (yes, this is a specialty) insist they can improve your chances of a dismissal of charges or perhaps a plea deal that reduces fines or eliminates points. At the very least, it's worth a call to a traffic lawyer before you pay a ticket—unless you want your teen driver to pay the fine and suffer the penalties as a costly teachable moment.

EXHIBIT 45: TEXTING AND SEXTING

We can argue about the benefits and costs that mobile phones bring to modern life. Actually, you can argue among yourselves; I love my smartphone. But indisputably, the mobile phone has ushered in an unprecedented era of teenage legal liability.

Let's start with cars. All the news about texting and driving is bad. How bad? So bad that cell phone service providers asked noted film director Werner Herzog to make a documentary about the perils of driving while using phones. (It's called *From One Second to the Next*, it's available online, and it will break your heart.) So bad that a study published by the *New England Journal of Medicine* found that teens who reached for a cell phone while driving increased their risk of a crash by more than 700 percent.

Does parental intervention, in the form of hypocritical nagging, help? No. An AT&T study reported that according to 77 percent of teens, adults tell kids not to text while driving, but adults do it "all the time."

Is texting while driving illegal? As of this writing, it's against the law in almost every state, with a few states banning it specifically for novice drivers.

Law enforcement, including judges, are understandably frustrated about the recurrence of text-induced accidents. In response, a New Jersey appeals court made a novel suggestion in a case involving texting teens.

When Linda and David Kubert were injured in an accident involving an eighteen-year-old texting driver (each lost part of a leg in the crash), they predictably sued the driver, Kyle Best. Then, a surprise: they also sought recovery from Kyle's friend Shannon Colonna, a seventeen-year-old who had sent Kyle a text while he was driving.

Was Shannon liable for the accident?

The New Jersey judges said no, because it wasn't clear that Shannon knew Kyle was driving when she sent the text. But a majority of those judges ruled that a texter who knows her friend is driving—even if the texter isn't in the car with his driving friend—has a legal responsibility to refrain from texting to keep that driver safe.

With a heavy heart, we turn now to texting's raunchy cousin, sexting (its heinous cousin, cyberbullying, can be found in chapter 18).

Sexting is the act of forwarding nude, sexually suggestive, or explicit photos on your phone or online. It's the dreadful offspring of the marriage of peer pressure, which has existed since the dawn of time, and up-to-the-minute technology.

At least twenty states have laws addressing youth sexting; other states have tried to criminalize this conduct. Even if your state doesn't have a sexting law, it is likely that sending images of a naked teen by phone violates state or federal laws that make it illegal to own or share child pornography—even if a teen sends a photo of herself. And no, the court will not be particularly interested in arguments about whether the poses are artistic, or the by-product of immature thinking. A note to your teens: apps that claim to share photos temporarily and then make them disappear can be thwarted by a screenshot of the incriminating pose. Assume everything lasts forever.

Sexting prosecution may seem appropriate, at least to deter teens from cruel sharing of intimate photos. But the decision to hold teens responsible for sexts, however well meaning, can run into constitutional roadblocks. For an example of a case with a twist that prosecutors may not have anticipated, we turn to the Tunkhannock Area School District in Pennsylvania. A high school student (later known in court as N.N.) had her phone confiscated because she used it on campus. Her principal looked inside and found nude and seminude photos, meant for N.N. and her boyfriend.

Off went the seized phone to local authorities, and on receipt, the local district attorney threatened to charge N.N. with child pornography unless she completed a course on sexual violence and victimization. Other students caught with similar images were given the same choice: classes or charges. Three students sued the DA, claiming the education program would violate their free speech rights, and a federal appeals court agreed.

With help from the local ACLU, N.N. decided to sue her school district, claiming the phone search was an invasion of her privacy. The district paid N.N. and her lawyers $33,000 to settle the case.

If you are a parent of a sexting teen, protecting that teen from prosecution may collide with your justifiable anger at her bad judgment. Nonetheless, N.N.'s legal battle shows that it can pay to defend your teen against overreaching school authorities who never should have examined the phone in the first place. N.N. learned an important lesson about privacy and the limits of government authority. You can—and should—punish a teen later, privately, for taking and storing nude photos.

FOR MORE INFORMATION

The Juvenile Law Center (jlc.org), cited earlier for its crystal-clear explanation of how teens and parents should respond to arrests, publishes exemplary guides for parents, children, and guardians; while the center is located in Pennsylvania and focuses on that state's law, its publications are a good starting point for understanding kids and courts (or look for a similar nonprofit in your state).

For comprehensive advice about prevention, intervention, treatment, and recovery from drug and alcohol abuse: drugfree.org. And socialhost.drugfree.org is an interactive site with state-by-state laws about parental responsibility for hosting parties where alcohol is served.

AAA offers information on teen driving, including licensing and other relevant laws, customized by state: teendriving.aaa.com.

The National Safety Council runs teensafedriving.org, which promotes improved teen and parent awareness of teen driving risks, and offers advice parents can give teens about safe driving. Another site, driveithome.org, pairs with corporate partners to promote safe teen driving. These sites offer a parent-teen driving agreement that lays down specific rules and consequences for failure to follow them.

And if you want to surreptitiously understand current slang: teenchatdecoder.com, netlingo.com, and noslang.com might help.

21

CAMPUS SAFETY

OPENING STATEMENT

I bet your search for the right college for your child was thorough—perhaps too thorough. Thorough, of course, is not a synonym for relaxing or fun. To ensure your child's enrollment in the institution of higher learning that best met her educational needs (and, be honest, satisfied your bragging rights), you trudged to different campuses, suffering through high-pressure tours and those irritating group information sessions that inevitably feature earnest parents posing obvious questions to patient admissions staffers. Possibly you risked humiliating your would-be student by shooting keepsake video. How industrious you were, reading, researching, totting up each school's career placement successes and calculating tuition costs. You scoured your address book in the hope of unearthing a back-channel connection to your child's top choices. Did I mention the tutoring costs? Or the parental root canal that is the "essay review," even if you outsourced it?

By the time your child enrolled, you probably felt smug about having covered every possible angle.

But you may have missed one.

Did you check to make sure your child's school is safe?

An embarrassing admission: I am 0-for-2 in checking on the safety of my children's colleges before they matriculated. I just assumed safety was everywhere improved since my own college experience at the University of Pennsylvania's urban campus in the late 1970s and early '80s, where dorm security seemed nonexistent and campus (and off-campus) crime reliably recurrent. (Not to single you out, Penn, since I know many campuses allowed similar conditions at the time, but ever since you rejected my daughter's application things haven't been the same between us. Two words, Office of Development and Alumni Relations: spam filter.)

So when I started to read up on the safety of college campuses, I felt the way I do when I check out a New York City restaurant's health rating only after dining there: better informed, but a little queasy about the establishment's shortcomings. When it comes to your student's safety in college, there's reason to be vigilant.

In 2014, the White House issued a report on rape and sexual assault, highlighting the problem on college campuses with alarming statistics: one in five women has been sexually assaulted while in college, and only 12 percent of student victims reported their assault to law enforcement.

When you start worrying about campus safety, here's one of the things you learn: there is a magazine called *Campus Safety*. *Campus Safety* is published nine times a year and reaches campus safety and security professionals. Surely they know how to keep a campus safe. So here are some questions the magazine suggests you ask to check on a school's commitment to do the same:

- Does the school engage in emergency planning? Are those plans tested and coordinated with local first responders?
- Is every staff member subjected to a background check?
- Does the school report its crime statistics to the U.S. Department of Education and publish an annual report?
- Does campus security receive adequate funding? (The norm is 2.5 to 3 percent of a school's annual budget.)

Safety-conscious mothers, and their college-bound children, owe an incalculable debt to a determined, grieving mother who, joined by her husband, helped revolutionize the way colleges approach security.

BOSSES OF THE BAR: CONNIE CLERY

Constance "Connie" Clery, Barnard '53, remembers her only daughter, Jeanne, as a happy freshman at Lehigh University.

"I was pleased to see her growing into a mature young woman. Jeanne would tell me stories of her time at Lehigh, like being thrown upside down in a trash barrel, and I would say kiddingly, 'Were you in slacks?' 'Of course I was, Mom.' . . . She was joy, total joy."

In family photographs, Jeanne is the embodiment of the typical 1980s college student: smiling face, fluffy hair, the look of a young woman galvanized by thoughts of her bright future.

Jeanne was raped and murdered by another student, a stranger to her, in her Lehigh University dorm in 1986. How did he get into her room? Connie and her husband, Howard, found out that Lehigh had had safety problems at dorms like Jeanne's, where locked doors were propped open—with empty pizza boxes. Lehigh had registered thirty-eight violent offenses, including rape, robbery, and assault, in a three-year period. But neither the Clerys nor other parents or students were ever informed, and the school was not required to tell them, either.

Jeanne's killer was convicted of murder, and a civil suit against the school was settled, but Connie and Howard were determined to protect other students.

They went to Capitol Hill to push for better disclosure of campus crimes, and in response to their efforts, Congress passed the Crime Awareness and Campus Security Act, which was later renamed in Jeanne's memory. Under the Clery Act, schools are required to publish an annual security report, keep a crime log, and follow procedures for emergency responses. And the Clery Center for Security on Campus trains college administrators about safety and prevention on campus.

Thanks to her parents' efforts, Jeanne Clery leaves a legacy of safer campuses. We could, for a minute, regret the passing of the era of open dorms where students and visitors could enter, unbothered, to socialize. But if we did, we wouldn't be thoughtful mothers or concerned adults. I prefer a campus with ID checks, and with the emergency plans that make it simple for schools to notify students about how to respond to danger or a threat. Today you can educate yourself about a school's security and safety and compare its system and protocols to other schools with a quick web search.

IT'S THE LAW

Here are the campus crimes schools must disclose (though not necessarily in those glossy, come-hither brochures they publish to mesmerize your children):

◆ Criminal homicide (murder and manslaughter)
◆ Sexual offenses
◆ Robbery
◆ Aggravated assault
◆ Burglary
◆ Arson
◆ Motor vehicle theft
◆ Arrests and disciplinary referrals for liquor and drug law violations and illegal weapons possession

Parents can find this information in the school's Annual Security Report (online and on paper), which contains three years of crime statistics, security policies and procedures, and the rights guaranteed to victims of sexual assault. Colleges also have begun to release data about domestic violence, dating violence, and stalking. In addition, schools are required to list the efforts they are making to prevent sexual violence on campus. In fact, you should consider reviewing the sexual harassment policies of the schools your child may attend; they may offer insight into whether the campus culture is permissive or more protective. (We'll look at campus sexual harassment in greater detail below.)

Can all this data help you keep your student safe? Not without your help. A beloved friend who is a mom, and a lawyer for one of the country's most prestigious universities, offers this advice: show the data to your student as a lesson in the ubiquity of campus crime. Whether students attend school in an urban setting or a pastoral one, they need to be careful: they can be assaulted, and their property stolen, on any campus.

CAMPUS SAFETY TIPS

Talk to your student about school safety before she goes to college and when she is home. Don't be deterred by any negative reaction from your worldly teen. Instead, consider eye-rolling a sign that your commonsense safety advice is registering in her brain, so replete with intellect but so short on judgment.

To get the conversation started, here is a summary of key tips campus police at Brandeis University and Tufts University offered to the *Boston Globe:*

- *Lock your doors.* Make sure your dorm room or apartment doors are locked at all times, especially if you are out or sleeping in. If you live off-campus, check the doors and windows to be sure the locks are good. If they seem wobbly, ask your landlord or building manager to replace them. Never prop open doors in residential housing.
- *Be aware of your surroundings.* Walk on well-traveled and well-lit paths. Get to know the locations of campus emergency phones. Remove earbuds or headphones so you can hear someone approach. Do not walk alone at night. If you are walking to a car, have your keys ready and check before you enter that no one is in the car or lingering nearby. If you feel unsafe, walk away.
- *Program campus security numbers into your cell phone.* This includes the number for your school's late-night ride service and the emergency and nonemergency numbers for

campus police. Use the late-night ride service if you ever feel unsafe.

- *Keep an eye on your belongings.* Don't leave your laptop, cell phone, or anything of value on a table in the library or a classroom. Zip up your purse or backpack before you walk.
- *Report suspicious people or activity.* Do not let strangers into your residence hall. If you see a stranger in your dorm or apartment, call the campus police, and do not confront that person.
- *Ask for help.* If you feel unsafe or stressed, reach out for campus support, whether it's an RA, health professional, or the police.

My university lawyer friend offers one more tip: make sure your student reads the school code of conduct and understands what's expected.

EXHIBIT 46: SEXUAL ASSAULT AND HARASSMENT

The sportier readers among you might remember Title IX (covered in chapter 18) for its requirement that schools provide men and women equal opportunities in athletics. Title IX, by barring sex discrimination in schools, also has been used to hold schools liable for sexual harassment and sexual assault, including student-on-student assault. Students are protesting inadequate enforcement of Title IX protections, and college administrators are taking pains to improve their supervision, increase educational efforts, and impose stricter punishment. It's not an easy task when, as one report put it, student-on-student sexual assault usually involves acquaintances, no witnesses, and an unclear memory of events due to alcohol abuse.

This is a sensitive and controversial topic, and one that absolutely deserves your attention. One way to educate your college-bound child about the risks of sexual assault is to review codes of conduct at your student's school together. You'll likely find a set of expectations that has changed dramatically from your own time on campus.

Duke University, where a false accusation of sexual assault against members of the 2006 men's lacrosse team roiled the campus and riveted the nation, adopted one of the nation's strictest college sexual assault policies in 2013, making expulsion, and not just suspension, a recommended punishment for a student found guilty of sexual assault. Duke also offers guidance for students accused of misconduct and, significantly, their parents. As the school says, "You will undoubtedly want to show support to your son or daughter. Listen to his or her perspective. Encourage him/her to accept responsibility for the role he or she played in a situation. And show that you still stand behind him or her."

As for sexual harassment, examples of prohibited behavior may look similar to the acts warned against in the workplace (we'll take a closer look at that topic in chapter 22). Unwelcome sexual propositions or flirting; unwanted physical contact; comments about a person's body, appearance, or dress; and repeated requests for a date are all among the types of conduct that could be construed as harassing.

If your student reports harassment to you, help bring her concerns to the attention of appropriate school officials; the Title IX coordinator is a logical first stop. The law affords you the right to bring a lawsuit against the school or file a claim with the Department of Education's Office of Civil Rights (OCR), which is the federal agency that enforces Title IX, but those are last-resort measures that may not yield the remedies you seek; if they do, it won't be quick. (A lawsuit can follow an OCR investigation.)

EXHIBIT 47: HARASSMENT ON THE FIELD?

Do Title IX's protections against sexual harassment extend beyond actions to words? Melissa Jennings thought so, and it took her almost ten years of litigation against a legendary coach whose school, along with some of Melissa's teammates, supported him every step of the way before she reached a settlement in her case.

Melissa was a reserve goalie for the Lady Tar Heels of the University of North Carolina at Chapel Hill. She was recruited to play for UNC by Anson Dorrance, a man whose sporting bona fides include coaching Mia Hamm and winning multiple NCAA championships. Along the way, he led the women's national soccer team from 1986 to 1994 and guided that team to a gold medal at the first women's World Cup tournament.

Good coaches have a keen grasp of human psychology, allied to a kind of instinctive salesmanship that allows them to bond with and rally their student athletes in the service of a common goal: winning. While their season is under way, a coach and his team are together for hours and under intense conditions, in locker rooms, on the road, and on the field. Might there be cussing? Sure. Unladylike comments? No doubt. Too much information? Inevitable.

But even taking that culture into account, Melissa still felt Coach Dorrance's behavior went too far. So far, in fact, that without his ever touching or propositioning her, Melissa believed that Coach Dorrance violated her Title IX rights by creating a sexually hostile environment.

Here are just some of the incidents Melissa alleged in her lawsuit. Do you think they amount to sexual harassment? (Apologies for some of the language that follows.)

- In front of the team, Dorrance asked one player nearly every day "who [her] fuck of the minute is, fuck of the hour is, fuck of the week [is]," whether there was a "guy [she] hadn't fucked yet," or whether she "got the guys' names as they came to the door or . . . just took a number."

- ◆ Dorrance called a member of the team, named Charlotte, Chuck because he thought she was a lesbian.
- ◆ When Melissa and Dorrance met for a postseason discussion of her performance—in Dorrance's hotel room—the coach asked Melissa, whose grades were sagging, "Who are you fucking?"

Melissa was cut from the team and then she sued. Dorrance and the university fought back, and the court battle lasted for a decade until Melissa reached a $385,000 settlement with the school.

Melissa's lawsuit proved controversial. UNC supported its coach. The court decision that kept her lawsuit alive included a spirited dissent that argued that while Coach Dorrance made vulgar and inappropriate comments, they often weren't even directed at Melissa and hardly amounted to a Title IX claim. When the settlement was reached, former players told the reporter they supported their coach and the program. Only Melissa's lawyer seemed to speak publicly on her behalf.

STUDENT PRIVACY

While schools continue to strive to protect students from wrongdoing, the law offers students strong protection in another realm: privacy.

Once they reach majority at age eighteen, your teens, even if they can't drink until they turn twenty-one, are the beneficiaries of a little-known federal privacy law that can prevent you, their parent, from accessing their student and, sometimes, medical records. The Family Educational Rights and Privacy Act, or FERPA, is meant to grant control over school records to students and their parents. Once students turn eighteen, that authority is the student's alone. That means you may have no right to see records of your freshman's academic performance in college unless your student grants you permission, though you will have access if you claim your child as a dependent for tax purposes. Many schools have even stricter privacy protections than FERPA provides, and do not allow parents to access student educational records under any circumstances without the student's permission. If, like me, you feel that your tuition payments entitle you to a nodding familiarity with your child's GPA, make sure your student signs the appropriate waivers to give you those rights by the time you move her into school.

This law contains a health and safety exception that allows a school to contact parents in the event a student is considered a threat to herself or others. Since individual schools interpret that exception differently, don't count on a college to alert you when something is wrong. It's exceedingly hard to ferret out information about a college student's behavior, but there's no real substitute for your own curiosity. Keep communications open with your child. Get to know her roommates; maybe one of them will feel comfortable telling you that something's wrong. Meet her RA, and even her dean, at the start of each school year. While schools have limits on sharing educational records, a dean or RA can speak to concerns about your student. The school can initiate that conversation; so can you. (These are not protected "records," thus the opportunity for more candor.) That said, make sure to balance your inquiries with your student's need to strike out on her own—in other words, stop hovering.

FOR MORE INFORMATION

The Clery Center for Security on Campus (clerycenter.org) offers resources for parents and students to gauge how universities are dealing with security. The center notes that schools that report higher numbers of incidents in their annual security report may be those that are effectively encouraging students to report crime, and suggests how you can look "beyond the numbers" to assess safety.

The Centers for Disease Control and Prevention (cdc.gov) offer tips on college health and safety, including advice about mental health, substance abuse, campus security, and sexual violence, with links to much more guidance about these important topics.

The National Institute on Alcohol Abuse and Alcoholism publishes multimedia warnings about the dangers of college drinking, including an interactive graphic that shows alcohol's journey through the body and its deleterious effects, and calculators to compute calories, blood alcohol content, and cost: collegedrinkingprevention.gov.

Advocacy organizations with more information about students and safety include SAFER (Students Active for Ending Rape; safercampus.org) and Know Your IX (as in Title IX; knowyourix.org).

PART FOUR

EMPLOYMENT ISSUES

22

ON THE JOB

OPENING STATEMENT

My father was a hardworking—and working-class—immigrant. Forced by bad timing and worse circumstances to forgo a formal education, Dad learned his trade, auto mechanics, during his involuntary stay at a displaced-persons camp in Germany after World War II. Once he landed in Newark, New Jersey, after the war, he set out to ply that trade and eventually ran his own gas station in downtown Paterson, starting just before I was born.

City Hall Service (the station sat just a block or two from Main Street, near City Hall) was the source of many valuable work lessons for an impressionable firstborn daughter who bore the full weight of her immigrant parents' ambitions. Along with access to the plastic-handled steak knives and golden presidential coin sets that gas stations gave away to attract customers, I also saw what it meant to run your own business. Based on what I saw, none of it seemed appealing.

In retrospect, I came to realize that the Shell station, with its mechanic's tools, oil-soaked cloths, scruffy desk, ancient radio (tuned to all-news stations, of course), and permanent floating crew of men who liked to pass the time kibitzing about politics and cars, was a fantastic treasure chest of characters and commerce. At the time, though, my nascent middle-class sensibilities abhorred the grease and grime. I wanted an office job, with a clean desk and an even tidier restroom. I wanted a place where peace and quiet would prevail, along with polite people in conformist office attire who typed and filed.

And so I got my wish one college summer, with a position in midtown Manhattan as a receptionist at a small advertising agency.

I have only one memory of that summer job, and it's vivid. I was stationed at my desk, minding the phone and my own business. In flew the creative director of the firm, presumably fresh from a three-martini lunch or a successful pitch, or both. I didn't know him at all, but I'm sure I gave him a polite hello. In response, he strode toward me and in full public view gave me a robust kiss on the mouth.

IT'S THE LAW

Times have changed. Decades after that drunken smooch, unwanted advances are now a violation of federal law meant to protect women against discrimination at work. You can't be treated differently, sexually harassed, offered different shifts, jobs, pay, or promotions, fail to get a job, or be fired because you are a woman. Nor can you be punished with a demotion or pay cut, or be fired, for reporting sex discrimination.

If your employer does any of this to you, it's a violation of Title VII of the Civil Rights Act of 1964. It's the same landmark Civil Rights Act that addresses voting rights and school desegregation, and bars hiring, promoting, and firing because of race, color, religion, and national origin. Legend has it that a Virginia congressman, Howard Smith (a Democrat and a conservative, back when that combination was possible), added the word *sex* to the list of protected groups to try to kill the bill (though Smith later claimed he added the word to support the National Women's Party). Whatever his motivation, the bill passed, and along with it, the Equal Employment Opportunity Commission, or EEOC, was born to enforce the law. (Laws passed later prohibited discrimination because of age and disability.)

For some real-world examples of sex discrimination, we turn to a list offered by Equal Rights Advocates, a San Francisco–based civil rights organization. If you find yourself in these situations, or variations of these situations, you may be the victim of illegal sex discrimination:

- You apply for a job as a sales executive. Although you have experience and excellent qualifications, you are not hired because some of the company's longtime clients are more comfortable dealing with men.
- You want to be a firefighter. The department is taking applicants, but the job description states that all candidates must be able to lift one hundred pounds. You believe such a feat is not necessary to carry out the duties of a firefighter, and serves instead to keep women from applying.
- You are told that you are laid off due to company cutbacks and reorganization. However, men in the same position and/or with less seniority keep their jobs.

◆ Your boss is the vice president of the company. He repeatedly makes unwelcome comments about your body and routinely puts his arm around your waist when discussing work-related matters. You tell him his behavior makes you uncomfortable and ask him to stop. He says, "Maybe you are too uptight for this job. I probably should never have hired you." You now are afraid of losing your job if you don't "loosen up."

◆ You are a woman who works in the sales department of a major retail chain. You have short hair and dress in pants most days. Although you meet deadlines and sales quotas, you receive poor performance evaluations, which include comments about your lack of femininity and your "aggressive" nature. Men with similar personality traits and equally or less impressive sales records than your own receive above-average performance evaluations and are promoted more quickly.

You might read this list and think: Hey, I never went to law school, and even I can spot these hypothetical situations as obvious examples of discrimination. What about more ambiguous ones? For example, what if an employee "voluntarily" has sex with her boss? How can she later claim harassment?

To take your more specific question first, sex that seems voluntary might still be harassment if the harassment prompted the consent, or if a relationship began as voluntary and then a boss pressured an employee to keep having sex or else face workplace consequences.

These situations are what lawyers call "fact specific." In other words: frequently nuanced, often confusing, beset by "he said, she said" disputes. One person's sense of unfair discrimination might bewilder a colleague who sees a merit-based management decision.

In every instance, though, a viable discrimination claim has to involve treatment at work that negatively affects terms and conditions of employment. To begin a closer look, let's dive right into the treacherous topic of the office romance.

OFFICE ROMANCE

Workplace romances tend toward the intense, the short-lived, and, usually, the ultimately destructive, especially if they are clandestine.

Some employers have tried to ban them, but those efforts are tough to police; it's very hard to regulate love, or at least attraction. For their own protection, some companies have floated the notion of a "love contract," which is even less romantic than it sounds. In this document, the happy couple admits to a work-based romance, affirms that it is consensual and not in exchange for professional advancement, and can even agree to arbitration if they bicker. It's like a prenup for work, and can be an employer's dream.

In a fascinating twist on this notion, the incoming president of Alabama State University, Gwendolyn Boyd, signed an employment contract that gave her $300,000 a year, a car, and a place to live—but barred her from sharing the presidential residence with a theoretical long-term lover. Specifically: "For so long as Dr. Boyd is president and a single person, she shall not be allowed to cohabitate in the president's residence with any person with whom she has a romantic relation." While lawyers speculated about how on earth ASU could enforce the provision, or whether it precluded her from living with someone in a relationship she deemed unromantic, Boyd told an education reporter that because she lived alone, she didn't have a problem signing the contract.

With or without contracts, people working together in adjacent cubicles or other shared spaces will remain reliably flirtatious, so the question remains: when does semi-innocent banter evolve into actionable conduct? To better answer that question, here's a refresher tutorial (courtesy of Equal Rights Advocates) about some of the unwelcome behavior that can constitute sexual harassment and lead to legal trouble:

Verbal or written:

◆ Commenting about a person's clothing, personal behavior, personal relationships, or body
◆ Making sexual or sex-based jokes or innuendoes
◆ Requesting sexual favors or dates
◆ Spreading rumors about a person's personal or sexual life
◆ Threatening a person for rejecting or refusing sexual advances or overtures

Physical:

◆ Impeding or blocking someone's movement
◆ Inappropriate touching of a person's body or clothing
◆ Kissing, hugging, patting, or stroking
◆ Assaulting (touching someone against her will or without her consent)

Nonverbal:

◆ Looking up and down or staring at a person's body
◆ Making derogatory gestures or facial expressions of a sexual nature
◆ Following a person around

Visual:

♦ Displaying or sharing posters, drawings, pictures, screen
savers, or emails of a sexual nature

What do you do if these bullet points reflect your real-life work
situation, or if you think you are the victim of another form of sex
discrimination at work?

EXHIBIT 48: FILING A TITLE VII CLAIM

If you think you are the victim of discrimination at work, you should
not have to put up with behavior that the law bans. On the other
hand, do not charge ahead with a case against your employer without
carefully weighing the pros and cons, fully understanding whether
you have a claim, and seeking advice from a lawyer with relevant experience about whether you can prevail. For example, harassment and
hostile work environment are, believe it or not, technical terms of art:
behavior by your boss that seems indisputably hostile may not be il-
legally hostile. Also, this is your job, and unless you are employed for
fun, you will need to eat and pay bills while you mount your battle.
Plus employers tend to defend themselves energetically, and almost
always with resources that are more powerful than yours.

Let's assume you've checked, and it seems you are a victim of behavior that violates the federal law, Title VII. (Your state and town
may offer additional legal protection.)

To make the claim, you'll need notepaper, colleagues, and a calendar.

First, the notepaper. The consensus view on employment issues
(this is true if you are the employer, too) is that you should write everything down and save all relevant documents (including printouts of

emails or memos). When did it happen? Where? Who was there who might have heard or seen the wrongdoing? Write it all down and take your notes home.

Check the employee handbook, if there is one. It should explain the process to follow for making a complaint, including to whom you should report the wrongdoing. Generally, that would be your boss, or supervisor—unless he or she is the person about whom you have the complaint—or the human resources department. Enlightened employers take these claims seriously, and there's a chance your report will stop the problem. Even if it doesn't, there's a good legal reason to speak up: if you fail to report the discrimination or harassment, your employer may have some legal defenses to damages or liability if the company has antidiscrimination procedures in place that you bypassed.

Federal law will protect you only if you are employed at a workplace with fifteen or more employees (twenty employees for an age discrimination claim, fifty for those under the Family and Medical Leave Act). These rules apply to private employers; government workers have different requirements.

Now, about that calendar. Before you can sue an employer in federal court, you have to file your complaint (called a charge) with the EEOC and follow its process. So these filings are crucial. They also have unforgiving deadlines. In general you have 180 calendar days after a discriminatory act to file your charge; 300 days if a state or local agency has a parallel antidiscrimination law that applies to your situation. Federal law gives you 300 days after the act of discrimination—or harassment—to file, but some states want you to file sooner. If you missed a deadline, check the laws in your state or city for a local civil rights law; you may be able to sue in state court anyway.

Once you file a complaint with the EEOC, the agency will usually ask the parties if they wish to mediate the discrimination charge. If either party declines, or if mediation fails, the EEOC will investigate. If the agency does so and finds reasonable cause to believe your story—something that occurs only rarely—the agency will try to settle with your employer through a process it calls conciliation. If that fails, the agency can issue you a "right to sue" letter. (In rare cases, the agency will sue on your behalf.) If the investigation will take too long, you may be able to get permission to sue before the EEOC finishes its work. And if the agency doesn't find cause, you can appeal the decision, although it's rarely done and almost never successful.

Easy, right? Wrong.

EXHIBIT 49: TIGHT DEADLINES

Can you believe we are still fighting for equal pay for women?

Believe it, alas. The National Women's Law Center reported that in 2013, women were paid, on average, 77 cents for every dollar paid to men.

Pay discrimination has its very own federal law, the Equal Pay Act, which requires employers to pay men and women equally for doing the same work. Women often sue under that law, as well as Title VII, for a pay discrimination claim.

Just like other Title VII discrimination claims, if you have been the victim of pay discrimination, you'll need to pay attention to the calendar. But thanks to Lilly Ledbetter, you can at least start the clock when you find out that your paycheck is too skimpy, instead of when your boss first decided to shortchange you.

BOSSES OF THE BAR: LILLY LEDBETTER

Lilly Ledbetter almost certainly is the most famous daughter of her hometown, Possum Trot, Alabama. Lilly secured a management post at the Goodyear tire plant in Gadsden,

Alabama, and worked there for almost twenty years before learning (via an anonymous note disclosing the pay of three male managers) that she had been underpaid. How underpaid? The anonymous tipster helped Ledbetter learn she was making $3,727 a month while men doing the same job pulled down $4,286 to $5,236 a month. She filed an EEOC complaint and then sued, and a jury awarded more than $3 million in damages.

On appeal, the U.S. Supreme Court decided that her claims were filed too late, so Lilly deserved zero. Why? The time limit for filing a Title VII complaint, said the court, is 180 days after your employer first discriminates against you. Since Lilly didn't know she was underpaid until years after it started, the clock had run out, and she was plumb out of luck.

Justice Ruth Bader Ginsburg, our hero and longtime champion of women's rights, implored Congress to correct this injustice and in 2009 Congress passed, and newly elected President Obama signed, the Lilly Ledbetter Fair Pay Act. Thanks to them, the time frame for pay discrimination suits has widened to allow you to sue 180 days after the most recent skimpy paycheck you receive.

As a nonlegal aside, can we all vow to do everything in our own power to fatten our take-home pay? A recent study showed that when women are offered a job, only 7 percent negotiate the first salary offer; more than 55 percent of men take that confident, bank-account-fattening step.

EXHIBIT 50: WORKING WHILE PREGNANT

Are you pregnant, or did you just give birth? Are you on maternity leave or getting ready to take that time off? Congratulations! I'd love to swap remedies for morning sickness and leads on flattering maternity wear (hint: there is none), but instead, let's be practical and focus on the law.

Once again, federal (and a few state) laws stand ready to protect you. The Pregnancy Discrimination Act is part of Title VII, and it bars workplace discrimination of women who are pregnant or who gave birth. Translation: pregnancy-related medical conditions must be treated the same way as all others. (Need a doctor's note to get leave or sick benefits for that heart condition? Same rules apply if you are expecting.)

Yet another law—the Family and Medical Leave Act—sensibly gives unpaid time off to new parents, even if your child is adopted, and protects your job, or at least promises you an equivalent job with equivalent pay and benefits when you return. The FMLA applies to employers who have at least fifty workers within seventy-five miles, and applies only if you've worked at your employer for at least twelve months. (It gives equal protection to dads, and to you if you want to care for an ailing relative, or have a serious health condition of your own.)

We pause and wonder: Is this all really necessary in the twenty-first century? Can employers really be so backward as to think it appropriate to discriminate against pregnant women, rather than help make their (temporary, after all) change in circumstances joyful and easy?

Which brings us to Charles Sisson.

Charles, the head of HCS Medical Staffing in Milwaukee, was ordered by a federal judge to pay $148,000 to settle a claim of pregnancy discrimination against employee Roxy Leger. What did Charles do that led the judge to label his behavior "inherently humiliating and . . . degrading"? Where to start? According to the EEOC, which brought the lawsuit, Charles referred to Roxy's pregnancy as a joke and said maternity leave should last only a couple of days. He suggested Roxy was taking time for prenatal appointments as a ruse for additional time or money. The icing on the malevolent cake? When the beleaguered Roxy was recovering from her Caesarean section, her boss fired her and ended her health insurance. By certified mail.

To recap: a woman who works in the United States, in the medical industry, in the twenty-first century was subjected to embarrassment and ridicule and lost her job and benefits . . . while pregnant and immediately afterward. Roxy prevailed in her claim, but other mothers who think they've suffered discrimination have not succeeded in court, even with the weight of the EEOC behind them. Such was the fate of Angela Ames, a loss mitigation specialist with Nationwide Mutual Insurance in Iowa. Angela took issue with the way her department head, Karla Neel, reacted to her pregnancy and then her return to work. (As recounted in the appellate court decision in this case, Karla "rolled her eyes" when Angela discussed her need to go on bed rest, under doctor's orders. Legal, perhaps, but not cool.)

According to the decision, on Angela's first day back from leave (the baby, her second child, was premature) she was unable to use the company's lactation room because she hadn't completed the necessary paperwork for access. While Angela waited for a "wellness room" to open up, her day got worse. Angela's boss told her she had two weeks to complete the work that had piled up during her maternity leave, none of which had been touched in her absence, even though Nationwide had trained a replacement while she was away. If Angela couldn't get it done in time, her boss expected her to work overtime; if the work was still incomplete, Angela would be disciplined.

At this point, you will be unsurprised to learn that Angela became visibly upset. Karla, her department head, handed Angela paper and a pen and dictated the text of her resignation, saying it would be best for Angela to go home with her babies.

Angela sued Nationwide, alleging sex and pregnancy discrimination. The EEOC filed a brief supporting her claim. But a federal court didn't see it that way, and an appellate court agreed. The appellate court panel ruled, unanimously, that Nationwide did not force Angela to resign. Rather, the company "sought to accommodate [Angela's] needs." Moreover, there was nothing discriminatory about the lactation paperwork, since every nursing mother had to fill it out. Said a presumably relieved Nationwide: "Nationwide is fully committed to supporting the health and wellness needs of all of our associates, including providing lactation space when needed."

Angela, of course, is hardly the only new mother who has looked to the law for support while feeding a new baby.

BREASTFEEDING BATTLES

Breastfeeding is beautiful, and its health benefits to baby and mom are beyond dispute: babies drink in antibodies that protect them from viruses and infections; mothers can reduce their risk of premenopausal breast cancer and osteoporosis, not to mention reclaim their pre-baby shape sooner.

If you have ever cared for a baby, you know babies love to eat, at times and places of their choosing, not yours. This means moms need the ability to breastfeed in public. Even today, unfortunately, too many people still see breastfeeding as inappropriately exhibitionist, if not slightly obscene. As one human rights expert put it, "It's ironic that it's fine to use a woman's breast in advertising . . . but using them for their natural purpose is considered taboo."

Here's where the law can make a difference. Under federal law, employers with more than fifty workers have to provide a nursing mother with a private place (specifically not a toilet stall) and reasonable time to express breast milk.

That's federal law; about half the states also have laws protecting nursing mothers at work. And about half the states specifically exempt breastfeeding mothers from public indecency prosecutions. In Florida, for example, a nursing mother can't be charged with lewdness (in public, or while using a computer), indecent exposure, or sexual conduct— you know, because nursing moms feel so, um, indecent and sexual? Virtually every state (forty-five plus the District of Columbia) makes it legal for moms to nurse in any public or private location.

All these excellent legislative assists notwithstanding, nursing mothers still find themselves fighting for their feeding rights. A passenger on a Freedom Airlines flight sued after she was kicked off a plane for nursing her daughter and refusing to cover herself with a blanket a flight attendant provided. The case settled for an undisclosed amount (and Freedom has since shut down). In a related development, a nursing mom settled her lawsuit against the Transportation Security Administration; she alleged that TSA officers in Phoenix forced her to X-ray or toss bottled breast milk, rather than (consistent with agency policy) offer another way to check the milk so she could board her flight and feed her son.

EXHIBIT 51: WEIGHT AT WORK

Weight discrimination seems to be one of the few biases employers can still entertain without much worry about legal recourse. Employees suffer the consequences, with one study finding that obese workers earn about 2.5 percent less (and obese women, as much as 6.2 percent less) than their fitter counterparts.

As I type, one state—Michigan—and several cities bar discrimination at work based on weight and height. The state representative who wrote the law said he was "flabbergasted" at the number of cases of women who tried to land office jobs, and had the right skills, but failed because they were overweight.

The reassuring news is that overweight workers may be able to find protection in other laws. For example, a worker may be able to claim her obesity gives her protection under the Americans with Disabilities Act. But in general, overweight employees have little to no protection against workplace prejudice, even when weight has nothing to do with their ability to perform their work.

BOSSES OF THE BAR: MELISSA NELSON

A dental assistant in Iowa, Melissa Nelson became a feminist hero after she was fired by her boss, dentist James Knight.

James fired Melissa, his longtime and well-regarded employee, after telling her that even though she had done nothing wrong, James had grown too attached and feared he might want to embark on an affair. This manly defense of marital morals took place after James's wife found out that he and Melissa had been texting, and insisted that Melissa was "a big threat" to their marriage. Melissa, presumably unimpressed by James's self-control, saw her sacking as sex discrimination and went to court, claiming James had violated the state's Civil Rights Act.

In their first opinion on the matter, the all-male panel of state supreme court judges ruled that James was entitled to fire Melissa because he viewed her as "an irresistible attraction." A twenty-first-century legal opinion branding a married mother and professional as some sort of demonic seductress drew an appropriate reaction: widespread media ridicule. The men withdrew their opinion (pun fully intended) and issued another, losing the "irresistible attraction" phrase, but still finding for James.

What a dispiriting mess. The notion that a woman could do a great job at work but drive her boss to such illicit distraction that he has the legal right to fire her for that reason, and no other, makes me want to deposit all of our makeup, tailored skirts (yes, even the slightly outdated but still comfortable one you bought on sale and can't quite give away), and higher heels into a giant locked warehouse. Shall we hold our collective breath until one of us fires a hot guy simply for being too hot, and wins a court challenge before a group of male judges? I didn't think so.

EXHIBIT 52: HIRING, FIRING, AND BEING FIRED

I write from New York, which is an "at will" employment state, as is every other state except, currently, Montana. (Hey, Montana: your Wrongful Discharge from Employment Act—which says nonunion workers who are not under contract but have been on the job for at least six months cannot be fired unless there is good cause—sounds eminently fair and protective. Other state legislatures, I'm talking to you: any takers?)

What at-will employment means is that unless you, the worker, have an employment contract that says otherwise, or a collective bargaining agreement, your boss can dump you at any time, for any reason, or no reason, unless it's an illegal reason (such as discrimination). Oh, and your boss can demote you, change your salary, and reduce or end your benefits or paid time off. On the bright side, you also can leave at any time for any or no reason.

This means most of us run the risk of being fired, or needing to fire someone, along the path of our work life.

So what if you're on the chopping block? With any luck, management has at least "managed" your expectations so you already know your bosses haven't been dazzled by your work. This isn't always the case, however, and sometimes you can feel blindsided by the news, even with fair warning.

If you are hustled into your supervisor's office and see her HR person at the ready, stay calm, listen, and do not sign any agreement before you think it over. You want to be sure you have access to the best severance deal you can get; sometimes that requires negotiations you will not want to undertake on your own behalf.

As is so often the case where law is involved, when it comes to the possibility that you might be let go, a little bit of proactive effort on your part can reap meaningful rewards.

Workplace Fairness, a nonprofit advocacy group focusing on employee rights, suggests looking for an employment lawyer if any of these situations apply to you:

- ◆ You have concerns about how you are being treated in the workplace or whether your termination or layoff was legal.
- ◆ You are considering quitting your employment because of your employer's apparently unlawful conduct.
- ◆ You do not want to or cannot negotiate with your employer regarding severance pay.
- ◆ You do not clearly understand your rights or are unsure of the proper action to take after your termination.

- You are nearing the end of your "statute of limitations," or deadline for filing suit, and are still unsure of how or where to file a claim.
- You are being pressured to sign a complicated and lengthy "release of claims" that you do not fully understand.
- You want to file a lawsuit in state or federal court.
- You know of many other employees who want to bring the same type of claim against the same employer.
- You are dissatisfied with a government agency's (such as the EEOC) investigation of your complaint.
- You have powerful evidence that your termination was illegal.

For more guidance on selecting a lawyer, turn to chapter 29.

THE COBRA FILES

If you worked for a company with twenty or more employees and were let go, you almost always can keep your company-supplied health insurance for eighteen months (and sometimes longer, depending on the state) thanks to the clumsily named COBRA law. (Do you really need to know? Okay, it stands for the Consolidated Omnibus Budget Reconciliation Act.)

COBRA covers you in most circumstances whether you are fired, your work hours are reduced, or even if you quit. And while it's enormously helpful, and sometimes necessary, to hold on to your current insurance until you land a new job, be prepared: chances are your company was subsidizing your health insurance premium, so you'll have sticker shock, at the worst possible time, when you get that new bill. Remember to check local law: some states may allow you to maintain that coverage for a longer period.

Given the cost, if COBRA applies to you, you should investigate alternatives for health insurance. For example, if you are married and both you and your spouse had insurance under your plan, you may be able to enroll in your spouse's group health plan right away, without waiting for the annual enrollment period. Ongoing national health insurance reform may provide other options for affordable, appropriate care.

What if you have to fire someone yourself? It's the flip side of the discussion we've just had. And—no surprise—I recommend you talk to a lawyer at your workplace, who can identify possible issues and offer advice on how to reduce the possibility of a lawsuit.

Good bosses make sure their workers know where they stand. If your employee is falling short, she should know about her shortcomings—and have a chance to correct them—long before she is let go. Your HR colleagues can give you advice about how best to keep a record of those conversations and accrue evidence that an employee isn't meeting your expectations.

You will want company when you deliver the bad news, and you will want to deliver it succinctly. You want to explain why: was it performance, or a layoff as part of a larger budget-cutting effort? If you are this person's boss, you should deliver the news yourself, rather than punt: if you don't, your employee may wonder if you agree with the decision. This is no time for ambiguous management messages. There's nothing more suspicious to a fired worker than an explanation that doesn't sound credible, especially if she's in a position to wonder whether discrimination is the real reason for the sacking.

When you've explained the decision, stop and listen. Letting an unhappy person vent is one of the best ways I know to reduce the risk of litigation later—sometimes people just need an opportunity to explain their position, and if they don't get one, the hostility can spawn bigger problems.

You should consider whether a severance package, coupled with an agreement not to disclose information or malign the company, would be fair and protect you from legal action. At the very least, the meeting should include an explanation of benefits, like remaining vacation time.

EXHIBIT 53: ALL ABOUT INTERNS

Occupying a workplace gray zone between volunteer and employee is the intern who, despite her traditional status as a barely noticed short-term office mate who soaks up experience and fetches coffee, has become the focus of an increasingly pitched legal battle. At issue: is it legal to hire interns and pay them nothing? Under federal law, internships can be unpaid if the work meets certain criteria, including whether the internship is educational for the intern (it should be) and whether the intern displaces regular, paid employees (she cannot).

A series of court challenges to unpaid internships already have encouraged some companies to start compensating interns (though at minimum wages that will bring me no closer to my dream of a child-funded second home). Unpaid internships still dominate at nonprofits and in government, where they are generally permitted. Even Sheryl Sandberg, patron saint of ambitious women, got dragged into the intern controversy when an editor at her Lean In organization posted an ad for an unpaid intern, only to change the job description to "volunteer" when online opprobrium poured in. The organization later said it would create a formal, paid internship program.

Once on the job, unpaid interns may have few of the protections that paid employees enjoy. A federal court in New York, for example, dismissed a sexual harassment claim that an unpaid intern, Lihuan Wang, filed against a television company, Phoenix Satellite TV, after she claimed her supervisor somehow turned a lunch to discuss her performance into a hotel visit (he had to "drop off a few things"), where he asked her, "Why are you so beautiful?" then reinforced those thoughts with an attempt to kiss her. Because she was an intern, the court held, Wang had no rights to sue under New York law. (The company denied any discriminatory activity took place; the New York City Council later passed a bill to protect future interns against sexual harassment.)

I have mixed feelings about this issue. Friends who launched successful careers with a stint as an intern slaving without compensation bemoan the legal attack on unpaid internships. They look to interns as a source of future talent and fear that these challenges will block a traditional entry point into fields like publishing and television. On the other hand, it's hard to understand why successful companies can't shell out a minimum wage for highly motivated young workers, especially those from families that cannot underwrite a child's dress rehearsal in the work world. All that said, I always have a soft spot for young women who are willing to challenge an entrenched system, like Lucy Bickerton.

BOSSES OF THE BAR: LUCY BICKERTON

Wesleyan graduate Lucy Bickerton had an internship that would be the envy of any aspiring reporter. She worked for the *Charlie Rose* show for twenty-five hours a week from June to August 2007. According to Lucy, she had some meaningful work (preparing background research on guests, assembling press packets), some glamorous responsibilities (escorting hosts through the studio), and some inevitable scut tasks (tidying up the greenroom).

The salary for her toil? Zero dollars.

Lucy sued the show, claiming this lack of pay violated state and federal labor laws. She wasn't alone: interns at other prominent companies, including Fox Searchlight Pictures, Hearst Magazines, and Condé Nast, filed suits for lack of payment. The companies all denied doing anything wrong. Rose's show settled the suit with Lucy and other interns, paying them up to $250,000 in back wages and legal fees.

Federal courts are reconsidering the issue, and their decisions should offer more specific guidance for companies to determine when interns can work without pay. Thanks to Lucy's legal challenge, it's likely more interns can expect a paycheck in exchange for their labor. But it's also likely there will be fewer interns; not long after Lucy's lawsuit, Condé Nast pulled the plug on its internship program.

FOR MORE INFORMATION

The U.S. Equal Employment Opportunity Commission (eeoc.gov) publishes a useful summary of legal (and impermissible) employment practices for every stage of the hiring process.

The National Employment Lawyers Foundation (nela.org) supports employee rights and offers a Find-A-Lawyer service for employees who feel they've been treated unfairly on the job.

The National Women's Law Center (nwlc.org) is an advocacy group for women and families; its website offers reports and toolkits about employment issues women face.

A Better Balance (abetterbalance.org) advocates for working families; its website has news and information about legal issues facing women at work.

Equal Rights Advocates (equalrights.org) is a national civil rights organization focused on economic and educational issues for women and girls.

Workplace Fairness (workplacefairness.org) seeks to advocate for fair treatment of workers; its website publishes practical tips on sexual harassment, among other resources.

ProPublica, the independent, nonprofit investigative journalism organization, has published a fascinating series about the revolt against unpaid internships at propublica.org/series/internships.

23

HOUSEHOLD HELP

OPENING STATEMENT

On our toughest days, during that challenging, bittersweet period of my daughter's senior year of high school, only one activity seemed to bring us together: watching the film *The Help*.

I am ambivalent about *The Help* in book and movie form. Both versions of the wildly popular story are lovingly presented, the movie has a great cast, and I'm cheered by any narrative that gives an underdog her just revenge. On the whole, though, it's a sentimental take on a serious historical matter—civil rights and race relations—and sentimental is not my style. But that's just me. My daughter has no qualms about the story and loves it in every medium. She especially relates to the bond between the devoted maids and their adorable charges, and sees parallels to her relationship with her beloved longtime babysitter. (Given the attributes of the employing mothers, which range from stereotypically slutty to unspeakably hostile, I've decided not to ask which character I resemble.)

When pressed, my daughter will allow that I've been a good boss to our gifted, indispensable caregiver. But have I been a legally appropriate one?

Before various Nannygates made this issue clear, most otherwise law-abiding adults ignored the legal responsibilities that attach to home workers. We've already looked at some of the rights you enjoy as an employee at your job. Let's now switch sides and examine your responsibilities as an employer.

IT'S THE LAW

You may think: if someone works for me, they are an employee, full stop. But the law divides workers roughly into two classes: employees, and independent contractors, who roughly speaking are closer to freelancers. The way your employee works for you will put her in one of these categories and determine your legal responsibilities.

To explain the difference, let's borrow a sort of charming example from the IRS; specifically, its Publication 926, Household Employer's Tax Guide:

> *You pay Betty Shore to babysit your child and do light housework four days a week in your home. Betty follows your specific instructions about household and child care duties. You provide the household equipment and supplies that Betty needs to do her work. Betty is your household employee.*

(Note that at four days a week, Betty is not a full-time worker but she's still your employee.)

An independent contractor, by contrast, is someone whom you

hire for a certain result, but that person decides when and how it gets done. Take it away, IRS example:

> *You made an agreement with John Peters to care for your lawn. John runs a lawn care business and offers his services to the general public. He provides his own tools and supplies and he hires and pays any helpers he needs. Neither John nor his helpers are your household employees.*

Got it? If not, here's a pop quiz, using examples from my own household:

Beloved babysitter/housekeeper? Employee. She has to work at certain times, I set her salary, and I buy the products she uses at my home.

Electrician or plumber? Independent contractor, and I mean independent. No control over when he is available, he brings all sorts of complicated tools, and it goes without saying that I don't, much less can't, tell him how to fix the short or the leak. Painters, plasterers, and even all those workers whose jobs don't begin with the letter *P* are independent contractors if they work on a freelance basis in a manner you don't necessarily control.

What does it mean if your household employee is an employee under federal law? In a word, taxes. And another word, benefits, as in those your employee, legally paid, can collect from Social Security long after you part company.

To summarize your tax obligations: If you pay your household worker—who is an employee—more than a certain amount ($1,800 in a year at the time of this writing), you are required to pay Social Security, Medicare, and, possibly, state income taxes, and also withhold taxes for your employee. (If you are so inclined, you can pay your employee's share of those taxes yourself.) You may owe unemployment taxes as well if you pay more than a certain amount ($1,000 as I write this) during a three-month period.

In general, these rules don't apply to your babysitter if he or she is under the age of eighteen. They can apply, though, if you hire your adult children or your own parents for pay.

So how do you comply with the law? As a starting point, you'll get your very own EIN, or employer identification number, from the government. I've done it, and (perhaps since the request will draw revenue into our government's coffers) the IRS makes it easy. If you go to irs.gov, you can do it online. You also can read the IRS's own delightfully straightforward documents for guidance. Two favorites: the aforementioned IRS Publication 926: Household Employer's Tax Guide, and IRS Publication 15 (Circular E): Employer's Tax Guide, each of which has its own web page with updates.

I think of Publication 926 as a sort of Declaration of Independence for household workers. When employers comply, and pay taxes, those workers can collect the Social Security they deserve in retirement.

At the end of the year, you have to generate a W-2 form for your employee to file with the IRS; you also file that information yourself with the Social Security Administration and relevant state tax authorities.

It's worth noting that many household workers are covered by the minimum wage and overtime laws passed right after the Great Depression, though some of those employees (such as "casual babysitters," workers who care for the elderly and sick, and live-in employees) have only limited protection under those laws.

Along with taxes, you have another obligation as an employer: making sure your employee is eligible to work in the United States.

You might think this requirement sprang up after the events of September 11, 2001. You would be wrong. It is the by-product of a round of immigration reform that led to the Immigration Reform and Control Act of 1986. Under the law, only U.S. citizens, noncitizen nationals (such as natives of American Samoa and Swains Island—I've never heard of it, either), lawful permanent residents (who hold a green card), and aliens legally authorized to work (under pretty specific circumstances) can be hired. If you hire someone, she must show you that she falls into one of those categories, and you must send a form, the U.S. Citizenship and Immigration Services Form I-9: Employment Eligibility Verification, to the federal government to prove you checked.

You are not required to check the eligibility of a worker who performs "casual domestic work in a private home on a sporadic, irregular, or intermittent basis." As we've discussed, if you have a full-time babysitter or housekeeper, it's hard to justify describing that person as working "sporadically" in any way.

To add a wrinkle to this already complex issue (bear with me—we are almost there), undocumented workers can pay taxes if they apply to the IRS for an individual taxpayer ID number, and you can withhold on their behalf. That is a move born of trust, which some experts assert is legitimate, that the IRS won't call the Department of Homeland Security and turn the worker in.

What happens if you employ an undocumented immigrant—someone born overseas who doesn't have a legal right to live in the United States—and get caught? If you are in line for a prominent government post, nothing good. Which brings us to the origins of that consciousness-raising term: Nannygate.

EXHIBIT 54: NANNYGATE

The year was 1993. I was a junior associate at a high-powered New York law firm, and all around me Ivy League–trained baby lawyers were plotting their ascent to the top of their profession, not merely as well-compensated partners in private practice, but as leaders in public life. In their minds, undaunted by the odds, they were soon to become federal prosecutors, judges, perhaps, someday, even attorney general of the United States.

How do I know my colleagues were so wildly ambitious? I know because the minute "Nannygate" made headlines, they started asking around for babysitter recommendations.

These young lawyers were as taken aback by the situation as President Bill Clinton, who clearly did not anticipate a controversy when he chose Zoë Baird, an accomplished corporate lawyer, as his nominee for attorney general in 1993. Zoë's nomination went awry because she and her then husband (a constitutional law professor at Yale) had hired a Peruvian couple, undocumented immigrants, to work as their driver and nanny and had failed to pay their Social Security taxes until just before the nomination. Even though the Peruvian couple was in the process of applying for citizenship with Zoë's help, and even though Zoë and her husband had consulted an immigration lawyer, who told them (incorrectly) that they did not need to pay Social Security taxes, the disclosures couldn't be reconciled with the fact that as attorney general, Zoë would supervise the Immigration and Naturalization Service.

Zoë Baird withdrew, and the president quickly found another candidate: Kimba Wood, another accomplished lawyer and mother. (Law geeks: she specialized in antitrust law, which, to my mind, puts her in the pantheon of great legal minds; antitrust law is essentially incomprehensible.)

But the well-credentialed Kimba also fell afoul of the new national stringency toward hiring undocumented immigrants. In the past, Kimba had hired an undocumented immigrant as a sitter. That Kimba had hired the sitter when it was still legal to do so, paid the requisite taxes on her salary, and later helped her sitter become a legal resident didn't alleviate political concerns, and she was summarily axed from consideration for the post. In her place, Clinton selected a safe choice: Janet Reno, a Florida prosecutor who had no children.

These high-profile exceptions (and there are others) aside, the IRS doesn't catch too many taxpayers who fail to pay taxes on their household help. The agency does offer amnesty for household employers who have not paid taxes but decide to come clean. A new program called the Voluntary Classification Settlement Program (way to name programs so laypeople have no idea what they are, IRS) invites employers to reclassify employees correctly, and then eliminates interest and penalties for prior years' taxes that should have been paid.

EXHIBIT 55: NANNY SURVEILLANCE

Should you spy on your nanny?

I am not a fan of this practice, which I'm not sure yields enough information for the mistrust it could create between worker and boss.

But if you can't resist the power of technology, here are two basic rules:

1. Install the camera in a room where your nanny does not expect privacy. Living room may be okay; bathroom is another story.
2. Be careful about audiotape. While you may live in a state where videotaping another person without their permission is legal, that state is likely to have stricter rules about audiotaping without consent. (In general, it's illegal to record a conversation when you are not participating and can't overhear it.) Besides, chances are you are less concerned with what your employee is saying than what he is doing.

If you proceed, rather than taping surreptitiously, consider telling your nanny first. That conversation eliminates the possibility that your nanny will find out you were snooping behind her back, a trust buster. And in any event, don't most people behave better when they know they are being watched?

EXHIBIT 56: HOUSEHOLD HELP BEST PRACTICES

At a time when any signs of life in organized labor are a pleasant surprise, it's rewarding to know that housekeepers are trying to band together and demand rights they surely deserve. So if you are about to employ household help for the first time, or just want to be a more enlightened employer, a great way to get oriented is to consult organizations dedicated to their well-being.

One group is called Hand in Hand, and it offers a manifesto about household employment practices that is a thoughtful road map to consider as you hire. Hand in Hand recommends that employers of nannies, housecleaners, or other caregivers take "one step up" to make these relationships more professional, and therefore treat these invaluable employees with respect. These are its guidelines, and I reprint them here, slightly edited, for you to consider:

DO YOU COMMUNICATE CLEARLY AND OPENLY?

- Have you clearly defined your employee's responsibilities in the form of a contract or written agreement, so that both parties understand their obligations and responsibilities?
- Do you have a defined schedule for evaluation that includes a review of employer and employee expectations and experience and a plan of action to respond to any concerns?
- Do you negotiate a trial period with a new employee after which either party can terminate an agreement?
- Have you negotiated a standard termination notice period, stating that an employer or employee would need to provide two weeks' notice prior to terminating any employment arrangement?

DO YOU PAY FAIR WAGES?

All employers:

◆ Do you provide semiannual or annual raises?

◆ Do you have a plan to pay severance in accordance with number of years worked?

Full- or half-time employers:

◆ Do you pay the living wage of $15 to $18 per hour (+ $2 supplement if you do not provide health benefits)?

◆ Do you provide overtime pay for every hour over 40 hours per week?

Part-time employers:

◆ If you employ someone for four hours or less per week, do you pay at least $50 for the first three hours and $15 for every subsequent hour?

◆ Do you provide overtime pay if the work in a given week takes longer than the mutually agreed-upon amount of work time?

DO YOU PROVIDE BENEFITS, TIME OFF, AND OTHER PROVISIONS OF A HEALTHY WORKPLACE?

All employers:

◆ Do you provide health coverage (insurance, $2 wage supplement, or another mutually agreed-upon way)?

Employers of direct care workers (such as home health aides or nannies):

◆ Do you provide petty cash for activities, transit, or meals?

Employers of housecleaners:

◆ Do you provide protective gear and offer the option of non-toxic supplies?

Full-time employers:

◆ Do you provide a mutually agreed-upon number of paid sick and/or personal days?

◆ Do you provide two weeks or more of paid vacation days at times chosen by the employee?

◆ Do you provide paid days off on the standard eight paid government holidays?

◆ Do you provide meals and breaks?

Part-time employers:

◆ Do you pay your employee regardless if you cancel for any reason or if they are sick?

CELEBRITY LAW LESSON: LADY GAGA

Let's say you are a global pop star, famous for your outrageous stagecraft, flamboyant fashion, and elaborate videos. You can even really sing. Let's say you have a personal assistant named Jennifer O'Neill whom you pay $75,000 a year. Let's say your assistant thinks she deserves overtime pay for being on call "every hour of every day" for nearly a year, and that your dispute over Jennifer's pay lands in federal court. And let's say that, when asked about the time commitment you expected from your assistant, you testified (yes, testified, as in under oath, at a deposition):

You don't get a schedule. You don't get a schedule that is like you punch in and you can play fucking Tetris at your desk for four hours and then you punch out at the end of the day. This is when I need you, you're available.

It's safe to conclude that no matter how her career progresses, Lady Gaga should stay very far away from providing testimony of any sort, particularly in her own defense. The judge hearing the case declined Lady Gaga's request that it be dismissed and sent it to a jury to determine whether Jennifer deserved pay for her on-call time; before it delivered a decision, Gaga and Jennifer settled for an undisclosed sum.

FOR MORE INFORMATION

Along with the publications mentioned in this chapter, the IRS publishes yet another guide, Form 1779, with advice about determining whether a worker is an independent contractor or an employee, at irs.gov.

Hand in Hand: The Domestic Employers Association (domestic-employers.org) seeks better working conditions for nannies, housekeepers, and home attendants and offers employers tips on communication, fair wages, and benefits.

The International Nanny Association (nanny.org) seeks to guide employers and employees in screening, hiring, and paying nannies.

PART FIVE

PROTECTING YOURSELF

24

ONLINE ESSENTIALS

OPENING STATEMENT

Have you ever hired someone and hated their work? Did you retaliate by posting a critical rant on an online review site? Did you feel better, even self-righteous about sharing your experience with innocent would-be customers? Well, before you post again, consider the fate of Virginia homeowner Jane Perez.

In 2011, Jane hired local contractor Christopher Dietz, a high school friend, to spruce up her home.

Despite their school ties, the transaction went sour; Jane was unhappy with Dietz's work. Homeowner-contractor relationships have a high failure rate, and in that regard Jane and Dietz conformed to type. But in the Internet era, Jane was able to broadcast her dissatisfaction far and wide. She took to Yelp and awarded Dietz the dreaded single star, claiming that his work damaged, rather than improved, her home. Also, as she explained to Yelp readers, he trespassed on her property. Typed Jane: "Bottom line do not put yourself through this nightmare of a contractor."

For Dietz, the review was a business-choking disaster. He accused Jane of costing him $300,000 in lost revenue and sued her for defamation, seeking $750,000. At the same time, missing the point of his own lawsuit, Dietz took to the web to retaliate with complaints about Jane, prompting her to sue him.

The case of the competing complaints went to a jury, which decided to call it a draw, finding that Dietz and Jane had defamed each other, but that neither should collect a dime as a result.

Ah, the web, that irresistible cesspool of unreliable information, porn, argument-settling stats, instant-gratification shopping, and ever-expanding opportunities for credit card fraud and identity theft. Anarchic? By its very nature. Can it be tamed? Not without colliding with important principles of free speech.

On the other hand, the web is hardly the Wild West. As Jane and Dietz learned, traditional laws still apply. If you publish a false statement about someone that harms their reputation, they can sue you for defamation, whether you publish online or in print.

The Internet and the law make an awkward pair: a mismatched couple of technology, sprinting forward, and law, limping behind. To stay out of trouble online, we need to understand where they intersect.

IT'S THE LAW

Let's take an armchair trip across the ocean to see just how difficult it is to regulate online activity.

Our destination: Europe, where privacy receives more protection than it does in the freewheeling former colonies. In 2014, European legislators wanted to help people who Googled themselves and found something they didn't like. So the European Union passed a law, dubbed the "right to be forgotten," that forces Google to remove some search results (though not the underlying articles) on request. The result: immediate controversy and confusion. British news organizations cried foul when they learned that links to material they had published would be removed. And critics noted that the links Google removed in Europe could be easily found on Google's U.S.-based site.

Yikes. Well, at least the Europeans tried. In the United States, by comparison, lawmakers have barely dipped a toe into the legislative waters. It's fair to say that if you want to be "forgotten" on the web in the United States, your best recourse is not to seek a legal remedy, but to see if a reputation management company can help you downplay negative material. (One hint: the more times you search for that humiliating bit of web data, the higher that unsavory material might rise in search results.)

Clearly, we are watching the web—and the law—evolve, and so let's keep our goals for this chapter modest: let's learn how to maintain our dignity, avoid inadvertent online theft, and keep our jobs.

PROTECTING (WHAT'S LEFT OF) YOUR PRIVACY ONLINE

We live in an age of depressing revelations about government spying, but also one of epic, narcissistic oversharing. As a result, our formerly unremarkable behavior has been memorialized and shared worldwide, often against our will, and not just by the National Security Agency but by our thoughtless relatives and friends.

I, for one, preferred to break out my awkward Elaine Benes dance moves at a wedding reception without fear of being tagged and held up to permanent ridicule.

Is there any recourse for those of us who feel nostalgic about personal privacy?

Ironically, social media offers a glimmer of hope. Let's look at Facebook. Because of its reach and enduring popularity, Facebook sits in the crosshairs of our ongoing debate about Internet privacy. That's why checking out the site's fine print can be instructive. Facebook explains all the ways it might use the information that you shoveled into its virtual storage facility. But Facebook also offers ways to limit where the information you post can go. So why not conduct a Facebook privacy checkup? Go to the site's Interactive Tools, where you can review what you allow the public and advertisers to see and mine, and then to its account and privacy settings, where you can make adjustments to those boundaries. A single change, like untagging yourself from photos your friends post, lets you exert more control over your online profile. Then repeat this exercise for other social media sites you frequent: find the fine print, then exercise online discretion.

Happily, the Internet itself serves up lists of advice for Internet privacy protection. Sure, they all require more work than mindlessly clicking videos, but it's worth the effort—you should consider protecting your sensitive data as important to your well-being as putting cash in the bank or locking your car. So what can you do?

- Use a password manager to generate strong passwords that you can change (and store for retrieval when, if you are like me, you quickly forget them).
- Enable privacy-protecting settings on your web browser, add software that allows you to restrict how your information is collected (such as Lightbeam, which lets you

manage the so-called cookies that track your online reading habits), and switch to a search engine that lets you surf the web without tracking your information (popular alternatives include DuckDuckGo and Ixquick).

- Limit the amount of personal information you and your children provide; tactics can include creating fictitious answers to those pesky security questions and using fake names online.

EXHIBIT 57: POSTING WITHOUT STEALING

You didn't need me to warn you that the Internet is perilous, and now you know that it can be reckless and even legally actionable to post a negative comment online. But what about sharing an enviable graduation photo? Cat videos? Thoughtful content analyzing important geopolitical issues? Surely those items can't cause legal trouble, right?

Think again.

In the words of the Digital Media Law Project, "Every time you publish something online, whether it's a news article, blog post, podcast, video, or even a user comment, you open yourself up to potential legal liability."

In part, that's because federal law gives content owners the power to sue people who use their material without permission.

To put it bluntly, when you post someone else's article, photo, or music without their permission, you may be stealing. It's the digital equivalent of purse-snatching, because you are potentially making it harder for the owner to earn money from the sale of her work.

Lawyers call this protected content *intellectual property*, even though the term includes material that no intellectual would be caught dead reading or watching. From a comic book to the artwork on a box of Cocoa Puffs, if it is the by-product of creativity, the creator usually has the right to decide how it is used.

So, for example, take your beloved photo collection. Here's a legal fact that should be better known: the photographers own it, not you. The yearbook photo that memorialized my indefensible perm? Those wedding photos in which you look impossibly slim and are surrounded by guests whose presence you can no longer explain? The photographer is in charge, unless she signed away her rights. In short, you are not legally permitted to repost and share those photos without permission. For sites that encourage you to share content, the safest route is to post your own.

Don't panic—I'm not saying you'll get sued when you post your sister's vacation photos, but technically speaking, you need permission. And plenty of times, you'll have it: many people want their work to get a wider audience.

Plus, the law doesn't protect everything. We are free to reuse federal government publications. Under certain circumstances, you can use chunks of other people's work to comment on it, or create new works; that's called *fair use*.

And intellectual property protection isn't permanent. Eventually, work falls into what's called the *public domain*, where it can be freely used. This is why publishers love to repackage editions of literary classics: no pesky payments to long-dead authors. And it's why epic battles are fought over whether a profitable work has crossed the line from protected to free. Take Sherlock Holmes. The editor of a three-volume *New Annotated Sherlock Holmes* squared off against the estate of Holmes's creator, Sir Arthur Conan Doyle, which had been collecting licensing fees for use of the characters. Were Holmes and Dr. Watson still protected property, or available for use for free? A federal judge here ruled that the sleuth had become public property in the United States. (Unsolicited advice to all parties: carefully lower those dusty volumes and legal papers, fire up Netflix, and watch Benedict Cumberbatch instead. Ah, much better.) And the song "Happy Birthday"? Can't we all use it for free? Although nobody's likely to come after you for singing it at your nephew's birthday party, the song is not in the public domain. An American publishing company, Warner/Chappell Music, claimed ownership in a lawsuit against filmmakers and musicians who balked at paying for permission to use the song.

Intellectual property law is super specific and replete with exceptions that are truly beyond the scope of this book. So if you are starting your own blog or website or want to know what you can do if you think your intellectual property has been pilfered online, go to the Digital Media Law Project website, dmlp.org, for in-depth explanations of intellectual property rights. The site has a wealth of practical information about other digital media topics and even offers a legal referral service along with Harvard's Berkman Center for Internet & Society.

By the way, do you blog, or maintain a robust social media presence, and make money doing it? Maybe I am a little jealous of your effortless output of latticed pies, stylish interiors, and suspiciously well-groomed children. Still, I salute your creativity and diligence. And I urge you to obey the law. Take a look at the legal guide offered by the Electronic Frontier Foundation, eff.org, which covers some of the topics we've reviewed and more, all with a goal of protecting your free speech rights.

EXHIBIT 58: WEB V. WORK

A list of people canned for inappropriate social media use would quickly fill this book. So I'll share one example to illustrate the hazards of posting about your job. Katie Duke, a New York nurse who gained a following when she appeared on a reality TV show about the emergency room where she worked, lost her job the same day she posted a photo on Instagram of an emergency room. The room was empty and in disarray; Katie noted it had just been used to treat a patient. While Katie said the firing wasn't prompted by a breach of privacy, and the hospital wouldn't comment, let's apply the law of common sense: is it a good idea or a questionable one to share images of a recently used emergency room, even one that's empty?

Lots of law is complicated. This is simple. With limited exceptions, your employer can fire you for work-related content you post online, even if you post on your own time and to your personal site. And if you think your company isn't interested in your online activity, think again: one study suggests that in 2015, 60 percent of corporations will have programs to watch their workers' social media behavior.

How can you avoid this fate? Exercise discretion. You remember discretion, that abandoned attribute that encourages us to think before we type? It's good to pause before complaining about your employer online. Other sensible tips:

- If your company has a social media policy—and many do—read it and follow it.
- Do not post confidential information about your company or its clients. This happens much more often than it should.
- Similarly, protect work-related information by keeping passwords secret and otherwise following company security policies.

As law (and human behavior online) continue to evolve, you'll need up-to-the-minute information about how to comport yourself. Some resources follow, and as always I invite to you watch my website, lisagreenlaw.com, for updates.

FOR MORE INFORMATION

Julia Angwin is an investigative journalist who specializes in technology. Her website offers comprehensive (and alarming) reporting about the scope of digital tracking and what you and your children can do to protect your privacy: juliaangwin.com.

The Privacy Rights Clearinghouse (privacyrights.org) is a California-based nonprofit that provides consumer advocacy and publishes a Social Networking Privacy guide.

For guidance on keeping the web safe for your children and yourself, the National Crime Prevention Council publishes material (some featuring its iconic canine, McGruff the Crime Dog) that covers web safety and security for issues that include social networking and identity theft, for parents, kids, and teens, at ncpc.org.

The U.S. Copyright Office, at copyright.gov, offers guidance on copyright, including FAQs and a Copyright Basics fact sheet. The Library of Congress also publishes copyright materials, including cartoons featuring Cop E. Wright, who raps about the law to a group of creative kids, at loc.gov.

An interesting guide to fair use for video comes from the Center for Social Media, which offers a Code of Best Practices in Fair Use for Online Video at centerforsocialmedia.org/fairuse.

DOMESTIC VIOLENCE

OPENING STATEMENT

So many statistics, all of them grim.

Let's start with a government report, the National Intimate Partner and Sexual Violence Survey. The survey, released by the Centers for Disease Control and Prevention in 2010, found the following:

- Nearly one in five women has been raped in her lifetime.
- Almost half of those rapes occurred before the victim turned eighteen.
- One in four women has been the victim of severe physical violence by an intimate partner.
- One in six women has been stalked or has feared that either she or someone close to her would be harmed or killed by a stalker.

This is a global problem. The World Health Organization says that 30 percent of women worldwide have been victims of intimate partner violence.

Are men also victims of domestic violence? Yes, and more often than you might expect. Are men our concern here? No, and not just because this is a book for women, but rather because women are disproportionately victims of violence at the hands of a significant other, spouse, or ex.

Domestic violence, despite its pervasiveness and upsetting frequency, has mostly been relegated to the shadows of public attention. Every once in a while, a famous woman's horror story surfaces and we pause, make appropriate expressions of sympathy and distress . . . and then return to our presumably nonviolent lives. Photos published worldwide exposed beautiful best-selling cookbook author Nigella Lawson and her handsome and phenomenally wealthy husband Charles Saatchi in the midst of a public fight, with Charles holding a weeping Nigella by her throat. Charles spun the incident as merely "playful" and then announced plans to divorce Nigella to a British tabloid. A judge granted their divorce after a seventy-second hearing, and the issue receded from public view, soon eclipsed by testimony about Nigella's drug use from two of her former personal assistants who were tried for (and acquitted of) fraud.

In our information-saturated world, already crowded with round-the-clock news of disasters and atrocities, these small-scale problems don't sustain our attention. Then again, domestic violence is so prevalent that to pay constant attention would be like obsessively monitoring traffic reports for evidence of car accidents. But I think its relative invisibility is also a side effect of our simply not wanting to admit its existence. As women, we skew toward blaming ourselves for our problems, and publicly admitting to domestic violence can feel like exposing your own, epic failure. Also, more practically, a woman who is under attack often fears losing

her partner, and the economic support that partner offers, or repri-
sal, or worse.

Since domestic violence almost certainly has touched you, your
friends, your daughters, or your female relatives, I want you to be in
a prime position to help. You may make a huge difference in another
woman's happiness, safety, even life span.

As we are about to learn, this is a legal matter in which you can
aid yourself without a license to practice law. If you are a victim, know
a victim, or even see a victim, you can speak up, share information,
and launch protective legal processes. Our careful, womanly organiza-
tional skills can be employed to keep logs for ourselves or for a friend,
accompany a friend to a police station, or find a shelter. And our in-
herent nosiness means we can ask a question that, even if based on a
hunch or assumption, may still yield a disclosure that can lead to legal
help.

So let's review the laws meant to keep women safe and think about
what we can do, each of us, to reduce the outrageous volume of domestic violence.

IT'S THE LAW

Most laws protecting women against domestic violence are state
specific. But a federal law, the Violence Against Women Act (yep,
VAWA), first passed in 1994 and since reauthorized, toughens pun-
ishments for some crimes and offers support to improve legal, law enforcement, and community support for domestic violence victims and
to develop and fund protection and prevention programs.

The federal government also runs the National Domestic Violence
Hotline for victims to get help. The hotline, which has answered more
than three million calls, receives more than twenty-two thousand
calls a month—a month!—and responds in more than 170 languages.

The government says the law has reduced domestic violence and improved state responses.

If you are the victim of domestic violence and you want advice about your next steps, you should call the hotline for advice. It is open 24/7 and the calls are confidential. (Its website will warn you, as do all domestic-violence-related sites, that your web surfing can be monitored by an abuser; it may be safest to log in from a borrowed computer or call from a borrowed phone.) As I write, the number is 1-800-799-7233 (or 1-800-799-SAFE).

In domestic violence law, the relationship between victim and perpetrator matters—it must be construed as "personal." Depending on the state, that personal relationship can range from spouses and exes to couples who live together, or did, and are dating, or broke up, or even parents who never lived together. It's not domestic violence if the parties are strangers.

DO YOU KNOW A VICTIM?

If you think a woman you know and love is a victim, consider these suggestions adapted from those offered by Family Tree, a wonderful organization in Denver that aids both men and women struggling with domestic violence (along with child abuse and homelessness).

10 Helpful Things to Do or Say to Someone
Who Is Being Abused

1. Open a dialogue. "Are you ever afraid of _____ 's temper?"
2. Show concern. "I am afraid for your safety."
3. Appreciate the danger she is in. "I'm afraid the danger will get worse."

4. Commit to being supportive. "I will always be here for you."
5. Listen. "If you ever need to talk, I will just listen and not give advice."
6. Value the victim. "This is not your fault and you do not deserve to be abused."
7. Compliment the victim. Help to counter the toll that the verbal abuse may be taking on her self-esteem.
8. Make observations, not judgments. "I'm worried about you; you don't laugh as much anymore."
9. Offer to help in ways you can. Set clear and fair boundaries you are comfortable with.
10. Ask questions that focus on her feelings. "That sounds scary to me—how do you feel about it?"

5 Things Not to Do or Say

1. Don't say "Just leave."
2. Don't give an ultimatum. This helps the batterer isolate the victim further and cuts off her support system.
3. Don't bad-mouth the batterer. This may cause the victim to be defensive of the batterer and will make it seem unsafe to confide in you.
4. Don't disbelieve or demand proof of the abuse. You are not a judge. If she feels unsafe, that is all that should matter to you.
5. Don't tell the victim what she "has to do." Domestic violence is about power and control, and if a victim is going to heal, she must regain control herself. Do not give advice, or tell the victim what she needs to do, or what you would do. It is good to help the victim discover her options, but the decision must be hers alone.

EXHIBIT 59: RESTRAINING ORDERS IN ACTION

In the legal fight against domestic violence, restraining orders (sometimes called protective orders or injunctions) are the first line of defense. Depending on the state and the situation, an order can require an abuser to stop the abuse, and/or require the abuser to stay away from you at work, home, or school, or to cease all forms of contact. If children are involved, the order can restrict or stop contact and set custody and support payments.

A restraining order establishes a record of abuse, and will make it easier to pursue official help. If an abuser violates the order, the person who has the order can call authorities who can arrest and jail the abuser for violating the order.

The problem with court orders is that a victim is often left wondering whether her abuser will obey or retaliate against her for seeking one in the first place. As a Justice Department study put it: "victims face a dilemma—staying or leaving, and securing, maintaining or dropping a protective order may all result in reabuse."

The evidence on whether restraining orders work is mixed. The Justice Department took a look in 2009 and concluded that while restraining orders do not prevent all abuse, they don't seem to increase risk. They have been shown to improve the well-being of victims, who at least feel that they have legal support. Some evidence suggests that the harsher the terms of the order, the more protection it will offer, as will an order coupled with criminal prosecution.

How bad does behavior need to be to qualify for a restraining order? It's what lawyers call fact specific. Each state will have different standards and then look at the petition to see if the behavior applies.

Two court cases in North Dakota illustrate the range of responses courts might have to domestic disputes.

Case 1. A husband and wife concluded a bitter divorce fight; a court found the ex-husband had alienated their children from his ex. The court granted the ex-wife physical custody of their kids and allowed the ex-husband limited, supervised visits and two twenty-minute phone calls a week, which their mom could monitor. Two days after a court affirmed the judgment, the mom was in her car at a stoplight. The dad pulled up alongside her, and according to her, screamed, "I'm going to kill you, you fucking bitch." This incident, coupled with a cell phone message he left calling her a "cheap whore" and a supervised visit he had with the kids that was halted by a supervisor because of his behavior, led a court to grant the mom a restraining order. The order was affirmed on appeal because she made a credible showing that she feared imminent harm.

The dad did not help his case when, as the hearing wrapped up and his ex-wife's lawyer asked if the judge would bar her ex from possessing firearms, he said, aloud, to his lawyer, "I tell you what . . . if it can get any worse, it will."

Judges really hate open-court challenges to their authority.

In response, the judge made a firearms ban part of the restraining order.

Case 2: A husband and wife had an argument. During the argument, the wife told a court, her spouse called her a "bitch," treated her "like a child and a baby," and said he would burn down their home if he couldn't keep it.

She secured a temporary order of protection and, on appeal, it was reversed. Why? Because she could not show she feared imminent harm from her husband. The threat that he "would" burn the house down was closer to a "perceived possibility" that he might set it on fire. Also, the wife admitted that the husband had not been physically violent, and described a fight where she slapped him.

It's no surprise that when women seek protective orders, results vary widely. Different states have different laws. Different judges hear requests in different ways. At bottom, this is a situation where a woman needs to persuade a fact-finder—the judge—that she has been threatened or has suffered abuse. It's Lawyering 101, but in a situation much more fraught than the usual legal disputes. A consistent story, well told, is the place to start; credible witnesses and physical evidence (photos, objects, even bruises) may not be necessary but will bolster a case.

EXHIBIT 60: STALKING

A sixty-four-year-old woman identified in court papers as L.M., retired as a protocol officer from the Department of Defense, took to a dating site after her husband died in 2009. There she met another federal employee, Kenneth Kuban, sixty-one, who worked for the Library of Congress. They dated, she broke it off, and he pursued her so relentlessly that she eventually secured a restraining order in 2011.

That's when the Internet stalking began.

Kuban, according to prosecutors, took to the "Casual Encounters" section of Craigslist to pose as L.M. Using her name, he invited men to visit "a senior lady who is looking for some fun and adventure" and wanted to meet "a gentleman in his fifties that . . . can give me some pleasuring."

One hundred men felt they fit the bill. Drawn by the lure of easy middle-aged action, they trekked to L.M.'s Virginia home from as far away as North Carolina. L.M. was forced to install cameras and security gates at her home to turn back the tide of horny Romeos, and local law enforcement sometimes made several visits a day to send the men away.

Kuban's posts were traced back to his Library of Congress computer. He was charged with stalking, pled guilty, and was sentenced to five years in prison.

Why do I share this story? Because it seems so random, so awful, and so difficult to prevent or address. One minute, you are looking for a date. The next, you are hoping federal authorities imprison the man you met, dated, and rejected, meaning no harm.

What, exactly, is stalking? The Justice Department offers a working definition: "a course of conduct directed at a specific person that would cause a reasonable person to feel fear."

Just like those for domestic violence, which of course is an intersecting problem, stalking statistics are mind-boggling. By a common estimate, 6.6 million people are stalked every year in the United States. Most victims are stalked by someone they know, and two-thirds of female victims are stalked by a current or former romantic partner.

For years, no laws were on the books to bar stalking. Then, in 1989, a young actress, Rebecca Schaeffer, was shot to death by an obsessed fan who showed up at the door of her home. The next year, four Orange County, California, women were murdered by ex-boyfriends, estranged husbands, or rebuffed love interests. All four victims had restraining orders and all thought their exes would kill them, but police had no power to intervene. California passed the first antistalking law in 1990 and by 1992, twenty-seven states had antistalking laws on the books. Today, stalking is a crime in every state.

WHAT TO DO IF YOU ARE BEING STALKED

I'm sure I do not need to underline how serious this situation is. So let's review some concrete advice from the Stalking Resource Center, which is part of the National Center for Victims of Crime, a national advocacy organization:

1. Trust your instincts. Victims of stalking often feel pressured by friends or family to downplay the stalker's behavior, but stalking poses a real threat of harm. Your safety is paramount.

2. Call the police if you feel you are in any immediate danger. Explain why even some actions that seem harmless—like leaving you a gift—are causing you fear.
3. Keep a record or log of each contact with the stalker. Be sure to also document any police reports.
4. Stalkers often use technology to contact their victims. Save all emails, text messages, photos, and postings on social networking sites as evidence of the stalking behavior.
5. Get connected with a local victim advocate to talk through your options and discuss safety planning. Call the National Domestic Violence Hotline at 1-800-799-SAFE.

CYBERATTACKS: THE RISE OF REVENGE PORN

We all know the Internet is awash in porn. Researchers are only beginning to tally the effects that an all-access pass to lewd imagery may have on developing minds. As if that isn't worrisome enough, what if a revealing photo on the web is yours?

That is a possible, horrible outcome thanks to a nasty Internet publishing subculture known as revenge porn, which earned that name because angry former suitors are so often the perpetrators. These jilted lovers post naked images of their ex-girlfriends, along with personal information, on websites purpose-built to attract anonymous, savage online commentary.

Since 2013, thirteen states have passed laws to block distribution of a sexual photo (some laws say "private" or "intimate") without its subject's consent. In other states, victims might be protected by invasion of privacy laws, and sometimes copyright violations (if the woman shot a selfie, she owns copyright of the photo). It's not an easy attack to stop, though, because the purveyors of this porn can be hard to track down, and more established website operators can defend a lawsuit thanks to federal law that grants them broad protection for user-posted speech. In short, it can be a battle between personal privacy and free speech.

An organization called Without My Consent seeks to help victims of revenge porn combat these egregious invasions of privacy. Its website, withoutmyconsent.org, is collecting state-by-state information that can help victims and their lawyers fight back.

EXHIBIT 61: COMBATING ABUSE

If the bad news is that domestic violence—overwhelmingly suffered by women—continues to plague us in many forms and venues, the good news is that an increasing number of dedicated professionals are pushing back.

The federal government has offered grants to encourage a coordinated and multidisciplinary focus on violent crime against women so that the criminal justice system is better equipped to solve these unique, if common, crimes.

One program, the Domestic Violence High Risk Team, in Newburyport, Massachusetts, has been lauded for its hybrid approach to preventing violence. Teaming members from a local crisis center, hospital representatives, the district attorney's office, and police and parole officers, the group meets to review cases and share information (within confidentiality limits, which can be delicate).

Does the approach work? A data point suggests it does: in 106 high-risk cases that were aided by the program, only eight women had to take shelter; prior to the formation of the program, estimates were that 90 percent of the women in those cases would have sought shelter.

Perhaps close coordination between authorities in different disciplines, coupled by attention from loving friends, will help more victims get the help they need.

FOR MORE INFORMATION

The National Coalition Against Domestic Violence (ncadv.org) and the National Center for Victims of Crime (ncvc.org) have robust resources and information. You can call the National Domestic Violence Hotline, 1-800-799-SAFE, for assistance (always make sure you are in a safe place before placing a call or doing web research).

Love Is Respect provides a safe space for young people to discuss dating violence, and offers information and resources: loveisrespect.org.

PART SIX

LATER LIFE ISSUES

TAKING CHARGE I: MEDICAL DECISIONS AND POWERS OF ATTORNEY

OPENING STATEMENT

This is a sad story about my father, Jack Green.

At age seventy, my beloved, hardworking dad learned he had lung cancer. His awful diagnosis came with one advantage: while he had tough decisions to make about treatment, he had enough time to think about his immediate future, along with the opportunity to do some paperwork. As the lawyer member of the family, I was able to persuade my father to sign a living will and health care proxy that outlined his preferences about care and put me in charge of carrying them out.

Thanks to these documents, we were in a much better position to execute Dad's wishes when his condition worsened after his surgery. After all, we had his signature on papers that gave us the authority to make plans about his final years.

Our family, led by my heroic mother, suffered through scary months of tough choices and uncertain outcomes until Dad died. We didn't always agree on what was best. But those documents helped us fulfill our obligation to care for someone who had cared so well for us. Our difficult time was made easier because we had a snapshot, however imperfect, of Dad's own preferences and some authority to tell doctors how Dad wanted to live, and die.

I learned a lot from that searing experience. While we did some things correctly, we missed other obvious needs, including planning for the fate of Dad's small business before it was too late. Let me help you understand the many ways the law allows family and trusted friends to come to the aid of someone who is incapacitated.

IT'S THE LAW

If you are going to make a plan for your own illness and death, you need to engage in profound, searching thought about issues much more personal and sensitive than the scope of this book allows. But law conveys authority, and part of planning for the end should include exercising your authority to influence these deeply personal—and inevitable—events.

For health issues, you can do that by signing a document called an advance health care directive. The contents vary from state to state but generally can include two sets of instructions: a living will and a durable power of attorney for someone to make health care decisions for you.

In a *living will,* you offer guidance about what level of end-of-life care you want if you are unable to communicate. Typically, the living will lays out what treatments you want to undergo, or forgo, with as much specificity as you can bear. Do you want to be resuscitated if your heart stops beating? Do you want mechanical ventilation to help you breathe if you can't? Fluids or food intravenously or through a tube in your stomach? Would you want these treatments under any circumstances? And do you want palliative care so you are not in pain?

By granting *health care power of attorney*, meanwhile, you have appointed a person to be your agent (sometimes called a health care proxy) and carry out the medical decisions you would want when you are unable to make those decisions on your own. Think of your living will as an end-of-life map and your health care proxy as a conductor who has authority for both those issues and other medical situations that may arise before you are terminally ill or incapacitated.

What powers will your agent be able to exercise? The most dramatic is the power to decline medical treatment and stop lifesaving procedures, including artificial respiration and feeding. You can give your health care agent authority to admit or discharge you from a hospital, to agree to pain medication, and to donate your organs and tissues. That's why it's important to talk to your health care agent, with as much specificity as you can muster, about what you would want, and why.

Your health care power of attorney also should make it clear that your agent has authority to look at your medical records.

A broader and somewhat controversial alternative has its own acronym: POLST, or Physician Orders for Life-Sustaining Treatment.

The POLST form is a comprehensive checklist of patient preferences for the seriously ill, covering everything from antibiotics and artificial nutrition to resuscitation and respiration. It's signed by a doctor and meant to be carried around as a sort of portable guide to your own end of life.

These decisions are sobering. Mortality is sobering. No one wants to think about this topic in advance. But the consequences of inaction can be catastrophic.

EXHIBIT 62: WHEN COURTS HAVE TO DECIDE

Three unexpected medical emergencies, three young women in peril, three families forced to divine what those young women would want them to do while strangers second-guessed their decisions and motives. The Quinlan, Cruzan, and Schiavo cases provide unassailable evidence that you and your loved ones should draft health care directives.

In 1975, Julia and Joseph Quinlan, a self-described average middle-class family in New Jersey, got the 2 A.M. call every parent dreads. Their twenty-one-year-old daughter, Karen Ann, was in a local hospital, unconscious and, soon, comatose, after mixing alcohol and sedatives at a party. Eventually, Karen fell into a "persistent vegetative state" and had to be tethered to machines to live.

After careful consideration and prayer, her parents eventually decided they wanted to remove Karen from her ventilator. But that decision required court approval. Karen's parents lost their first round, but a unanimous New Jersey Supreme Court ruled that Joseph could serve as Karen's guardian and make decisions about her care. Karen was removed from her respirator but lived for another nine years before dying of pneumonia in 1985.

Karen Quinlan's family famously began a national conversation about living wills, and Nancy Cruzan's family brought that conversation to the attention of the U.S. Supreme Court. They had good reason.

In 1983, Joyce and Lester Cruzan's daughter, grievously injured after a car accident, never regained consciousness and, like Karen, she ended up in a persistent vegetative state. Nancy's parents eventually concluded that she should have her feeding tube removed. (She was able to breathe on her own.) But hospital employees refused to listen. Nancy's parents took their case to courts in Missouri, which denied their request, then to the Supreme Court. The Supreme Court's 5–4 decision recognized a right to die but required Nancy's parents to amass clear and convincing evidence that their daughter would want her tube removed. Nancy's parents found that evidence, her feeding tube was removed, and she died soon after that, eight years after the crash.

One more case completes this sad medical trinity. In 1990, Theresa Marie Schiavo collapsed in her Florida home after her heart stopped beating, and she suffered severe brain damage. Her husband, Michael, sought permission to remove Terri's feeding tube; her parents, Bob and Mary Schindler, who tried to unseat Michael as Terri's guardian, disagreed. Their dispute found its way to court, and her tube was removed, then reinserted, more than once. As the Schiavos' situation gained national attention, Congress weighed in, passing a controversial law transferring authority for the case from state to federal courts to keep Terri alive. Other laws were passed, courts ruled, the Supreme Court rejected opportunities to intervene, and finally, Terri died in 2005, almost two weeks after her tube was removed.

Together, these wrenching cases speak with a single voice and ask the same question: what would these young women have wanted their loved ones to do? But searching for that evidence, so central to each court's ruling, turned out to be like looking for a lost earring on a sandy beach: lots of exhausting activity and little to show for it. What these cases also had in common, and why I raise them here, is that none of the young women had expressed their end-of-life preferences in writing.

Obviously, it's unrealistic to expect young, healthy people to think to write down their end-of-life preferences. Nonetheless, talking specifically with your loved ones is a massive step in the right direction. You certainly should commit your own preferences to writing. For you, but also for your family, to save them from confusion and from battling with one another or with the courts (and, in the Schiavo case, outside groups, Congress, and the president), who may fight them fiercely to deny you, and them, a peaceful passing.

EXHIBIT 63: ASSISTED SUICIDE

A handful of states allow terminally ill patients to get fatal drug prescriptions from their doctors. These laws are complicated, with multiple steps, consultations, and waiting periods built in to be sure the patient is both sufficiently ill and mentally competent. And their use is still rare: seventy-seven patients in Oregon used drugs to end their lives in 2012. Are they an important advance in civil rights, or an unconscionable intrusion into the sanctity of life? I'll let you decide.

EXHIBIT 64: FINANCIAL AND PERSONAL AID

If you become disabled, you may need help with more than health care decisions.

A common solution, and one you should address at the same time you draft the health care documents we just discussed, is to grant someone a durable power of attorney to look after your personal and business needs. (Once again, the particulars of this document will vary by state; it's ideal to have an experienced lawyer help you.)

What's a durable power of attorney? The word *durable* means the power you grant while healthy remains in effect after you are incapacitated. (*Power*, of course, is authority.) The word *attorney* is a bit misleading: your durable power of attorney need not be granted to a lawyer; the designation really means you've chosen an agent to make decisions for you.

What can your agent do for you? You have the power to set limits, but the scope of authority can include the following:

1. Paying your expenses
2. Collecting Social Security, Medicare, and other government benefits
3. Collecting insurance payments
4. Managing your investments
5. Accessing your safe-deposit box
6. Managing your retirement accounts
7. Managing your property
8. Filing your tax returns

In short, power of attorney can mean a lot of power. Unlike guardians and conservators, whom we will discuss in a moment, these agents act without court supervision. As my experienced trusts and estates lawyer warns his clients, "The good news is that he/she can sign for you, and the bad news is that he/she can sign for you." So you want to be sure you choose someone you trust—someone who ideally has demonstrated loyalty and levelheadedness over time. Some advisers suggest choosing one person for your durable power of attorney and another as a health care proxy, to decentralize decisions and reduce the risk that the one person you selected turns out to be untrustworthy or worse. Be sure to select a successor agent, just in case something happens to your primary choice.

CALL OF DUTY: MANAGING SOMEONE ELSE'S MONEY AS A FIDUCIARY

What if a relative or friend chooses you to serve as her fiduciary, entrusted with looking after her finances, perhaps to prepare for prolonged illness or old age?

Congratulations. With fiduciary power (the power you obtain as agent for your family member or friend, who is legally known as the principal) comes great fiduciary responsibility.

The Consumer Financial Protection Bureau, the federal agency created in the wake of the 2008 financial crisis, summarizes four core fiduciary duties:

- *Act only in your principal's best interest.* Read the power of attorney document and follow it, including the circumstances under which it becomes effective; involve your principal in decision making if possible; avoid possible conflicts of interest, such as hiring a family member to work for your principal; do not borrow, lend, or give your principal's money to yourself or others. Significantly, do not pay yourself to act as a fiduciary unless the power of attorney document (or state law) gives you permission.
- *Manage your principal's money and property carefully.* Keep a detailed list of your principal's assets and debts; protect her property and make sure real estate is kept in good condition; invest carefully, perhaps more conservatively than you invest your own savings; pay bills and taxes; cancel unnecessary insurance; collect debts; see if your principal is entitled to benefits.

- *Keep your principal's money and property separate from yours.* Avoid joint accounts; maintain title to money and property in your principal's name; learn how to sign checks and other documents as an agent; pay your principal's expenses from her funds, not yours.
- *Keep good records.* Maintain a detailed list of money you receive and spend for your principal; keep all receipts, even if for small expenditures; avoid paying in cash; and if you are being paid, keep records of the work you did for pay.

EXHIBIT 65: TAKING FULL CONTROL

What if a loved one no longer can make decisions, and didn't identify and empower anyone to help?

Under these dire circumstances, courts can appoint guardians (or conservators) to manage that person's affairs. Before making that appointment, the court will investigate whether the incapacitated person—known as a ward—meets the state's test to prove incompetence.

Once appointed, a guardian operates under court supervision and may have wide-ranging authority over the ward that can include:

1. Choosing where to live
2. Choosing medical treatment, including end-of-life decisions
3. Driving
4. Owning property
5. Marriage or divorce
6. Voting

A court also can appoint a guardian for an estate—or property—that the guardian will manage on a ward's behalf. While a guardian can be a relative, it can also be an institution, such as a bank.

Guardianship disputes can be costly, emotional, and slow. And when relatives fight across state lines for control of an incapacitated relative, the proceedings can seem a sad mirror image of epic child custody battles.

To illustrate that point, we need look no farther than the war that erupted between two children of Lillian Glasser, an octogenarian widow suffering from Parkinson's disease and Alzheimer's.

Lillian lived in New Jersey with her husband, Ben, a doctor, who left her a $25 million fortune. So far, so peaceful. When Lillian visited her daughter in Texas, her daughter, who said she was alarmed by her mother's incapacity, applied for and won guardianship over Lillian in the Lone Star State. But should Texas have granted the request? Her son, resident in Florida, fought the guardianship appointment. And Lillian told a reporter she wanted to live in New Jersey. The battle over Lillian's future—which was paid for out of Lillian's assets—reportedly cost more than $3 million and lasted for years, even after Lillian died in 2011. Cases like these have prompted calls for a unified law governing which state has jurisdiction over these claims. As of this writing, thirty-seven states and the District of Columbia adopted the law; Texas was not one of them.

FOR MORE INFORMATION

The American Bar Association (americanbar.org) publishes a comprehensive, multistate health care power of attorney form.

The ABA also publishes a Consumer's Tool Kit for Health Care

Advance Planning, which includes self-help worksheets, state-specific advance planning forms, and guides and forms to help you grant power of attorney. It's worth reading even if you hire a lawyer to help with these matters.

TAKING CHARGE II:
ESTATE PLANNING

OPENING STATEMENT

If I maintained a blog, I would call it Confessions of a List Maker. I cherish my lists, and I bet you do, too. The to-do list I compile at the end of a workday. The grocery list I post, and continually update, on my refrigerator. The running list of errands that surfs into my brain whether I'm in "relaxation pose" in yoga or nestled in bed with my attentive boyfriend. (Shhh! Our secret.)

Women are compulsive, fabulous list makers. Lists order our world, fend off bouts of forgetfulness, and ensure that every event conforms to our precise specifications.

So for purposes of this chapter, think of a will as a list. Not just any list, but arguably the most important list you will ever write. After all, when you send your significant other to the market and he "accidentally" forgets the shopping list, it's easy enough to remind him of the items you need. Not so with a will, for obvious reasons.

By most estimates, fewer than half of American adults bother to write a will. We are not going to be among that sorry cohort. So let's begin planning for the afterlife right now.

IT'S THE LAW

The basic rules for creating a valid will—the crucial document that will distribute your property and assign care for your children—are this simple:

1. You must be at least eighteen years old.
2. You must be mentally competent.
3. The document you create has to state that it is your will.
4. Two witnesses need to sign it (they should be adults who are not going to inherit anything from your estate).
5. You must identify an adult to act as executor of your estate; in other words, the person who will carry out your wishes.

This may all seem beyond elementary, but before you scrawl your last wishes on a cocktail napkin or email them to your kids after a dark night of contemplative thought about your mortality, remember that your state will have particular requirements about language, witnesses, or other formalities. Of course, a lawyer who knows your state's estate laws can guide you through those details.

But you may be asking a common question: can you do it yourself?

EXHIBIT 66: THE DIY WILL

If you have complicated plans for distributing your assets or a large estate that might be subject to extra taxes, or sense the potential for family battles after you're gone, you need professional help. If you are the type of person who is more likely to create a will with the help of a lawyer than on your own, ditto. The cost of a lawyer's help need not be exorbitant—one estimate is $500 to $1,200 for a will and the living will and power of attorney documents we discussed in chapter 26. After all, even lawyers can start their work by referring to form documents and then tailoring them to meet your needs.

If you insist on self-help, however, DIY websites abound, and even your local library could offer forms to get you started. Since estate laws are state specific, be sure you select a form that is good to go in your home state. You don't want to sign a will that can't be enforced the way you planned because you missed a technicality, a problem that trusts and estates lawyers say they see all too often, and often too late for repair.

Bottom line: a DIY will may be better than nothing; an investment in specialized help is the safer course.

ESTATE PLANNING BASICS

If the prospect of estate planning seems daunting, consider this must-do list (adapted from one published by Charles Schwab). It has only five parts; once they are completed, you can feel secure that you've made a good start at helping your family manage its future:

1. Tell your loved ones where to find your important documents; make a list of accounts, assets, and insurance policies.

2. Draft your will and a final letter of instructions (offering guidance on everything from funeral planning to distributing special items not mentioned in the will).
3. Establish durable powers of attorney and health care directives (see chapter 26).
4. Update the titles and beneficiaries for accounts such as retirement accounts, pensions, and insurance that are not distributed by a will.
5. Consider creating a revocable living trust along with a pour-over will to make sure other assets are placed in the trust (more on that below).

EXHIBIT 67: ESTATE PERSONNEL

In addition to carefully distributing your assets in your will, you need to identify the person—the *executor*—who will make sure your wishes are met. Your executor can be a relative, including an adult child; some people prefer to name a person with no family or personal ties, such as a lawyer, accountant, or even a financial institution. You can name co-executors, and you should name a successor executor, in case something happens to your first choice.

An executor is different from an *administrator;* that is the person a court names to manage your estate if you don't have a will—in legal terms, if you die intestate. At which point your property is distributed according to state law, and not your preferences. Which is not going to happen . . . right?

EXHIBIT 68: ALL ABOUT PROBATE, OR: WHAT HAPPENS TO YOUR WILL?

Probate is one of those off-putting legal terms that sound more ominous than they are. Simply put, probate is the way a court makes sure a will is valid. (Naturally, it comes from the Latin; *probare,* or "to test or prove.") A judge reviews the will and then appoints the executor to distribute assets as the will instructs.

Wills require probate review, and probate used to have a reputation for taking forever, which presumably didn't matter to the decedent but could be a problem for beneficiaries. Many states have streamlined the process. That said, probate is not free; your estate will have to pay court fees to get it done. Nor is it private, since your will is filed in court for anyone to see.

For those two reasons, and sometimes for more complicated estate planning purposes, it can make sense to adopt probate-avoiding strategies.

One strategy is simple: distributing nonprobate property. Some significant assets, including life insurance, pensions, and retirement savings, are ones you pass along by naming a beneficiary; no need to include in your will so no need for probate. (But take care to coordinate your retirement plans and your estate planning; make sure the beneficiary forms you may have filled out long ago reflect your family situation and direct those assets to the right people.) If you own your home or any accounts jointly (specifically as joint owners with right of survivorship), those assets pass to your co-owner after your death, no will required.

Another way to avoid probate is by setting up a trust.

EXHIBIT 69: WILLS V. TRUSTS

Should you consider a trust instead of (or alongside) a will? It's a question you can answer with the help of an estate lawyer. Before you do, let's examine the basics.

With a trust, you appoint a trustee (a family member or friend, or a bank or law firm) to manage and distribute the assets you place in the trust. You can set up a *living* trust that takes effect immediately, or a *testamentary* trust that goes into effect after you die. Another key distinction: a trust can be *revocable* (easily changed) or *irrevocable*. A revocable living trust is popular as a tool to avoid probate. And it's a good approach if you want to have your trustee manage your assets if you fall ill or become disabled.

Irrevocable trusts, on the other hand, can be powerful tax planning tools. Since they contain assets that cannot be reclaimed, those assets can be shielded from estate taxes.

Trusts also suit people who require privacy, because trusts skip the probate process, which is public, and save time in states where probate remains a drawn-out affair.

But trusts do not manage themselves, and managing a trust means costs and fees that come from your assets. Trusts do not work unless they contain assets, and that is why a pour-over will might accompany a living trust, since it "pours over" assets into the trust at death. Also, a trust will not provide instructions a will can offer, including naming guardians for your children.

In short, if you think a trust should be part of your estate plan, you'll want a lawyer (and a financial planner, probably) to help guide you.

SPECIAL NEEDS TRUSTS

If you have a child or grandchild with special needs, you will want to consider a particular kind of trust. When set up properly, a special needs trust (sometimes called a supplemental needs trust) can allow you and other family members to put away money for the child's care, even once that child reaches adulthood, without exceeding limits that would deny that child Social Security or Medicaid help. The trustee for the special needs trust may also have the authority to hire a care manager or other expert to help look after that child.

A special needs trust has to meet specific criteria under federal and state law, so it's critical to have a lawyer who specializes in this issue help you set one up.

To make sure that the trustee (who can be a relative, a professional adviser such as a lawyer, or a bank or financial services company) provides the specific care a special needs child deserves, parents also should draft a letter of intent that explains, in detail, the child's schedule and preferences, their own preferences for education, and medical care.

EXHIBIT 70: YOUR DIGITAL ESTATE

So you've written your will, and distributed your assets with care. Jewelry to one family member, art to another; even your ironically curated snow globe collection will find a proper home, as will your books, letters, and mementos.

But what about your music collection? What about your vast digital photo albums? Or, if you roll this way, those jewels or game pieces you can collect while killing time online?

Did you mention your digital cache in your will? And even if you did, how will anyone collect your password-protected prizes?

The disposition of digital assets is rocking the ordinarily stodgy world of trusts and estates, with families and friends who want access to their loved one's online accounts facing stiff resistance from sites that claim a commitment to maintaining user privacy.

Scattered early skirmishes in this battle have yielded inconclusive results. The family of a Marine killed in Iraq, Justin Ellsworth, made headlines when they asked Yahoo to let them see Justin's email account, then went to court when Yahoo declined because of its privacy rules. Yahoo eventually granted the Ellsworth family permission, and since then has revised its rules, which, at the time of this writing, say that users agree that "any rights to your Yahoo! ID or contents within your account terminate upon your death."

We all accrue vast digital reserves, some valuable, some useless; some public, some personal. And as time passes, the number of these accounts is growing. It's been reported that millions of deceased persons already have left Facebook accounts behind. Facebook's policy, by the way, is to "memorialize" the account of a deceased Facebook user, so it's secured but impossible to log into. But Facebook also allows immediate family to contact the site and remove the account.

Google, meanwhile, developed an "Inactive Account Manager" that allows you to designate someone to retrieve some of your Google data, including mail and photos, if you haven't used your account for a predetermined amount of time.

While service providers begin to make accommodations for their users, the law is scrambling to keep up. Only a handful of states have laws allowing estate representatives access to digital assets. And when the organization that drafts uniform laws for states to adopt started its review of the situation, the group encountered some thorny questions.

Who is the custodian of work emails, and should those be shared after death? How much access should a personal representative have to digital assets: the right to see them, or the right to maintain the accounts?

No doubt law in this area will develop through test cases and state legislature attention. (I'll keep you posted on my website, lisagreenlaw.com.) In the meantime, when you're drawing up a will, what can you do to protect and share your digital assets? At the very least, make an inventory of your online assets, including usernames and passwords, choose someone you trust to look after them, and then reference that plan in your will and trust. (Don't put your passwords in your will, since it is a public record.)

EXHIBIT 71: PET (AND PLANT) PROVISIONS

Thanks to advances in the animal rights movement, which are among the most interesting in all of modern law, most states now recognize "pet trusts" that allow you choose a caregiver for your pet after you go and to set aside funds to make sure your pet is treated to your specifications.

That's right, you can now lower the full protection of our legal system onto the cute, hairy head of your Rex or Daisy, and meet your maker serene that no matter how your human descendants behave, your pet will be cared for after you've gone. (Since animals are often considered property, a trust is better than a will; you won't be around to convince a skeptical judge that Bo should be a beneficiary of your estate.) Obviously, to ensure your pet's happy future, you should identify a caretaker who loves and understands your pet—maybe even consider a backup—and talk to him in detail about your plans.

It's worth noting a limit to your efforts at posthumous pet control: don't expect a court to enforce your wish that your pet be euthanized after you pass. Pet owners try this from time to time, perhaps out of fear that no one can look after their pet as well as they did. You won't be around to enforce the edict, and it's unlikely anyone else will want to act on your behalf. Georgia Lee Dvorak tried to have Boots, her cat, euthanized after she died because she worried Boots might be abused. (She also left $1.3 million to pet-related causes.) When Georgia passed, the trustees at a local bank elected not to enforce the euthanasia provision, and instead were able to place Boots with a pet advocate.

Meanwhile, if trusts and estates lawyers ever launch a Client Hall of Fame, I nominate Ronna Scoratow, who took estate planning to a new level when she allocated $5,000 in her will so a friend could care for her giant philodendron. Ronna gave special legal protection to the plant, in its forties at the time of the bequest and showing no signs of slowing down, because she expected it would outlive her. As she explained to the *Wall Street Journal*, "after I pass, I don't want her to go unloved."

EXHIBIT 72: HAPPY BEQUESTS

In addition to family, friends, pet, and plants, you can bequeath your assets to organizations and charities that deserve support; it's a beautiful way to aid a good cause long after you're gone. And when that bequest is cleverly made, the results can be wonderful.

Consider Benjamin Franklin. At the time of his death in 1790, this fiscally sophisticated founding father left 1,000 pounds each (about $4,400 at prevailing rates) to Boston and Philadelphia with the provision that they could not be spent for two hundred years. Fast-forward, and behold the power of compound interest: the trusts were worth millions of dollars by the time they were redeemed. Delighted city fathers invested the proceeds toward a noble cause: education.

Franklin's gift was the acme of patient, well-designated planning. But other beneficiaries have had the lucky treat of a windfall that arrives out of thin air. Consider actors Kevin Brophy and Peter Barton. Brophy may be best known for his starring role in the 1977 television series *Lucan*, where he portrayed a boy raised by wolves and then civilized. Barton played the title role in *The Powers of Matthew Star*, about a superpowered alien prince turned high school student.

These two interpreters of teen angst had nothing to fret about when they learned in 2012 that an eccentric Illinois farmer, Ray Fulk, left them the bulk of an estate that was estimated to be worth almost $1 million. Apparently Fulk, who never married and was childless, was a fanboy par excellence and kept a *Lucan* poster on his wall. It was seemingly enough for Fulk that both actors had written kind, if generic, notes in response to his fan letters.

EXHIBIT 73: EPIC ESTATE BATTLES

The last thing you need in your life is more drama, right? Not only should we all settle down, but I believe our constant quest for Zen surely should extend to the afterlife, which is why we want to think ahead and make our estate plans smart, clear, and unambiguous.

Even with a sensible plan, though, the parceling out of assets among loved ones can spark hurt feelings. Remember your keen interest in which sibling got the largest slice of cake at a family meal? Take that ancient emotion, then stretch it throughout a lifetime of love, competitive feelings, and who knows what other issues, and you'll understand the underpinnings of many family estate wars.

I am a lawyer, and not a therapist, but I can share some wise advice about how to minimize hurt feelings about estates.

P. Mark Accettura, an estate planner and author of the aptly named *Blood & Money: Why Families Fight over Inheritance and What to Do About It,* made several suggestions in the *Journal of the American Association of Individual Investors,* among them:

◆ Address personal property separately. Make a detailed list of your possessions and who should inherit them (in many states, this list can be included in your will).

◆ Update your plan regularly. Take account of changes in your life and the lives of your beneficiaries.

◆ Hold a discussion about special assets. Vacation homes and family businesses can be especially stress producing.

◆ Prearrange your funeral details. This spares family disputes about a very sensitive topic.

◆ Make logically defensible choices. Did you choose your eldest child as your executor, or the child who lives closest to you? Those are choices that make objective sense. If you make unconventional bequests, you may upset children and other family members, especially if they are surprised.

◆ Balance the needs of second spouses and children. No matter how much you love your children, you should think about providing for your spouse, who may need resources after you go. On the other hand, don't encourage kids to take up a "death watch" if they won't inherit anything until their stepparent passes.

◆ Leave to children equally; disinherit as a last resort. Think hard about favoring needier siblings, or rewarding successful ones. Unequal bequests can activate fierce rivalries. Think carefully about the repercussions of disinheriting a child (unless a serious condition, such as addiction, makes that option appropriate).

◆ Keep estate planning private. Accettura suggests you refrain from sharing your plan (except for health care power of attorney), since it may change. Other experts believe that sharing the plan ahead of time, if you can bring yourself to discuss it, minimizes hard feelings.

One more tactic to keep tempers from erupting? The no-contest clause, which is enforced in almost every state. It disinherits a beneficiary who tries, and fails, to challenge a will or trust. To make it work, you need to bequeath something of value to the potential challenger; otherwise, she has nothing to lose if she mounts a legal fight.

And apropos of disinheritance, remember that it's very difficult to disinherit your spouse, but in almost all states (except Louisiana, as of this writing) you can disinherit your children. If you are inclined to leave a child (or other relatives who you think expect a handout) out of your will, here's a simple step: write it down. Putting your decision in writing, in your will, means a judge won't think you inadvertently forgot that particular relative.

Another source of estate friction: second marriages that pit newlyweds against children from prior unions. Couples contemplating a second (or third) marriage should coordinate estate planning with a prenup, where one spouse can agree to forgo a claim to the other's estate in exchange for another benefit, such as being named a beneficiary to a life insurance policy. Couples can also reiterate that they want to maintain property as separate, even after they wed. (See chapter 6 for much more about prenups.)

CHALLENGING A WILL

Sometimes an expectant heir or heiress gets an unpleasant surprise: they were cut out of a will. Is there any chance to redress something that seems so wrong?

Here are four legal arguments that might overturn a will:

1. *Undue influence.* Was the decedent pressured?
2. *Fraud.* Was the will the product of trickery? Maybe the signer thought she was signing a different document?
3. *Improper execution.* Does the will suffer from a technical flaw?
4. *Lack of capacity.* Did the signer have an adequate understanding of her assets and beneficiaries?

Those are the potential grounds for a battle, but waging one will cost a lot and, if the will is properly created and signed, rarely succeed.

Before we leave the arena of estate wars, it's time to revisit one of the most public, most famous, most outrageous will wars ever. It was packed with drama, sex, money, court battles, paternity fights, and arguably the most prominent breast implants in American history. Who else could it concern but Anna Nicole Smith?

CELEBRITY LAW LESSON:
ANNA NICOLE SMITH

What passed through the minds of the justices of the Supreme Court of the United States as they prepared to consider arguments in the matter of Anna Nicole Smith's bid to collect a chunk of her late husband's fortune—for the second time—is anyone's guess. Did they rue the day they granted review to a case about a surgically enhanced former Playmate of the Year who met her multimillionaire husband while performing at Gigi's, a strip club in Houston? Were they secretly satisfied that one of the cases on their otherwise mostly esoteric docket proved as interesting to readers of *Us Weekly* as to readers of the Supreme Court–chronicling SCOTUSblog.com?

To someone like me, whose daily news diet contains equally healthy portions of refined high court analysis and juicy web gossip, the gift of the Anna Nicole Smith estate fight lies in its unusual, and satisfying, blend of sophisticated law and low culture. Impressively, while disintegrating from statuesque, self-made beauty to the embodiment of why we should be ashamed of ourselves for watching reality TV, Anna Nicole was able to nurture an improbable claim: that she deserved a share of her late husband J. Howard Marshall's estate, even though she wasn't mentioned in his will. Because Anna Nicole's fight was joined on many battlefields, including a Texas probate court, a California bankruptcy court, and the Ninth Circuit Court of Appeals, her quest for money morphed into a complex procedural fight. I'll spare you details of the so-called probate exception to federal jurisdiction and the exact grounds under which Chief Justice John Roberts decided, after sixteen years of litigation, that a bankruptcy court lacked the authority to award Anna Nicole more than $400 million from Marshall's estate. Inevitably, and appropriately, Roberts likened the proceedings to Bleak House, Charles Dickens's ur-text about a ruinous inheritance fight. Anna Nicole, her husband, and his son, E. Pierce Marshall, who fought Anna Nicole in court, all died before the Supreme Court announced its decision. Did those deaths end the arguing? Nope. Years later, a federal judge in California rejected Anna Nicole's estate's attempt to sanction the estate of Marshall's son. To make matters worse, Anna's own will was a tangled mess, suggesting that she didn't incorporate lessons she might have learned from her own estate battle.

As we shake our heads at the disaster that Anna Nicole's life became, what can we take away from her time in court? Simply this: when it comes to estate planning, ambiguity is the enemy. You can never be too clear, too explicit, or too organized. Time invested in a will yields not only monetary returns, as in maximizing the amount of money that heirs can keep, but emotional returns as well. Good parenting, as it turns out, doesn't end at the grave.

FOR MORE INFORMATION

Financial institutions are a great source for plain English advice about estate planning. Charles Schwab (at schwab.com) offers "Why You Need an Estate Plan. Now."

You know that list you've been meaning to make of essential documents your loved ones should know about after you're gone? Here's a good template, courtesy of my trusts and estates lawyer's firm (other examples abound online): http://www.dmlawyers.com/docs/Danziger_Markhoff_LLP_(00314692).pdf.

The American Bar Association's Section of Real Property, Trust, and Estate Law publishes a clear and useful explanation of wills, trusts, and related issues (including Estate Planning FAQs): americanbar.org.

The ABA and AARP together publish guides like their *Checklist for Family Survivors: A Guide to Practical and Legal Matters When Someone You Love Dies*.

For more on pet estate planning, look to the Animal Legal & Historical Center, Michigan State University College of Law: animallaw .info; and the Humane Society: humanesociety.org.

28

MANAGING MOM, DAD, AND OTHER OLDER LOVED ONES

OPENING STATEMENT

Way back in 1963, our nation's youthful president, John F. Kennedy, designated May as Senior Citizens Month. Back then, America had a population of 17 million adults who had reached their sixty-fifth birthday. Fast-forward fifty years and in 2013, America's senior population reached more than 41 million. In recognition of this age-quake, the United States Senate rebranded May as Older Americans Month and, with only slight condescension, lauded our gray lions and lionesses for "play[ing] an important role by continuing to contribute experience, knowledge, wisdom, and accomplishments."

Along with their undeniable wisdom, the most impressive characteristic of the seniors I encounter is that age has rendered them impervious to shame. Consider my mother, who after a lifetime of Sisyphean housekeeping, arguing with my late father, and nagging her kids about problems real and imagined, in her golden years morphed into a fun-loving singleton prone to departing, unannounced, for swinging gambling vacations with her boyfriend.

Mom and her age-appropriate beau are poster children for the new face of aging, tristate-area edition. Out: early bird dinners, sensible shoes, carefully curated porcelain figurines. In: lingerie shopping, months-long disappearances to a cozy Florida condo, and enthusiastic berating of waitstaff at popular boîtes who can't indulge their bewildering, particularized food preferences. Do these lovebirds care what my siblings and I think of their late-stage escapades? Certainly not. Ever since the boyfriend (or is it senior friend?) arrived at a family dinner in an expensive New York steakhouse rocking a pair of Bermuda shorts, white sneakers, and knee-high compression socks, we, the younger generation, have recognized gods of mature indifference in our midst.

Spry and hilarious as these seniors may seem, we know all good things come to an end. For some seniors, a shift from fully functioning to acutely dependent is abrupt. For others, it's a gradual shift that younger relatives don't notice or prefer to ignore.

If you have older adults in your life who once looked after you, it's time to prepare to return the favor. What, if anything, can you do to ensure their well-being and perhaps lighten your caregiving load?

A wise elder-care lawyer I know offers this practical advice: speak up now. Don't be afraid to raise care issues with Mom and Dad; chances are they are thinking about them, but reluctant to raise them with you.

When you do, review the information about power of attorney, health care proxy, and living wills in chapter 26. Don't delay. If your loved one loses the legal capacity to sign these agreements, you may end up forced into court for a guardianship hearing. An outcome that would have cost a few hundred dollars will be one you reach, if you're lucky, after spending thousands and sharing family matters with a judge.

If your impressively frugal parents opted for DIY documents in these matters, ask them if you can check them out. Do-it-yourselfers (not just elderly ones) might have relied on an incorrect or outdated form; when it comes to these issues, a court (or bank) might not accept these papers, nor any with execution errors. Before you or your elders go it alone, consider the value of having an experienced lawyer review your paperwork.

IT'S THE LAW

As your parents age, they likely will need care, either at home, in assisted living, or at a nursing home—or, in stages, at each one. It's beyond the scope of this book to offer guidance about making those choices, but as you do, remember that legal rights and responsibilities attach to each of them. Care options, and some legal issues to keep in mind, include:

> *At-home care:* Under new federal law, home health aides now qualify for minimum wage and overtime protection. This means you need to obey applicable laws on hours, disability insurance, and payroll taxes for your home health aide just as you do for other qualifying household employees (for more information, see chapter 23).
> *Agency help:* If you hire help through an agency, you (or your family member) have some legal protection for your patient through laws that cover Medicare-approved agencies; you should ask for a copy of those rights, in writing. (The National Association for Home Care & Hospice lays

out a model patient bill of rights: http://www3.nahc.org/
haa/attachments/BillOfRights.pdf.)

Assisted living: Assisted living is meant for people who
cannot live alone but don't require constant medical care.
However, a federal survey found that almost 40 percent of
residents in these facilities had Alzheimer's disease or other
dementia, which suggests they do need careful oversight.
These facilities are not federally regulated, but states are
stepping into the breach, which is helpful given the soaring
growth of this residential care option.

Continuing care retirement communities (CCRCs): CCRCs
are facilities that have varied housing and levels of care, so
that residents can either live on their own, in assisted living,
or in a nursing home. If a senior moves in and her situation worsens, she may be required to use the CCRC's own
nursing home. Like assisted living facilities, CCRCs are
not federally regulated, and state regulation varies.

Hospice care: Hospices are facilities for the terminally ill
and their families that, while they have doctors and nurses
available, intend to provide comfortable living conditions,
rather than a cure. Medicare covers hospice care, and the
agency has become more attentive to the condition of hospice patients, who can be covered if they are likely to die
within six months. Patients who stabilize sometimes find
themselves discharged.

Respite care: Some facilities, such as adult day care centers,
offer part- or full-day programs for older adults; other programs, based in assisted living facilities or nursing homes,
offer overnight, weekend, or longer stays so that caregivers
get a break.

Nursing homes: I know these two words strike fear in the
heart of every senior. As a lawyer, I will say this in their de-

fense: because nursing homes are subject to federal regulations, you can compare nursing homes that are certified by Medicare and Medicaid through a site called Nursing Home Compare (www.medicare.gov/nursinghomecompare), which offers data about inspection results, staffing levels, medical treatment of residents, and penalties, all compared to state and federal averages. Residents have specific rights to a certain quality of care and quality of life.

None of these regulations mean you can skip your own fact-finding efforts before you choose a destination for your loved one, nor rest on your laurels once you make a placement decision; as we all know, nothing substitutes for personal attention, unscheduled visits, and the other time-consuming, necessary data gathering we do to satisfy ourselves that Mom and Dad are well treated.

PATIENT PRIVACY

The Health Insurance Portability and Accountability Act (HIPAA) was passed in 1996 with good intentions: to protect patient privacy in an age of electronically stored (and easily shared) records.

Years after its introduction, HIPAA continues to confuse medical professionals who misunderstand its scope. Under the law's privacy provisions, medical professionals can share a patient's health information with family and friends as long as the patient doesn't object. Permission to share doesn't need to be in writing under the law, but some doctors and institutions will want that permission anyway. To be sure you will have necessary access to your elder's care, make sure she has signed a medical power of attorney and names you on any privacy agreements the doctor or facility seeks. The U.S. Department of Health and Human Services has excellent online information that is worth printing and sharing with medical professionals if necessary, at hhs.gov.

EXHIBIT 74: CONTRACT FOR CARE

As we've seen, government and nonprofit organizations can help you navigate the emotional journey to a new home for your senior, so let's focus our attention on a particular legal matter: the contract your patient or her agent will sign when she chooses an assisted living facility or nursing home.

AARP offers some commonsense suggestions about how to review the contract:

- Compare the contract to any sales or promotional material you received. Are the care and benefits you were promised reflected in the document?
- Look at discharge policies. Some homes charge for departures if they aren't given proper notice.
- Never sign the same day you visit.
- Consider asking a lawyer and a financial adviser to review the contract. (Unless your senior is able to pay out of pocket, financing her stay at a nursing home or other facility requires a level of familiarity with federal health insurance that most of us try to avoid at all costs.)

To summarize an issue so complicated, and so fraught with potentially costly mistakes, would be doing it—and you—an injustice. I urge you to hire a lawyer and financial adviser to help, if possible. But for an introduction to the issues you'll be facing, let's look at the two major social insurance programs your senior can qualify for, and how they pay—if at all—for nursing home care.

Medicare covers a wide range of medical costs for people who are sixty-five or older (and some younger people with disabilities), but not long-term nursing home care beyond a short period of time.

Medicaid covers health care, including nursing home care, for low-income patients. Because nursing home care is so expensive (one recent estimate puts the national median cost at almost $84,000 a year) it is common for patients to pay for it themselves at first, with savings or insurance, while "spending down" their assets enough so that they qualify for Medicaid coverage.

How much of a "spend down" is enough? While Medicaid is a federal program, states administer Medicaid with their own rules. So the answer will depend on where your senior lives; it may also change as national health care reform unfolds. In general, a senior trying to qualify for Medicaid can keep about $2,000 in assets (which usually does not include her home) and collect about $2,000 in monthly income. (Once the Medicaid patient and her spouse both die, Medicaid can seek reimbursement from the patient's estate for some of the money Medicaid spent on care—unless the couple leaves behind a child who is under twenty-one, blind, or disabled.) If a spouse is heading to a nursing home for more than thirty days, federal law meant to prevent "spousal impoverishment" allows that person's husband or wife (known as the community spouse, since he stays behind in their community) to keep a certain amount of the couple's income and assets within limits set by federal and state guidelines.

What if your mom has assets that put her above that very low Medicaid qualification threshold? She will have to spend them to pay for her care until she qualifies and perhaps try—under the careful eye of a reputable elder-care lawyer or counselor—to put some of them aside in a way that doesn't disqualify her from Medicaid coverage. In the past, if a nursing home stay looked probable, seniors would give money and other assets away to friends or relatives for safekeeping, so that they could shrink their holdings enough to qualify for Medicaid and not lose everything they had worked so hard to save. Medicaid caught on, so now the government reviews any asset transfers a senior makes five years before applying for assistance. If the transfers seem fishy—and fishy can include anything from outright gifts to kids, to selling property for less than it's worth, to paying for a grandchild's education—Medicaid will delay the start date for coverage to offset the loss of those assets to pay for care. This is why any senior money transfers should be carefully reviewed even if no one is contemplating a nursing home stay, and ideally with the assistance of an elder-care lawyer familiar with the law in your state.

A word about second marriages and Medicaid. Couples who are considering marriage later in life can sign a prenup that declares that they have no obligation to support each other, but Medicaid will not honor that provision. They will each be responsible for the other, without protection short of the "spousal impoverishment" allowances we just reviewed.

EXHIBIT 75: ON THE HOOK?

We've learned just enough about Medicaid spend-downs to deserve a big, frosty vat of our favorite refreshing grape-based beverage.

But before you take that first sip of pinot grigio, pour a backup glass. We are about to explore the little-known, lightly invoked concept of "filial responsibility." Not the general sense of looking out for ailing moms and dads, but as it relates to law that in close to thirty states can hold children responsible for their parents' sky-high bills for long-term care.

When these laws were passed, they were meant to model Olde English poverty laws that made blood relatives liable for poor members of the family. Those laws predated the passage of Social Security, Medicare, and, most important for this discussion, Medicaid, which covers a senior's nursing home care without concern about the assets of a senior's children. Thanks to our modern government safety net, nursing homes seldom look to these filial laws to force children to pay a parent's bills.

But there are—no need to pretend to be surprised—exceptions.

In 2007, John Pittas's mother was injured in a car accident and, after rehab, moved to the Liberty Nursing & Rehabilitation Center in Allentown, Pennsylvania, where she spent about six months before moving to Greece without paying a large part of her bill, which eventually approached $93,000. With the mom an apparent deadbeat, the nursing home invoked Pennsylvania law, which holds children financially liable for "indigent" parents, and sued John. A judge held John liable for the bill under the law, and an appeals court agreed.

Elder-law observers stress this situation is rare, but this case serves as a reminder that families need to address the prospect of nursing home financing carefully and as early as possible.

The attorneys at Elder Law Answers raise another good point: do not sign a nursing home contract as a "responsible party" on behalf of a patient unless you are acting as that person's agent or, in other words, have power of attorney to act on behalf of that patient. If you don't have that authority, but you sign a contract as a responsible party, or "guarantor" or "financial agent," you might be agreeing to pick up the (considerable) tab for payment.

EXHIBIT 76: THE FINE PRINT

A contract for nursing home or assisted living residency is long, complex, and the last thing anyone needs to worry about while making a fraught decision about the future.

That's why I hate to add one more issue to consider, but it's an important one: in case something goes horribly wrong at the facility, try to make sure your loved one has not signed away her rights.

Nestled deep within nursing home paperwork, you are likely to find an arbitration clause that denies your parent (or, the "Resident . . . or respective successors, assigns or representatives," as the agreement will rename your mom and those around her) the right to a jury trial if you later want to challenge the quality of care. Companies that are sued tend to like arbitration, in part because it removes the risk of outsize jury verdicts. If a grieving family seeks redress for what it considers bad care, an arbitration award probably won't seem adequate.

You can try to negotiate the removal of that clause, but if the home stands firm, you may be stuck. Some state courts have struck down arbitration agreements, but that is rare. And in what must be a very faint note of solace in an otherwise tragic situation, some state courts will allow grieving relatives to sue a nursing home for wrongful death, even if the deceased patient signed an arbitration agreement and the home is pushing for it to be upheld.

EXHIBIT 77: ELDER FRAUD

Writing this book turned a once-vibrant social urbanite (me) into a bit of a shut-in. Don't feel bad: passing up tickets to that enticing Beck concert and missing virtually every movie released in a fifteen-month period were sacrifices I'd be happy to make again.

My writerly home confinement did confer a few benefits for the book. One of them was an education in the tenacity of telemarketers, who liked to ring my home phone while I tried to work. The calls came in all forms: the prerecorded, disembodied voice that insisted I was paying too much for car insurance (I don't have a car). The caller who managed to mispronounce my last name, Green, and whose voice had the anticipation of rejection built into its deflated sound. The perky student, earning work-study wages through phone bank calls, seeking donations to my alma mater. And all the calls I interrupted before the prefabricated robo-voice really got going.

It's Fraud 101 for rip-off artists to recognize that seniors are a ripe target for telemarketing scams. And they are fiendishly correct: the National Consumers League reports that nearly one-third of tele-marketing fraud victims are age sixty or older. Let's assume your parents know enough to distrust that unfamiliar voice at the other end of the line (unless you call home even less frequently than I do, and your mom claims to have forgotten the sound of your voice). But what about the Internet? Are your parents prepared for email attachments that can unleash a virus into their operating system? Or for messages, seemingly from their bank or another legitimate concern, demanding that they update information immediately?

How can we possibly monitor our parents to make sure they avoid costly, embarrassing senior scams? I have an idea. Remember all the articles Mom and Dad carefully cut out of the local newspaper and sent to you, on the incorrect assumption you would agree with a par-ticular op-ed, or care about the success of your long-loathed high school classmate?

It's time to return the favor. Go to the web and find one of the handy lists of common senior scams. Email or print and mail as needed. Craving contact from you, your parents are sure to read the list and, just maybe, avoid the potential for serious trouble. (The Na-tional Council on Aging offers a good one; you can find the link at ncoa.org.)

What if your parents are the victims of a scam? Obviously, chasing scam artists can be an exercise in futility, but it's worth contacting local authorities, if not the FBI, to report fraud. The new Consumer Financial Protection Bureau offers a course that teaches older adults how to avoid financial scams, along with plain-English advice about financial planning, retirement savings, and reverse mortgages—financial situations that can ensnare seniors.

FOR MORE INFORMATION

The Medicare website (medicare.gov) has easy-to-navigate resources for caregivers, including fact sheets about which services Medicare covers.

The U.S. Department of Health and Human Services offers longtermcare.gov with a wealth of information (even in video form) about long-term care options, payment, and a directory of local services.

The National Academy of Elder Law Attorneys (naela.com) offers an online directory of its member attorneys.

The National Association of Area Agencies on Aging can identify resources in your state for help with a wide range of topics, including legal ones; visit n4a.org.

For elder finance issues, the Consumer Financial Protection Bureau (consumerfinance.gov) offers advice relevant to older Americans, including tips on avoiding scams and information about reverse mortgages; the National Council on Aging (ncoa.org) offers financial and health advice, including a Savvy Saving Seniors toolkit.

PART SEVEN

FINDING LEGAL HELP

29

HIRING A LAWYER, OR DOING IT YOURSELF

OPENING STATEMENT

It was a rare New York City August, sunny but mild, with temperatures so bearably low you'd think God decided to let residents adjust the municipal thermostat. The sort of summer where I could scoop up gorgeously ripe produce from the farmers market and assemble a flavorful, virtuous feast for my young adults, one of whom was returning home for a break from his government internship in Washington, D.C., the other underfoot while serving our community at an inspiring nonprofit job. My home practically hummed with the lovely lo-fi combo of an evening breeze, the pleasure of feeding my offspring, the aroma of fresh herbs.

I got ready to settle in, serve, eat, and enjoy.

And then the phone rang.

It was my sister, alarmed. My seventy-eight-year-old mother, she of the trim figure, spry boyfriend, and full capabilities, had been hit by a car while taking a fitness walk and was now under the care of doctors in the intensive care unit of an out-of-state hospital.

This awful emergency really happened while I was writing this legal advice book for you. In my horror and confusion, my first concern was my mother, of course. But as our family gathered and helped her recover, I thought of you, and how we could learn from this experience, together.

Remember, we do not seek out these crises, but they find us anyway, just like a motorist collided with my mom in a quiet suburban intersection on a soothing summer evening. When these nightmares happen, you may find yourself looking not only for emotional support from friends and family, but sooner or later for legal help to cope with the consequences.

What should you do next? To be more specific: how do you find a lawyer?

Regrettably, the search for a lawyer has not evolved all that much since the days of Charles Dickens, who in his lawyer-skewering masterpiece, *Bleak House,* railed against members of the bar "mistily engaged in one of the ten thousand stages of an endless cause, tripping one another up on slippery precedents, groping knee-deep in technicalities, running their goat-hair and horse-hair warded heads against walls of words and making a pretence [*sic*] of equity with serious faces. . . ." So little has changed—save, thankfully, for the goat and horse hairpieces.

Incredibly, it's easier to access reliable online ratings for a Thai restaurant, nail salon, or mobile phone accessory than it is to secure guidance about suitable legal counsel. That's in part because of an ongoing standoff between the freewheeling web, where strangers share their views with impunity, and a clannish, straight-laced profession that hasn't quite adapted to the modern idea of being judged in public. To make the situation even less consumer-friendly, if a public judgment about a lawyer is negative, the bad-mouthed lawyer can try to retaliate in court. Thus you have Paul Nardini, the lawyer who sued the ex-spouse of his client after the ex posted a negative review of Nardini's firm on Google+. Conversely, you have Yelp suing a lawyer, Julian McMillan, who it claimed posted fake positive reviews about his own firm on the site. (He denied the charge, claiming Yelp was retaliating for his own claims against the company.) Even lawyers who simply want to tout their own ratings can run afoul of state ethics laws that limit exuberance in lawyer advertising. In New Jersey, for example, it took three years of litigation before lawyers could tell potential clients they were named as "Super Lawyers" or "Best Lawyers," because the state's lawyer regulators feared the accolades could be misleading.

Despite these obstacles, an Internet search for a lawyer can yield some useful results. Some enterprising websites offer lawyer lists. And, for what it's worth, the occasional lawyer review does find its way to online review sites like Yelp. You can even score Groupons for deals on legal services, though the American Bar Association cautions they should comply with its rules governing lawyers' professional conduct.

For the most part, however, if you are seeking learned counsel, you will do best to rely on the time-honored technique of referrals—either from family, friends, state bar associations, or organizations of lawyers who practice a particular kind of law, such as elder care or trusts and estates. Specifically, state bar associations run referral services that act as matchmakers between lawyers and potential clients. The American Bar Association offers a website, findlegalhelp.org, that collects every state's referral services. And if you have a particular type of claim, you may be able to find a qualified lawyer with the right experience directly from the associations of lawyers devoted to one topic (such as family law, or wills and trusts; the "For More Information" sections of this book identify some of these groups).

How will you find more personal lawyer referrals? The same way you find a good doctor, or hairstylist, or tutor: ask around. In the words of my favorite fictional lawyer, *Breaking Bad*'s Saul Goodman, you are looking for "a guy . . . who knows a guy . . . who knows another guy." Or girl. Ask for referrals, and then ask why your friend recommends this lawyer. Personal experience? Golf partner? My favorite: represented an adversary and did such an incredible job, your friend wished she could switch lawyers.

Even better: the reinforcing second reference. To use a candid personal example, when my husband and I divorced, we knew we'd found the perfect lawyer to represent our children (as was briefly required in our case) when our respective therapists both recommended the same one.

Once you have recommendations, I urge you to meet with your prospective lawyer in person before you hire her. You are building a relationship with someone under fraught circumstances. Affinities count, as does the sense that this person not only understands your problem, but sees a way to resolve it that you can stomach. You are not out to make friends, but it's useful to feel comfortable with your chosen lawyer's demeanor, her office, and how she treats colleagues and subordinates.

When I helped my mom hire her personal injury lawyer, the in-office visit was crucial, since I found Mom's lawyer through a referral. Who made the referral? Her excellent trauma surgeon, who suggested a personal injury lawyer during one of those bedside conversations that is a combination of reassuring and surreal. (The referral was seconded by a lawyer I know, who vouched for the lawyer's firm.)

FIRST PERSON: HOW A LAWYER HIRES A LAWYER

Normally, in the rough-and-tumble aftermath of my mom's accident, details of my meeting with her personal injury lawyer would have been lost to my fading memory.

But for you, I took notes on the experience, which was a first for me. Here's how it went down:

Inside a nondescript brick office building in Teaneck, New Jersey, not far from where Mom was injured, the law firm's lobby clearly intended to transport would-be clients to a different world, perhaps a movie studio, circa 1950. The place was resplendent with faux plaster columns, models of vintage sailing ships, legal-themed movie posters, and a surplus of Plexiglas awards proclaiming the status of various partners as a "Super Lawyer" or "Best Lawyer." (These distinctions are, I kid you not, conferred onto lawyers by other lawyers.) Had I stepped into a legitimate firm, or wandered onto the set for the not-yet-produced *Real Lawyers of New Jersey?*

The office of the partner I was to meet continued the twin décor themes of kitsch and promotional excess. It was all overwhelming and unfamiliar to my experience studying theoretical legal concepts in law school, then practicing arcane, Wall Street–related law at a fancy New York City firm.

But as I settled into the absurdly overstuffed leather client chair, something happened.

I began to feel absolutely secure.

And that is why I want to explain how, though I was a fish out of water in this garish, showy setting, I came to know that I had met the correct counselor for the job.

A sense of security is exactly what the right lawyerly

choice will provide you. That sense is especially important to someone in a situation like mine: shaken, out of her depth, and struggling with emotions that undermine any ability to think clearly and act in my mom's best interest.

The man who became Mom's lawyer listened to my description of the case, and then contacted a person whose job description—"accident reconstruction expert"—was one I'd never heard before. He explained that Mom should not speak to the cops without contacting him first, and then assigned us a case manager to deal with insurance companies (cautioning me not to work directly with any agents).

For 33 percent of any compensation it would secure for my mom, this firm, with its Vegas–meets–*People's Court* décor and lavish full-color brochures, was going to hold my hand, and my mother's, and shepherd us through a fraught process with potentially huge consequences. Were their interests purely mercenary? Who knows. But at the moment, I wanted my victimized mother to be able to afford the months of care she would clearly need; these lawyers were incentivized to deliver.

How can you be sure your lawyer can provide the reassurance and relief you deserve when faced with a fraught legal problem? The office visit is key, but it has to be productive (and most good lawyers are short on time). Before you go, take time to write down details about your legal problem. Check out your potential lawyer with the state bar association to make sure she is licensed and hasn't been disciplined for professional misbehavior. Ask if you'll be charged for the initial visit. Pull together a folder with key documents. And consider these questions, among those suggested by the North Carolina State Bar:

- What experience do you have handling legal matters like mine? (This is, to my mind, the key question. To put it another way: Have you handled a matter like mine before? How often? And with what results? Would you hire a heart surgeon new to heart surgery? I didn't think so.)
- Do you have any special credentials in this practice area?
- Do you carry malpractice insurance?
- Can you give me a reference from a former client?
- Do you have a written agreement for representation that I can read before we work together?
- How will you charge me: by the hour, with a flat fee, or with a contingency fee (a percentage of any settlement or judgment)? You will likely find consistent approaches within specialties, with personal injury lawyers seeking contingency fees, and trusts and estates lawyers billing by the hour.
- Will I be charged for expenses you incur while representing me (such as photocopies, phone calls, or private investigators)?
- Who will work on my matter?
- How will you inform me about developments in the case?

An important note: while I am an advocate for a careful search, do not take so long that you might miss deadlines for the type of suit you might bring. As a quick way to check, search the term *statute of limitations* (in other words, the time limit you have to bring a lawsuit for a particular claim), your state, and the nature of your claim. That said, civil lawsuits often take years to resolve, and you could be living with the consequences of a hasty choice for a *looong* time.

Even if you decide to call it quits.

EXHIBIT 78: BREAKING UP WITH YOUR LAWYER

None of us wants to contemplate a lawyer-client breakup. But you may reach the conclusion that your lawyer's services are falling short of what you need. In this relationship, a breakup should be a last resort; you first should make sure you've tried to repair and improve the situation.

Remember that if you and your lawyer are not working out, you can almost always replace her, but you'll have to pay the legal fees you owe, and then budget for a new lawyer who will need to spend (billable) time to learn your case. (You are entitled to retrieve and share your legal file with a new lawyer.) In some states, you can try arbitration or mediation to settle your differences with your lawyer. (Suing for malpractice is possible, but difficult: you are asking a lawyer to represent your claim against another lawyer. Awkward.)

What if it's worse, and you think your lawyer has behaved unethically or broken the law?

Every state bar has a disciplinary process for bad lawyers, through either the state bar association or state courts. Start there and register your complaint. It's not only potentially helpful for you, but in egregious instances your complaint could get a lawyer disbarred, protecting future would-be clients from harm.

EXHIBIT 79: HAVING SEX WITH YOUR LAWYER

Against my will, but not against my better judgment, here is some intimate advice.

Ladies, do not have sex with your lawyer.

No offense intended, and believe me, I do not want to know about your sex life. While we've grown close, sharing our legal problems and possible solutions, elevating our judgmental antennae and sharpening our problem-solving skills, we're not that close.

So why do I feel compelled to mention sex? Because lawyers and clients sleep together more than you might think. Take it from me, or, if you prefer, from the state bar associations that regulate lawyer conduct: it's a terrible idea.

For one thing, you want your lawyer to think clearly and dispassionately (in every sense of the word) about your situation. What if you have a losing claim? Do you want your lawyer to withhold judgment for fear of hurting your feelings? No, you do not.

Bar associations hate these relationships not because they are prudes, but because they have concluded that a lawyer who is representing a newly acquired sexual partner can run into trouble with conflicts of interest, candor, and professional behavior. (These problems may not occur if you established the intimate relationship first, then worked together.)

Even if you and your lawyer have hit it off and are planning a life together, your relationship as lawyer and client could create other problems. That's what happened when a lawyer we'll call B.W. was retained by a husband and wife for a medical malpractice claim. After B. was hired, the husband left home to look for film industry work in California and the lawyer and the left-behind wife started an affair. The couple divorced, the ex-wife married the lawyer, and they had a child.

Happy ending for the newlyweds? Not so fast. The deposed husband sued the new husband for alienation of affection, breach of contract, and intentional infliction of emotional distress because of the affair. A jury awarded the cuckolded ex $1.5 million and, when the new husband appealed, the state supreme court upheld the judgment.

After the supreme court ruling, the new husband—who, remem-

ber, is a lawyer—told a reporter, "I knew I was going to get screwed."
We can all cringe on his wife's behalf.

EXHIBIT 80: AVOIDING LAWYERS

I won't take it personally, promise, if some of you would like to
bypass the law office and find a simple way to write a will, start a
small business, or even, if you are incredibly lucky and brave, secure
a divorce.

While the Internet has a better selection of time-sucking entertainment than professional services, you can find help on the web.

Many state courts offer comprehensive and reliable online guidance, including downloadable legal forms. And some nonprofits have
a wealth of DIY material so clear that I recommend you review their
guidance even if you plan to hire a lawyer. The Texas Legal Service
Center, for example, offers a series of charming videos that walk a
litigant through all the steps she needs to follow to represent herself in
court. Sort of legal education, Etsy-style.

Companies such as Nolo, LegalZoom, and Rocket Lawyer offer
state-specific common legal forms, lawyer-penned articles, and referrals to local lawyers.

Each of these sites, whether state-run or commercial, has dis-
claimers sternly reminding you that it is providing legal information,
not legal advice, and that if you need specific guidance you'll have to
hire a licensed attorney in your state. State bar associations are jealous guardians of their licensed profession, and practicing lawyers and
these DIY sites have skirmished over the scope of what the sites can
provide.

I've never used DIY legal forms, and as I've warned, a civilian
can make a mess of a document that has to be precise, such as a will
or trust. But if you have a simple problem and want a low-cost legal

solution, you can at least take a look at these online options to see if they can help. (Be sure to look at a document that is drafted to work in your state.) At the very least, you can educate yourself about the services you then ask a lawyer to perform, which will save you time (and therefore money). And let's at least acknowledge the people who have sought to make a high-end professional service accessible to everyone who needs it.

FOR MORE INFORMATION

The American Bar Association collects lawyer referrals in all fifty states here: findlegalhelp.org. State bar associations also offer referrals and state courts, DIY forms, and help navigating the court system; that information is easily obtained online. And businesses like Nolo (nolo.com), LegalZoom (legalzoom.com), and Rocket Lawyer (rocketlawyer.com) sell forms and provide lists of local attorneys, along with articles about a variety of legal issues.

These organizations, among others, stand ready with lawyer referral services in the following areas of the law:

American Academy of Matrimonial Lawyers: aaml.org
American Academy of Assisted Reproductive Technology
    Attorneys: aaarta.org
American College of Real Estate Lawyers: acrel.org
American College of Trust and Estate Counsel: actec.org
National Academy of Elder Law Attorneys: naela.org
National Association of Consumer Advocates: naca.net
National Association of Consumer Bankruptcy Attorneys:
    nacba2.memberpath.com

AFTERWORD

Law as a Labor of Love

Well, here we are, nearing the end of our time together but ready to embark on a new, proactive approach to improving our lives through law.

Together, we've learned that a realistic outlook and thoughtful planning can make the difference between lurching toward a suboptimal resolution of a crisis and calmly handling a situation the same way you already deal with the challenges and emergencies that intrude on your work and home life.

The value of paying attention to the law is clear. It's easy to pretend law doesn't matter to our lives, and relegate it back to its place in the news and entertainment sphere: reading a crime procedural, scanning an online article about a sensational trial, thinking a quick sympathetic (or snarky) thought about a celebrity divorce or sibling battle over a special something a parent left behind.

But if you've learned anything from this book, it's that—as the saying goes—ignorance of the law is no excuse. To put it another way: there is no excuse for ignoring your responsibilities as a partner, wife, ex-wife, mother, or daughter.

To the contrary, conscientious compliance with the ideas in this book is an expression of love. Yes, I went there: law is love.

Law is love when you engage with it to make sure your family is protected and your savings are safe. Law is love when it helps a special needs child get the educational support she deserves, or your parent receives appropriate care at a state-supervised nursing home. Law is love when you and your fiancé take advantage of the opportunity a prenup discussion provides for a candid talk about finances, the cause of so many damaging marital arguments. Law is love when preparation of a health care proxy encourages you to speak to your spouse and children about how you want to be treated if something goes wrong. It's love because all these forms, contracts, and serious-looking documents contain precious information about your preferences, and therefore guidance that will remove a terrible burden from your loved ones: the burden of guilt that they haven't acted in accordance with your wishes.

I know it's daunting to plan for bad news. But we both know that avoiding reality is worse. Let's promise each other to build our confidence in the future, and our family's strength, through productive activity: not just power walks through the park, or editing our closets to rid ourselves of last season's jeans (the pair we keep just because it still fits), but systematic attention to the ways the law can help organize and improve every stage of our busy, rewarding lives.

Thank you so much for sharing your time with me. I miss you already. So please visit me online at lisagreenlaw.com for updates on the law and other information you can learn from, use, and share.

NOTES

INTRODUCTION: YOUR FRIEND AT THE BAR

2   *Soia Mentschikoff got the nod:* Cynthia Grant Bowman, "Women in the Legal Profession from the 1920s to the 1970s: What Can We Learn from Their Experience about Law and Social Change?" *Maine Law Review* 61 (2009): 1.

2   *Not a single woman graduated:* Alexandra N. Atiya, "Women Grads Mark 50 Years at Law School," *Harvard Crimson*, May 5, 2003, http://www.thecrimson.com/article/2003/5/5/women-grads-mark-50-years-at/.

CHAPTER 1: LAUNCHING A RELATIONSHIP: WHEN IS ONLINE OVER THE LINE?

10   *the company guaranteed introductions, not dates:* "Woman Says She Was Duped by Dating Service," *Trentonian*, June 11, 2012, http://www.trentonian.com/article/TT/20120611/NEWS01/120619982; Susanna Kim, "New Jersey Woman Sues Matchmaking Service After Date of 'Horror,'" ABC News, June 21, 2012, http://abcnews.go.com/Business/jersey-woman-sues-matchmaking-service-date-horror/story?id=16605678&singlePage=true.

10   *"For a generation of people . . .":* Sam H. Sanders, "Modern Dating Is a Group Sport for the Hashtag Generation," Digital Life (blog), NPR.org, March 14, 2013, http://www.npr.org/2013/03/14/174302979/modern-dating-is-a-group-sport-for-the-hashtag-generation.

12   *"HUMOR RAINBOW DOES NOT CONDUCT CRIMINAL BACK-GROUND CHECKS ON ITS USERS . . .":* "OkCupid Terms & Conditions," last revised October 11, 2013, http://www.okcupid.com/legal/terms.

12   *The case was settled out of court:* Jose Martinez, "Lawsuit Against Amy Laurent Dating Service Dropped After Two Parties Come to Agreement," *New York Daily News*, June 24, 2010, http://www.nydailynews.com/new-york/lawsuit-amy-laurent-dating-service-dropped-parties-agreement-article-1.180979.

12   *The service called the lawsuit baseless and it was ultimately dismissed:* Nate C. Hindman, "Kelleher & Associates Suit Dismissed in Case of Matchmaking Fail," *Huffington Post*, September 19, 2012, http://www.huffingtonpost.com/2012/09/19/kelleher-associates-matchmaking-lawsuit_n_1897898.html.

13 *Those lawsuits in California, New York, and Texas:* Julie Triedman, "Fifth Circuit Knocks Out Match.com Class Action," Litigation Daily (blog), *American Lawyer,* October 4, 2013, http://www.litigationdaily.com/id=1202622254981/rss=rss_tal_litdaily.

13 *Mary Kay sued Match.com:* David Knowles, "Woman Sues Match.com for $10 Million After Surviving Brutal Stabbing by Man She Met on the Dating Site," *New York Daily News,* January 25, 2013, http://www.nydailynews.com/news/crime/stabbing-victim-sues-match-10-million-article-1.1247969.

14 *40 million Americans have tried:* Meredith Broussard, "Dating Stats You Should Know," Match.com, *Happen,* http://www.match.com/magazine/article/4671/.

14 *daters need to exercise "common sense and prudence":* Erin Meyer, "Sexual Predators Turn to Web to Snare Victims," *Chicago Tribune,* November 22, 2012, http://articles.chicagotribune.com/2012-11-22/news/ct-met-online-dating-20121122_1_spark-networks-true-com-online-relationship-site.

14 *a helpful list published by Johns Hopkins University:* "Crime Prevention Tips," Campus Safety and Security, Johns Hopkins University, jhu.edu/security/crimeprevention_dating.html.

CHAPTER 2: COHABITATION: DOES PRACTICE MAKE PERFECT?

17 *According to the 2006 to 2010 National Survey of Family Growth:* Casey E. Copen, Kimberly Daniels, and William D. Mosher, First Premarital Cohabitation in the United States: 2006–2010 National Survey of Family Growth, National Health Statistics Report, April 4, 2013, http://www.cdc.gov/nchs/data/nhsr/nhsr064.pdf.

18 *a "no nup":* Jill Papworth, "Why a Cohabitation Agreement Is Essential for Non-Married Couples," *Guardian,* March 8, 2013, http://www.theguardian.com/money/2013/mar/09/cohabitation-agreement-essential-non-married-couples.

18 *and almost all do:* Natalie T. Lorenz, "Cohabitation Agreements After the Civil Union Act," *Illinois Bar Journal* 100 (June 2012): 308, http://www.isba.org/ibj/2012/06/cohabitationagreementsafterthecivil.

18 *what can your "no nup" include?:* Jeanne M. Hannah, "The Law and Living Together," *Law Trends & News: Family Law,* American Bar Association, Fall 2010, http://www.americanbar.org/newsletter/publications/law_trends_news_practice_area_e_newsletter_home/fl_feat3.html.

20 *"meretricious union":* Herma Hill Kay and Carol Amyx, "Marvin v. Marvin: Preserving the Options," *California Law Review* 65 (1977): 939.

20 *Michelle's case was dismissed by a lower court:* Marvin v. Marvin, 557 P.2d 106 (Cal. 1976).

21 *lived with Dick Van Dyke for thirty years:* Anahad O'Connor, "Michelle Triola Marvin, of Landmark Paternity Suit, Dies at 76," *New York Times,* October 30, 2009.

22 *judge Ned Rosenberg delivered:* Joiner v. Orman, No. FD-07-001086-13 (N.J. Super. Ct. 2013).

22 *played Gordon Robinson for decades:* Roscoe Orman's IMDb page, accessed February 7, 2014, http://www.imdb.com/name/nm0650207/?ref_=nv_sr_1.

22 *Roscoe's lawyer vowed to appeal:* Thomas Zambito, "Sesame Street's Roscoe Orman Loses Palimony Battle with Mother of Their Four Children," *Newark Star-Ledger,* September 24, 2013, http://www.nj.com/essex/index .ssf/2013/09/sesame_streets_roscoe_orman_loses_palimony_battle_with_ mother_of_their_four_children.html.

CHAPTER 3: MARRIAGE BASICS

26 *They may need permission to officiate:* Uniform Marriage and Divorce Act, Section 206, http://www.uniformdivorce.com/UMDA.pdf.

26 *couples to marry without an officiant:* 23 Pa.C.S.A. § 1502.

26 *as young as fourteen for young men and thirteen for young women:* N.H. Rev. Stat. § 457:4, gencourt.state.nh.us/rsa/html/XLIII/457/457-4.htm.

26 *covenant marriage:* Arizona (A.R.S. § 25–901), Louisiana (LSA–R.S. 9:272), and Arkansas (A.C.A. § 9-11-803).

27 *Covenant couples agree to undergo premarital counseling:* Diana Jean Schemo, "In Covenant Marriage, Forging Ties That Bind," *New York Times,* November 10, 2001, http://www.nytimes.com/2001/11/10/us/in-covenant-marriage-forging-ties-that-bind.html.

27 *Department of State's guide to overseas marriage:* "Marriage Abroad," U.S. Department of State, travel.state.gov/law/family_issues/marriage/marriage_589 .html.

28 *The judge agreed with D.S.:* Joel Stashenko, "Panel Declines to Void ULC Marriage Ceremony," *New York Law Journal,* April 29, 2013, http://www .newyorklawjournal.com/id=1202597713893/Panel-Declines-to-Void-ULC-Marriage-Ceremony?slreturn=20140226120632.

28 *dismissed Anya's request for a divorce:* Andrew Kershner, "Judge Finds Couple's 'Symbolic' Resort Marriage Invalid," *New York Law Journal,* June 6, 2014.

29 *he wrote* 100 Million Unnecessary Returns*:* Michael J. Graetz, *100 Million Unnecessary Returns: A Simple, Fair, and Competitive Tax Plan for the United States* (New Haven, CT: Yale University Press, 2008).

30 *agency received more than fifty thousand:* Sandra Block, "IRS 'Innocent Spouse' Rules Can Be Tough," *USA Today,* June 24, 2011, http://usatoday30.usatoday .com/money/perfi/taxes/2011-06-23-domestic-abuse-taxes-irs_n.htm.

31 *that number had doubled to eighteen:* Adam Liptak, "Utah Ruling Means No Respite for the Supreme Court on Same-Sex Marriage," *New York Times,* December 27, 2013, http://www.nytimes.com/2013/12/27/us/utah-ruling-means-no-respite-for-the-supreme-court-on-same-sex-marriage.html?_r=0.

32 *Margaret H. Marshall, then chief justice:* John Ellement, "Margaret Marshall, Author of Mass. Gay Marriage Decision, to Retire," Metro Desk, *Boston Globe,* July 21, 2010, http://www.boston.com/news/local/breaking_news/2010/07/ _the_listing_of.html.

32 *it's been incorporated into wedding ceremonies:* Todd Feathers, "State Ruling on Gay Marriage a Hit at Weddings," *Boston Globe,* January 8, 2013, http://www.boston-globe.com/metro/2013/01/08/landmark-mass-decision-gay-marriage-becomes-popular-text-weddings/Lx9UXfJA1XdA3jLOqpUHML/story.html.

32 *"Civil marriage is at once a deeply personal commitment . . .":* Goodridge v. Department of Public Health, 798 N.E.2d 941 (Mass. 2003).

CHAPTER 4: COMMON-LAW MARRIAGE

35 *The states are:* "Common-Law Marriage," National Conference of State Legislators, http://www.ncsl.org/research/human-services/common-law-marriage.aspx.

36 *a woman takes her common-law husband's surname:* "Common-Law Marriage," National Conference of State Legislators, http://www.ncsl.org/research/human-services/common-law-marriage.aspx.

36 *Requirements vary by state:* "Common Law Marriage Fact Sheet," Unmarried Equality, www.unmarried.org/common-law-marriage-fact-sheet.

36 *no common-law marriage existed:* Garrett v. Burris, 735 S.E.2d 414 (N.C. App. 2012), aff'd 742 S.E.2d 803 (N.C. 2013).

CHAPTER 5: CIVIL UNIONS AND DOMESTIC PARTNERSHIPS

39 *The court then directed lawmakers:* Jennifer Ritschel-Smith, "United States Survey on Domestic Partnerships," *Journal of the American Academy of Matrimonial Lawyers* 22 (June 10, 2009): 142–44.

39 *These legal contortions ended when Vermont:* Edith Honan, "Factbox: List of States that Legalized Gay Marriage," Reuters, June 26, 2013, http://www.reuters.com/article/2013/06/26/us-usa-court-gaymarriage-states-idUSBRE95P07A20130626.

39 *approved civil unions in 2013 after two failed attempts:* Jake Grovum, "Backers See Momentum as 6th State Allows Same-Sex Civil Unions," *Stateline,* March 21, 2013, http://www.pewstates.org/projects/stateline/headlines/backers-see-momentum-as-6th-state-allows-same-sex-civil-unions-85899461405.

39 *Reciprocal Beneficiaries law:* "Civil Unions & Domestic Partnership Statutes," National Conference of State Legislatures, June 26, 2013, http://www.ncsl.org/research/human-services/civil-unions-and-domestic-partnership-statutes.aspx.

39 *to offer domestic partner benefits to couples who could wed instead:* Joanne Sammer and Stephen Miller, "The Future of Domestic Partner Benefits," Society for Human Resource Management, October 8, 2013, https://www.shrm.org/hrdisciplines/benefits/Articles/Pages/Domestic-Partner-Benefits.aspx.

40 *fewer still will legally recognize a partnership forged in another state:* "Civil Unions and Domestic Partnership Statutes," National Conference of State Legislatures, February 26, 2014, http://www.ncsl.org/research/human-services/civil-unions-and-domestic-partnership-statutes.aspx.

40 *many states have residency requirements:* "Defining Marriage: State Defense of Marriage Laws and Same-Sex Marriage," National Conference of State Legislatures, December 23, 2013, http://www.ncsl.org/research/human-services/same-sex-marriage-overview.aspx.

40 *M.'s civil union was the functional equivalent of a marriage:* Elia-Warnken v. Elia, 972 N.E.2d 17 (Mass. Sup.Ct. 2012).

CHAPTER 6: PRENUPTIAL (AND POSTNUPTIAL) AGREEMENTS

43 *Overwhelmingly, it was to protect separate property:* "Increase of Prenuptial Agreements Reflects Improving Economy and Real Estate Market: Survey

of Nation's Top Matrimonial Attorneys Also Cites Rise in Women Requesting Prenups," American Academy of Matrimonial Lawyers, October 15, 2013, http://www.aaml.org/about-the-academy/press/press-releases/pre-post-nuptial-agreements/increase-prenuptial-agreements-re.

43 *"Marriage is not just a private love story . . .":* Laura Petrecca, "Prenuptial Agreements: Unromantic, but Important," *USA Today,* March 11, 2010, http://usatoday30.usatoday.com/money/perfi/basics/2010-03-08-prenups08_CV_N.htm?csp=hf.

43 *prenups remain relatively rare:* Sanette Tanaka, "The Growing Popularity of the Prenup," *Wall Street Journal,* October 31, 2013, http://online.wsj.com/news/articles/SB10001424052702303615304579157671554066120.

44 *all states enforce prenuptial agreements:* "Council of State Governments Includes New Uniform Act as 'Suggested State Legislation,'" Uniform Law Commission, September 19, 2013, http://www.uniformlaws.org/NewsDetail.aspx?title=CSG%20Includes%20Uniform%20Premarital%20and%20Marital%20Agreements%20Act%20as%20%22Suggested%20State%20Legislation%22; see also Ken Altshuler, "Postnuptial Agreements: The Prenup for Married Couples," *Huffington Post,* September 21, 2012, http://www.huffingtonpost.com/ken-altshuler/postnuptial-agreements_b_1902006.html.

44 *What Can You Put in a Prenup?:* Diana Mercer, "Premarital Agreement Issues Checklist," American Bar Association, March 2012, http://www.americanbar.org/publications/gpsolo_ereport/2012/march_2012/premarital_agreement_issues_checklist.html.

45 *spouses cannot be disinherited:* Liz Moyer, "Prenups and Estate Planning," *Wall Street Journal,* November 15, 2013, http://online.wsj.com/news/articles/SB10001424052702304868404579194383854682634.

45 *certain topics are technically beyond its scope:* Steve Weisman, "A Guide to Elder Planning: Asset Protection," *FT Press,* January. 17, 2013, http://www.ftpress.com/articles/article.aspx?p=2012470.

46 *Here are five sensible topics:* Daniel Lippman, "Financial Issues to Discuss Before You Get Married," *Wall Street Journal,* September 29, 2013, http://online.wsj.com/news/articles/SB10001424127887323308504579087483530489704.

47 *will reach approximately $305,000:* "Estimating College Costs," MassMutual Financial Group, http://www.massmutual.com/planningtools/educationalarticles/articledisplay?mmcom_articleid=df94531cb3a4a110VgnVCM100000ee6d06aaRCRD.

49 *rather than share it as community property:* In re Marriage of Facter, 212 Cal. App. 4th 967 (2013).

50 *Elizabeth would receive up to $25,000:* Kieran Crowley, "Wife of Millionaire LI Real-Estate Mogul Gets Judge to Rip Up Her Prenup," *New York Post,* March 11, 2013, http://nypost.com/2013/03/11/wife-of-millionaire-li-real-estate-mogul-gets-judge-to-rip-up-her-prenup/.

50 *Dire predictions abounded:* Cioffi-Petrakis v. Petrakis, 993 N.E.2d 1273 (N.Y. 2013).

51 *"scream inequity . . .":* C.S. v. L.S., 41 Misc. 3d 1209(A) (N.Y. Sup. Ct. 2013); Brendan Pierson, "Judge Rejects Prenup That Would Leave Wife 'Practically

Destitute,'" *New York Law Journal*, July 10, 2013, http://www.newyork
lawjournal.com/id=1202610121192?slreturn=20140117203233.

CHAPTER 7: FOUR-PRONG PROBLEMS: WHO KEEPS THE ENGAGEMENT RING?

54 *But when those laws faded in the 1930s:* Matthew O'Brien, "The Strange (and
Formerly Sexist) Economics of Engagement Rings," *Atlantic*, April 5, 2012,
http://www.theatlantic.com/business/archive/2012/04/the-strange-and-
formerly-sexist-economics-of-engagement-rings/255434/.

54 *the average cost of a ring in 2011 was $5,200:* 2011 Engagement and Jewelry Sta-
tistics Released by TheKnot.com and WeddingChannel.com, August 30, 2011,
http://www.xogroupinc.com/press-releases-home/2011-press-releases/2011-08-
30-2011-engagement-and-jewelry-statistics-released.aspx.

55 *Otherwise, it doesn't matter who is at fault:* Lindh v. Surman, 702 A.2d 560
(Super. Ct. Pa. 1997).

55 *repurposing an engagement ring into the "F-you ring":* Mia Walker, "After Divorce, What to Do with the Ring?," *San Francisco Chronicle*, February 10, 2008,
http://www.sfgate.com/style/article/After-divorce-what-to-do-with-the-
ring-3227206.php.

CHAPTER 8: SEPARATION WITHOUT ANXIETY

62 *here's the site's summary:* Sample Separation Agreement, FindLaw, http://
family.findlaw.com/divorce/sample-separation-agreement.htm.

63 *qualify for Social Security retirement benefits based on your spouse's earnings:* Retirement Planner: Benefits for Your Divorced Spouse, Social Security Administration, http://www.ssa.gov/retire2/yourdivspouse.htm.

65 *Since she never demanded more information from E.:* Smith v. Smith, 2010 NY
Slip Op 52002 (N.Y. Sup. Ct. 2010).

65 *separate for two years:* Sharon Jayson, "Splitting? 79% of Marital Separations
End in Divorce," *USA Today*, May 6, 2012, http://usatoday30.usatoday.com/
news/health/wellness/story/2012-05-06/Splitting-79-of-marital-separations-
end-in-divorce/54790574/1.

66 *turned out to be no more than a tentative step:* Casella v. Alden, 682 S.E.2d 455
(N.C. Ct. App. 2009).

CHAPTER 9: ALL ABOUT ANNULMENT

68 *Henry VIII of England secures the annulment:* BBC History, "Catherine of
Aragon," http://www.bbc.co.uk/history/people/catherine_of_aragon.

68 *Britney Spears secures the annulment:* Associated Press, "Judge Dissolves Britney's 'Joke' Wedding," Today.com, January 6, 2004, http://www.today.com/
id/3869708/#.UzMVh61dX11.

69 *untreatable disease of the blood and bone marrow:* "Myelodysplastic syndrome,"
Diseases and Conditions, Mayo Clinic, http://www.mayoclinic.org/diseases-
conditions/myelodysplastic-syndromes/basics/definition/con-20027168.

69 *tricked into remarriage by the lie:* In re Marriage of Farr, 228 P.3d 267, (Co. Ct.
App. Feb. 4, 2010).

CHAPTER 10: DIVORCE: GETTING STARTED

73 *women were hired as "correspondents":* Ilyon Woo, "Breaking Up Is Hard to Do," *Wall Street Journal,* August 13, 2010, http://online.wsj.com/news/articles/SB1 0001424052748704901104575423341295531582.

74 *became involved with the coach's wife:* Jean M. Cary and Sharon Scudder, "Breaking Up Is Hard to Do: North Carolina Refuses to End Its Relationship with Heart Balm Torts," *Elon Law Review* 4:3, http://www.elon.edu/docs/e-web/law/law_review/Issues/Elon_Law_Review_V4_No1_Cary-Scudder.pdf.

75 *the closest reformers got:* Michael Gordon, "Jilted Husband Sues Online Infidelity Service Ashley Madison," *Charlotte Observer,* December 12, 2013, http://www.charlotteobserver.com/2013/12/12/4540855/jilted-husband-sues-online-infidelity.html#.UwLNtkJdX10.

75 *the state ranked seventeenth:* "Massachusetts Has the Lowest Divorce Rate in the Nation," Floating Path, March 9, 2013, http://www.floatingpath.com/2013/03/09/massachusetts-lowest-divorce-rate-nation/.

75 *The ploy for divorce tourism dollars worked:* Priya Jain, "Betty Goes Reno," *Slate,* July 21,2010, http://www.slate.com/articles/arts/culturebox/2010/07/betty_goes_reno.html.

76 *competed with Reno as quick-divorce getaways:* See generally William McGee and Sandra McGee, *The Divorce Seekers* (St. Helena, CA: BMC, 2004).

82 *allows same-sex couples to undo their marriage:* Christiansen v. Christiansen, 253 P.3d 153 (Wy. 2011).

82 *residency requirements:* "Defining Marriage: State Defense of Marriage Laws and Same-Sex Marriage," National Conference of State Legislatures, http://www.ncsl.org/research/human-services/same-sex-marriage-overview.aspx.

82 *consult a state-by-state guide:* "Divorce for Same-Sex Couples Who Live in Non-Recognition States: A Guide for Attorneys," http://www.nclrights.org/legal-help-resources/resource/divorce-for-same-sex-couples-who-live-in-non-recognition-states-a-guide-for-attorneys/.

CHAPTER 11: DIVORCE: PROPERTY AND SUPPORT

85 *First, she wrote a pamphlet:* Custody Rights and Domestic Violence, http://www.parliament.uk/about/living-heritage/transformingsociety/private-lives/relationships/overview/custodyrights/.

86 *She arrived too late:* "Caroline Norton," Spartacus Educational, http://www.spartacus.schoolnet.co.uk/Wnorton.htm.

86 *They enjoyed about three months of married life:* Frances Wilson, "'Criminal' Mrs. Norton," *Times Literary Supplement,* August 15, 2012, http://www.the-tls.co.uk/tls/public/article1103919.ece.

87 *The Institute for Divorce Financial Analysts has a good starter list:* Fadi Baradihi, "Surviving Financially After Divorce," Institute for Divorce Financial Analysts, http://institutedfa.com/Professionals.php?Articles-Surviving-Financially-After-Divorce-27.

88 *For example, in Ohio:* Equitable division of marital and separate property, Ohio Rev. Code Ann. §3105.171 (West 2014).

88 *property must be divided fifty-fifty:* Cal. Fam. Code § 2550 (West 2014).

88 *the division might be more flexible:* See, for example, Arizona Marital and Domestic Relations, Ariz. Rev. Stat. Ann. §25-318.

90 *prequalify for a mortgage before the divorce is final:* Baradihi, "Surviving Financially After Divorce."

91 *"A 'qualified domestic relations order' . . .":* "Qualified Domestic Relations Orders," United States Department of Labor, http://www.dol.gov/ebsa/faqs/faq_qdro.html.

92 *collect Social Security benefits:* "How Does a Divorced Spouse Qualify for Benefits?," Social Security Administration, http://www.dol.gov/ebsa/faqs/faq_qdro.html.

93 *Citigroup offers some sensible tips:* "Separating Credit," Citicards.com, https://www.citicards.com/cards/wv/html/cm/managing-your-finances/handling-hard-times/separating-credit.html.

94 *Frank and Jamie met as undergraduates:* See generally Vanessa Grigoriadis, "A Major-League Divorce," *Vanity Fair*, August 2011, http://www.vanityfair.com/society/features/2011/08/mccourt-divorce-201108.

95 *That was Frank's argument:* McCourt v. McCourt, 2010 WL 5092780 (Cal. Sup. Ct. Dec. 7, 2010).

95 *Private jets at $12,500 an hour:* Ibid.

96 *threw out her case:* Bill Shaikin, "Jamie McCourt Loses Bid to Throw Out Dodgers Divorce Deal," *Los Angeles Times*, September 9, 2013, http://articles.latimes.com/2013/sep/09/sports/la-sp-dn-jamie-frank-mccourt-dodgers-divorce-20130909.

97 *the story of Michael Morgan:* Yamiche Alcindor, "Should Alimony Laws Be Changed?," *USA Today*, January 18, 2012, http://usatoday30.usatoday.com/money/perfi/basics/story/2012-01-05/alimony-law-reform/52642100/1.

97 *sending monthly checks to his ex-wife in Florida:* Julia Spitz, "Spitz: Eyes Turn to Senate for Alimony," *Milford Daily News*, July 24, 2011, http://www.milforddailynews.com/x371608054/Spitz-Eyes-turn-to-Senate-for-alimony.

97 *even Powerball winnings end after twenty years:* Geoff Williams, "Taking the 'Permanent' Out of Permanent Alimony," *US News & World Report*, January 23, 2013, http://money.usnews.com/money/personal-finance/articles/2013/01/23/taking-the-permanent-out-of-permanent-alimony.

97 *alimony limits:* Bella English, "New Mass. Alimony Law a 'Model'—But Is It Working?," *Boston Globe*, October 20, 2013, http://money.usnews.com/money/personal-finance/articles/2013/01/23/taking-the-permanent-out-of-permanent-alimony.

97 *$9,000 monthly checks to her ex:* Anita Raghavan, "Men Receiving Alimony Want a Little Respect," *Wall Street Journal*, April 1, 2008, http://online.wsj.com/news/articles/SB120700651883978623?mod=tff_main_tff_top.

98 *"mother, homemaker and corporate wife":* Wendt v. Wendt, 757 A.2d 1225 (Conn. App. Ct. Sept. 5, 2000).

99 *economic theory of the case:* "What a Wife's Worth," *Stanford* (March/April 1998), http://money.usnews.com/money/personal-finance/articles/2013/01/23/taking-the-permanent-out-of-permanent-alimony.

99 *her view of marriage:* "Valuing the Invisible Work of Women," *Christian Science*

Monitor, December 16, 1998, http://www.csmonitor.com/1998/1216/122198
.opin.opin.1.html/(page)/2.

99 *an even newer trend:* Meg Canby and Dylan Mitchell, "A Discussion of Lingering Gender Bias in Matrimonial and Family Law," *New York Law Journal,* July 29, 2013, http://www.newyorklawjournal.com/id=1202612433367/A-Discussion-of-Lingering-Gender-Bias-in-Matrimonial-and-Family-Law?slreturn=20140125122320.

101 *a court has powerful options: Divorce Manual: A Client Handbook,* American Academy of Matrimonial Lawyers, http://www.aaml.org/library/publications/415/divorce-manual-client-handbook/1-divorce-process.

CHAPTER 12: CHILD CUSTODY

103 *California led the pack:* Phil Bushard, Doneldon Dennis, and Denise McColley, "FAQs Separating and Divorcing Parents Ask About Legal Matters," Association of Family and Conciliation Courts, http://www.afccnet.org/resourcecenter/resourcesforfamilies/pamphletinformation/categoryid/1/productid/2.

103 *more than 95 percent of custody plans:* "Child Custody and Support," American Bar Association Division for Public Education, http://www.americanbar.org/groups/public_education/resources/law_issues_for_consumers/custody_options.htm.

103 *a parenting agreement worksheet:* "Parenting Agreement Worksheet, Minnesota Version," Minnesota Courts, 2004, http://www.mncourts.gov/documents/Parenting-Agreement-Worksheet.pdf.

104 *As one eminent family psychologist put it:* Robert E. Emery, "Emery's Alternative Parenting Plans (Child Custody Schedules)," *The Truth About Children and Divorce,* http://emeryondivorce.com/parenting_plans.php.

104 *One website that offers automated scheduling:* "Effective Visitation Schedules," Custody X Change, http://www.custodyxchange.com/schedules/visitation-schedule-effective.php.

105 *The guardian will likely want to meet your children:* "Guardian ad litem," Cornell University Law School Legal Information Institute, http://www.law.cornell.edu/wex/guardian_ad_litem.

105 *The older the child:* "Child Custody and Support: Deciding Factors in Awarding Child Custody," American Bar Association Division for Public Education, http://www.americanbar.org/groups/public_education/resources/law_issues_for_consumers/custody_childpreference.html.

106 *Some states do not hold sexual orientation against parents:* Leslie Cooper and Paul Cates, "Too High a Price: The Case Against Restricting Gay Parenting," American Civil Liberties Union, 2006, https://www.aclu.org/files/images/asset_upload_file480_27496.pdf.

106 *The idea of an alienation "syndrome":* David Crary, Associated Press, "Parental Alienation Not a Mental Disorder, American Psychiatric Association Says," *Huffington Post,* September 21, 2012, https://www.aclu.org/files/images/asset_upload_file480_27496.pdf.

107 *offers sensible advice: Divorce Manual: A Client Handbook,* American Academy of Matrimonial Lawyers, http://www.aaml.org/library/publications/415/divorce-manual-client-handbook/4-children.

109 *taking away custody:* Melody M. v. Robert M., 103 A.D.3d 932 (N.Y. App. Div. Feb. 14, 2013).

110 *she had a constitutional right to the relocation:* Bartosz v. Jones, 197 P.3d 310, (Idaho October 16, 2008).

111 *courts have relied on factors:* Jeff Atkinson, "The Meaning of 'Habitual Residence' Under the Hague Convention on the Civil Aspects of International Child Abduction and the Hague Convention on the Protection of Children," *Oklahoma Law Review* 63 (2011): 647.

112 *A less combative approach:* Susan Brown, "Family Crises Getting Gentler Handling," *Northwest Indiana Times,* September 17, 2013, http://www.journal gazette.net/article/20130917/NEWS07/309179938/0/NEWS09.

112 *Grandparents have the right in every state:* "Child Custody and Support: Issues Surrounding Visitation," American Bar Association Division for Public Education, http://www.americanbar.org/groups/public_education/resources/law_issues_for_consumers/visitation_grandparents.html.

113 *the desperate grandparents:* Warren Richey, "Do Grandparents Get Visitation Rights? Supreme Court Declines Case," *Christian Science Monitor,* February 21, 2012, http://www.csmonitor.com/USA/Justice/2012/0221/Do-grandparents-get-visitation-rights-Supreme-Court-declines-case.

113 *could not prevail in court:* Ex parte E.R.G. and D.W.G., 73 So.3d 634, (Ala. June 10, 2011).

CHAPTER 13: CHILD SUPPORT

115 *A 2011 U.S. Census Bureau report found:* Timothy Grall, "Custodial Mothers and Fathers and Their Child Support: 2011," October 2013, U.S. Census Bureau, pp. 9–10, http://census.gov/prod/2013pubs/p60-246.pdf.

116 *the number is fair and reasonable for your children:* Tom James, "Child Support and the Limitations on Private Agreements," Responsible Divorce, http://responsibledivorce.com/legal/child-support.htm.

116 *you will need to review the numbers more carefully:* "Child Custody and Support: Setting Guidelines for Child Support," American Bar Association Division for Public Education, http://www.americanbar.org/groups/public_education/resources/law_issues_for_consumers/childsupport_sharedcustody.html.

117 *you cannot split a child's exemption:* "May divorced or legally separated parents split the dependency exemption for a child?" Dependents and Exemptions, Frequently Asked Questions, Internal Revenue Service, http://www.irs.gov/Help-&-Resources/Tools-&-FAQs/FAQs-for-Individuals/Frequently-Asked-Tax-Questions-&-Answers/Filing-Requirements,-Status,-Dependents,-Exemptions/Dependents-&-Exemptions/Dependents-&-Exemptions-3.

117 *allow a working mother who remarries:* Irwin Garfinkel, Marygold S. Melli, and John G. Robertson, "Child Support Orders: A Perspective on Reform," *Children and Divorce* 4, no. 1 (Spring 1994): 90, fn 43.

118 *seven deadbeat parents:* Wayne K. Roustan, "Deadbeat Dads, Moms Arrested When They Go to Collect Prizes," *Sun-Sentinel,* December 12, 2011, http://articles.sun-sentinel.com/2011-12-12/news/fl-deadbeat-arrests-20111212_1_deadbeat-dads-deadbeat-parents-child-support.

118 *your ex can be held in contempt of court:* "Child Custody and Support: Setting Guidelines for Child Support," American Bar Association Division for Public Education, http://www.americanbar.org/groups/public_education/resources/law_issues_for_consumers/childsupport_forced.html.

118 *deadbeats who live in a different state than their kids:* "Child Support Enforcement," Office of Inspector General, http://oig.hhs.gov/fraud/child-support-enforcement/.

119 *financial planning website learnvest.com offers:* Lorelei Laird, "How Do You Get Your Child Support Money?," Learnvest.com, June 19, 2013, http://www.learnvest.com/knowledge-center/how-do-you-get-your-child-support-money/.

120 *Sand was sentenced to two and a half years:* Mosi Secret, "2-Year Term for a Father Who Avoided Child Support," *New York Times,* May 21, 2013, http://www.nytimes.com/2013/05/22/nyregion/man-labeled-most-wanted-deadbeat-parent-gets-2-year-sentence.html?_r=0.

120 *About fifty thousand people reportedly are incarcerated:* Carmen Solomon-Fears, Alison M. Smith, and Carla Berry, "Child Support Enforcement: Incarceration as the Last Resort for Nonpayment of Support," Congressional Research Service, http://www.ncsea.org/documents/CRS-Report-on-CSE-and-Incarceration-for-Non-Payment-March-6-2012.pdf.

CHAPTER 14: FIGHTING OVER FIDO: THE PAIN OF PET CUSTODY DISPUTES

123 Pets Weekly *magazine suggests you secure the following paperwork:* Maryann Mott, "Avoid a Canine Custody Battle," *Pets Weekly,* August 9, 2010, http://www.thedogdaily.com/pawsperouspets/happy/adoption/avoid_canine_custody_battle/index.html#.UxnTTOddX10.

123 *He ended up looking after Beanie and Kacey:* "Cat Lover Goes to Jail for Hiding Pets," ABC News, June 4, 2006, http://abcnews.go.com/GMA/story?id=126927.

124 *Linda won custody:* Sally Kalson, "In Pet Custody Battles, Courts Treat Animals as Property," *Pittsburgh Post-Gazette,* June 25, 2006, http://www.post-gazette.com/life/lifestyle/2006/06/25/In-pet-custody-battles-courts-treat-animals-as-property/stories/200606250136.

124 *The* Hollywood Reporter *compiled a list:* Jilian Aubin and Austin Siegemund-Broka, "The 5 Most Famous Pet Custody Wars in Hollywood," *Hollywood Reporter,* August 9, 2013, http://www.hollywoodreporter.com/news/celebrity-pets-hollywoods-5-famous-595723.

124 *PETA cited Britney's standing as "the overwhelming choice":* "Help Us Out, K-Fed," People for the Ethical Treatment of Animals, http://www.peta.org/blog/help-us-kfed/.

125 *granted custody of Grady the cat:* Zovko v. Gregory, Case No. CH 97-544 (Va. Cir. Ct., Arlington Cty. Oct. 17, 1997); Joyce Tischler and Bruce Wagman, "Lawyers Must Plan for More Pet Custody Cases," Animal Legal Defense Fund, August 18, 2006, http://aldf.org/press-room/press-releases/lawyers-must-plan-for-more-pet-custody-cases/.

125 *dogs can feel love and attachment:* Gregory Berns, "Dogs Are People, Too," *New York Times,* October 5, 2013, http://www.nytimes.com/2013/10/06/opinion/sunday/dogs-are-people-too.html?pagewanted=all.

126 *Surely they swap stories:* Amelia Glynn, "Fighting Over the Family Pet: 5 Crazy Custody Cases," *San Francisco Chronicle,* November 9, 2010, http://blog.sfgate.com/pets/2010/11/09/fighting-over-the-family-pet-5-crazy-custody-cases/.

CHAPTER 15: DIY, MEDIATION, AND COLLABORATIVE DIVORCE

130 *trained as collaborative lawyers:* "History of Collaborative Divorce," Collaborative-Divorce.net, http://collaborativedivorce.net/history-of-collaborative-divorce/.

130 *it allows a divorcing couple to negotiate sensitive issues:* Lisa J. Cappalli, "Commentary: The Client's Experience of Collaborative Divorce," *Connecticut Law Tribune,* September 3, 2013, http://www.ctlawtribune.com/id=1202617832665/Commentary:-The-Client's-Experience-of-Collaborative-Divorce?slreturn=20140207095139.

131 *Check a prospect's credentials and experience:* "Family Section," Association for Conflict Resolution, acrfamilysection.org.

131 *These ACR-approved mediators:* "The ACR Family and Divorce Mediator AP Designation," Association for Conflict Resolution, http://www.acrnet.org/familyap/.

131 *keep the details of their mediation private:* Monica Holzer Sacks, "Facilitative Mediation Is Better," American Academy of Matrimonial Lawyers, January 10, 2000, http://aaml.org/sites/default/files/Facilitative%20Mediation%20is%20Better.pdf; see also "What Is Mediation? How Does It Work?," Wrightslaw.com, http://www.wrightslaw.com/info/iep.disputes.popup.resp5.htm.

132 *He extols the process for encouraging feuding spouses:* Robert E. Emery, "Emery's Divorce Mediation Study," *The Truth About Children and Divorce,* emeryondivorce.com/divorce_mediation_study.ph.

132 *safeguards so that children don't misunderstand the process:* Abby Tolchinsky and Ellie Wertheim, "Focusing on the Child's Viewpoint in Divorce Negotiations," *New York Law Journal,* August 2, 2013, http://www.newyorklawjournal.com/id=1202613438429/Focusing-on-the-Child's-Viewpoint-in-Divorce-Negotiations?slreturn=20140207131833.

133 *issues related to children are always open to reconsideration:* "Certified Arbitrators and Mediators," American Academy of Matrimonial Lawyers, http://aaml.org/certified-arbitrators-mediators.

CHAPTER 16: MAKING BABIES

137 *According to the Centers for Disease Control and Prevention:* "Infertility," Centers for Disease Control and Prevention, http://www.cdc.gov/nchs/fastats/fertile.htm.

138 *up to six different adults can lay claim to a newborn:* "Parentage Act Summary," Uniform Law Commission, http://www.uniformlaws.org/ActSummary.aspx?title=Parentage%20Act.

139 *Father's Day also can be celebrated:* Meryl Rosenberg, "Myth or Fact: Are Egg Donor Agreements Necessary?," American Fertility Association, http://www.theafa.org/article/myth-or-fact-are-egg-donor-agreements-necessary/.

139 *result urged by the lawmakers:* UPA Section 702, http://www.uniformlaws.org/shared/docs/parentage/upa_final_2002.pdf.

140 *law that allows a sperm donor:* John Hanna, Associated Press, "William Marotta, Kansas Sperm Donor to Lesbian Couple, Fighting Child Support Payments," *Huffington Post,* January 2, 2013, http://www.huffingtonpost.com/2013/01/02/william-marotta_n_2395412.html.

140 *William reportedly handed over his sperm:* Steve Fry, "Court: Marotta Is a Father, Not Merely a Sperm Donor," *Topeka Capital-Journal,* January 22, 2014, http://cjonline.com/news/2014-01-22/court-marotta-father-not-merely-sperm-donor.

140 *that line of reasoning wouldn't apply to their case:* Engelking v. Engelking, 982 N.E.2d 326 (Ind. Ct. App. Jan. 15, 2013).

142 *the proposed law would upend a simpler test:* Patrick McGreevy, "Jason Patric Custody Case Inspires Sperm-Donor-Rights Legislation," *Los Angeles Times,* July 6, 2013, http://articles.latimes.com/2013/jul/06/local/la-me-sperm-donor-20130707.

142 *a donor needs to submit to ultrasounds:* "Thinking of Becoming an Egg Donor?," New York State Task Force on Life and the Law, New York Department of Health, https://www.health.ny.gov/publications/1127/.

142 *recommends payment to an egg donor be limited to $10,000:* "Financial Compensation of Oocyte Donors," American Society for Reproductive Medicine, Ethics Committee Report, vol. 88, no. 2, August 2007, http://www.sart.org/uploadedFiles/ASRM_Content/News_and_Publications/Ethics_Committee_Reports_and_Statements/financial_incentives.pdf.

143 *penalize a donor for backing out of the procedure:* Sanford M. Benardo, "Egg Donor Contracts: Concerns of Recipients and Concerns of Donors," *Albany Law Journal of Science and Technology* 21 (2011): 291.

143 *lawyer look at a written agreement:* "Thinking of Becoming An Egg Donor?," New York State Task Force on Life and the Law.

143 *secured an early victory in a Pennsylvania court:* J.F. v. D.B., 897 A.2d 1261 (Pa. Super. Ct. 2006).

144 *the couple had raised the twins together:* K.M. v. E.G., 117 P.3d 673 (Cal. 2005).

144 *underwrite the cost of egg freezing:* Julie Steinberg, "The Big Chill: A Financial Plan for Egg Freezing," *Wall Street Journal,* August 9, 2013, http://online.wsj.com/news/articles/SB10001424127887323997004578639861242029962; Sarah Elizabeth Richards, "Alimony for Your Eggs," *New York Times,* September 6, 2013, http://www.nytimes.com/2013/09/07/opinion/alimony-for-your-eggs.html?_r=0.

145 *maintains an online map:* Diane S. Hinson, "State-by-State Surrogacy Law: Actual Practices," Creative Family Connections, http://www.creativefamilyconnections.com/state-map-surrogacy-law-practices.

145 *potential parties to a surrogacy:* "Third-Party Reproduction: A Guide for Patients," American Society for Reproductive Medicine, http://www.reproductivefacts.org/awards/detail.aspx?id=12274.

145 *a master's thesis on the impact of surrogacy:* Mike Kelly, "Kelly: 25 Years After Baby M, Surrogacy Questions Remain Unanswered," *Record,* March 30, 2012, http://www.northjersey.com/news/kelly-25-years-after-baby-m-surrogacy-questions-remain-unanswered-1.745725.

146 *an uneasy blend of apprehension:* Associated Press, "'Baby M' Trial Weighs Views of Psychiatrist," *Los Angeles Times,* February 18, 1987, http://articles.latimes.com/1987-02-18/news/mn-2721_1_baby-m-trial.

146 *"The surrogacy contract is based on principles . . .":* In re Baby M., 537 A.2d 1227, 1250 (N.J. 1988).

147 *New Jersey law changed to bar payments to surrogates:* Allison Pries, "Whatever Happened to Baby M?," *Record,* January 5, 2010, http://www.northjersey.com/news/Whatever_happened_to_Baby_M.html.

147 *the New Jersey Supreme Court deadlocked:* Kate Zernike, "Court's Split Decision Provides Little Clarity on Surrogacy," *New York Times,* October 24, 2012, http://www.nytimes.com/2012/10/25/nyregion/in-surrogacy-case-nj-supreme-court-is-deadlocked-over-whom-to-call-mom.html?pagewanted=all.

148 *allowed each would-be parent more leeway:* See, e.g., A.Z. v. B.Z., 725 N.E.2d 1051, 1059 (Mass. 2001).

148 *children could inherit property:* Adam Liptak, "Children Not Entitled to Dead Father's Benefits, Justices Rule," *New York Times,* May 21, 2012, http://www.nytimes.com/2012/05/22/us/children-not-entitled-to-dead-fathers-benefits-justices-rule.html.

CHAPTER 17: ADOPTION

151 *Some states set a minimum age of eighteen:* "Who May Adopt?," Child Welfare Information Gateway, U.S. Department of Health and Human Services, https://www.childwelfare.gov/systemwide/laws_policies/statutes/parties.pdf#Page=2&view=Fit.

151 *A private adoption agency may impose other restrictions:* "Review of Qualification Requirements for Prospective Adoptive Parents," Adoption.com, http://adopting.adoption.com/child/review-of-qualification-requirements-for-prospective-adoptive-parents.html.

151 *a private adoption is conducted:* "Adoption Options," Child Welfare Information Gateway, U.S. Department of Health and Human Services, https://www.childwelfare.gov/adoption/.

152 *to find a "perfect" family:* FAQs, The Homestudy Process, Adoption & Child Welfare Lawsite, http://www.adoptionchildwelfarelaw.org/faq_detail.php?id=88; "Home Study Requirements for Prospective Parents in Domestic Adoption," Child Welfare Information Gateway, U.S. Department of Health and Human Services, https://www.childwelfare.gov/systemwide/laws_policies/statutes/homestudyreqs_adoption.cfm.

152 *an adoption decree (or certificate):* Adoption Laws, National Adoption Center, http://www.adopt.org/adoption-laws.

153 *qualify for the full tax benefit:* Adoption Benefits FAQs, Internal Revenue Service, http://www.irs.gov/Individuals/Adoption-Benefits-FAQs.

153 *they made up 12 to 25 percent:* "Can Single Parents Adopt?," Independent Adoption Center, http://www.adoptionhelp.org/single-parents.

153 *revised its standards a decade later:* "The Adoption History Project," University of Oregon, pages.uoregon.edu/adoption/topics/singleparentadoptions.htm.

153 *specific laws addressing LGBT couples:* "Parenting Laws: Joint Adoption," Human Rights Campaign, https://www.hrc.org/files/assets/resources/parenting_joint-adoption_082013.pdf; "Frequently Asked Questions from Lesbian, Gay, Bisexual, and Transgender (LGBT) Prospective Foster and Adoptive Parents," Child Welfare Information Gateway, U.S. Department of Health and Human Services, 2011, https://www.childwelfare.gov/pubs/factsheets/faq_lgbt.cfm.

153 *pursue a second-parent adoption:* "Second Parent Adoption," Human Rights Campaign, http://www.hrc.org/resources/entry/second-parent-adoption.

154 *same-sex marriages were not sufficient:* James C. McKinley Jr., "N.Y. Judge Alarms Gay Parents by Finding Marriage Law Negates Need for Adoption," *New York Times,* January 28, 2014, http://www.nytimes.com/2014/01/29/nyregion/ny-judge-alarms-gay-parents-by-finding-marriage-law-negates-need-for-adoption.html.

155 *Another 55 percent were open, and 40 percent were mediated:* Deborah H. Siegel and Susan Livingston Smith, "Openness in Adoption," Evan B. Donaldson Adoption Institute, March 2012, http://adoptioninstitute.org/old/publications/2012_03_OpennessInAdoption.pdf.

155 *some states limit the agreements:* "Postadoption Contract Agreements Between Birth and Adoptive Families," Child Welfare Information Gateway, U.S. Department of Health and Human Services, https://www.childwelfare.gov/systemwide/laws_policies/statutes/cooperative.pdf.

155 *the most radical remnant of a closed adoption era:* Deborah H. Siegel and Susan Livingston Smith, "Openness in Adoption," Evan B. Donaldson Adoption Institute, March 2012, http://adoptioninstitute.org/old/publications/2012_03_OpennessInAdoption.pdf.

156 *The group's name, of course, pays sly homage:* "What Is Bastard Nation?," Bastard Nation, http://www.bastards.org/what-is-bastard-nation/.

156 *mutual consent registries:* "Access to Adoption Records," Child Welfare Information Gateway, U.S. Department of Health and Human Services, https://www.childwelfare.gov/systemwide/laws_policies/statutes/infoaccessap.pdf.

156 *adoption records had been sealed since 1946:* 750 Ill. Comp. Stat 50/18.04 (2010).

156 *thousands of adoptees:* John O'Connor, Associated Press, "Unsealed Birth Records Give Adoptees Peek at Past," Yahoo.com, August 7, 2013, https://news.yahoo.com/unsealed-birth-records-adoptees-peek-past-152824281.html.

157 *signed on to the Hague Convention:* "Convention Countries," Intercountry Adoption, U.S. Department of State, adoption.state.gov/hague_convention/countries.php.

157 *the number of foreign adoptions plummeted:* "Statistics," Intercountry Adoption, U.S. Department of State, http://adoption.state.gov/about_us/statistics.php.

157 *seeks parents who are married:* Tara Bahrampour, "Adopting from Overseas, Once Easy, Now Brings Lengthy Waits and Sometimes Heartbreak," *Washington Post,* January 11, 2013, http://www.washingtonpost.com/local/new-rules-on-overseas-adoptions-leave-some-would-be-parents-waiting-for-years/2013/01/11/c488c3b0-4bbe-11e2-b709-667035ff9029_story.html.

157 *the State Department halted adoptions:* Kevin Voight, "International Adoption: Saving Orphans or Child Trafficking?," CNN, September 18, 2013, http://www.cnn.com/2013/09/16/world/international-adoption-saving-orphans-child-trafficking/.

158 *another 112 incomplete adoption cases:* Suzy Khimm, "Va. Family Together After 5-Year Adoption Delay," *Washington Post,* April 13, 2013, http://www.washingtonpost.com/local/va-family-together-after-5-year-adoption-delay/2013/04/13/d6ef30b8-a47c-11e2-82bc-511538ae90a4_story.html.

158 *a child adopted from abroad can benefit:* "Acquiring U.S. Citizenship for Your

Child," Intercountry Adoption, U.S. Department of State, http://adoption .state.gov/us_visa_for_your_child/citizenship.php.

CHAPTER 18: SCHOOL SUPPORT

161 *subject to endless adjustments:* Arne Duncan, "America's Kids Need a Better Education Law," op-ed, *Washington Post,* August 25, 2103, http://www .washingtonpost.com/opinions/americas-kids-need-a-better-education-law/2013/08/25/fb71add8-0a90-11e3-8974-f97ab3b3c677_story.html; "A Teacher's Guide to Fixing No Child Left Behind," U.S. Department of Education, May 24, 2011, http://www.ed.gov/oese-news/teachers-guide-fixing-no-child-left-behind.

162 *advice from the American Academy of Pediatrics:* "Caring for Your Teenager" and "Caring for Your School-Age Child," American Academy of Pediatrics, http://www.healthychildren.org/English/bookstore/Pages/default.aspx.

163 *should pipe down:* See generally, "Your Right to Free Expression," American Civil Liberties Union, July 17, 2003, https://www.aclu.org/free-speech/your-right-free-expression.

164 *"materially and substantially disrupt . . .":* Tinker v. Des Moines Independent Community School District, 393 U.S. 503 (1969).

164 *Sorry, foul-mouthed freshmen:* Bethel School District v. Fraser, 478 U.S. 675 (1987).

164 *administrators can censor:* Hazelwood School District v. Kuhlmeier, 484 U.S. 260 (1988).

164 *passed student free-expression laws:* "Understanding Student Free-Expression Laws," Student Press Law Center, http://www.splc.org/news/report_detail .asp?id=1351&edition=43.

164 *upheld the suspension:* Wynar v. Douglas County School District, 728 F.3d 1062 (9th Cir. 2013).

164 *off-campus cyberbullying:* See generally "Student Rights and Responsibilities in the Digital Age: A Guide for Public School Students in Washington State," American Civil Liberties Union of Washington State, January 2012, https:// aclu-wa.org/student-rights-and-responsibilities-digital-age-guide-public-school-students-washington-state.

166 *"not plainly lewd":* B.H. v. Easton Area School District, PICS No. 13-2306 (3d Cir. 2013); Lawrence Hurley, "Supreme Court Declines to Hear 'I (Heart Sign) Boobies' Case," Reuters, March 10, 2014, http://www.reuters.com/article/2014/03/10/ us-usa-court-freespeech-idUSBREA290SA20140310.

166 *bullying among students ages twelve to eighteen:* "Indicators of School Crime and Safety: 2012," National Center for Education Statistics, http://nces.ed.gov/ programs/crimeindicators/ crimeindicators2012/tables/table_11_1.asp.

167 *61 percent of elementary and middle school girls:* "Analysis of State Bullying Laws and Policies," U.S. Department of Education, 2011, https://www2.ed.gov/ rschstat/eval/bullying/state-bullying-laws/state-bullying-laws.pdf.

167 *All states ban harassment:* "Cyberbullying and the States," National Conference of State Legislatures, http://www.ncsl.org/research/civil-and-criminal-justice/cyberbullying-and-the-states.aspx.

167 *If your child is being cyberbullied:* "Get the Facts," A Thin Line, http://www .athinline.org/take-control#deal-with-it.

168 *suing two classmates for libel:* Greg Bluestein and Dorie Turner, Associated Press, "School Cyberbullying Victims Fight Back in Lawsuits," *Huffington Post,* April 26, 2012, http://www.huffingtonpost.com/2012/04/26/school-cyberbullying-vict_n_1457918.html.

168 *passed a law holding parents responsible:* Ashley Luthern, "Monona Anti-Bullying Ordinance Sparks Debate About Issue," *Milwaukee Journal Sentinel,* June 5, 2013, http://www.jsonline.com/news/wisconsin/monona-council-passes-anti-bullying-ordinance-b9927437z1-210307651.htm.

168 *authorities may respond with a harsher:* Emily Bazelon, "Sticks and Stones: De-feating the Culture of Bullying and Rediscovering the Power of Character and Empathy," Resource Guide for Parents, http://emilybazelon.com/wp-content/uploads/2013/02/SticksStones_Guide_Parents.pdf.

169 *there is no federal antibullying law:* "Policies and Laws," StopBullying.gov, http://www.stopbullying.gov/laws.

169 *to set up an antibullying policy:* Morrow v. Balaski, 719 F.3d 160 (3d Cir. 2013).

170 *all four were reportedly bullied:* Sabrina Rubin Erdely, "One Town's War on Gay Teens," *Rolling Stone,* February 2, 2012, http://www.rollingstone.com/politics/news/one-towns-war-on-gay-teens-20120202.

170 *The school district agreed to training:* Maria Elena Baca, "Anoka-Hennepin School District Settles Bullying Lawsuit," *Star Tribune,* March 6, 2012, http://www.startribune.com/local/north/141427303.html.

171 *Title IX bars discrimination:* "History of Title IX," Title IX.info, http://www.titleix.info/History/History-Overview.aspx.

171 *protect women and girls in education:* "It's Your Education: How Title IX Pro-tections Can Help You," National Women's Law Center, http://nwlc.org/sites/default/files/pdfs/NWLCItsYourEducation2010.pdf.

172 *athletic opportunities be available:* "Debunking Myths About Title IX and Ath-letics," National Women's Law Center, http://nwlc.org/resource/debunking-myths-about-title-ix-and-athletics.

172 *they accounted for only 43 percent of student athletes:* Christine Brennan, "Title IX Needed Now More Than Ever," *USA Today,* June 20, 2012, http://usatoday30.usatoday.com/sports/columnist/brennan/story/2012-06-20/brennan-title-IX-needed-now-more-than-ever/55715430/1.

172 *96 percent of the women:* "Women Athletes Business Network: Perspectives on Sport and Teams," EY, http://www.ey.com/BR/pt/About-us/Our-sponsorships-and-programs/Women-Athletes-Global-Leadership-Network---perspectives-on-sport-and-teams.

172 *Here's a quick list:* "Play Fair: A Title IX Playbook for Victory," Women's Sports Foundation, http://www.womenssportsfoundation.org/home/athletes/for-athletes/know-your-rights/parent-resources/play-fair-a-title-ix-playbook-for-victory.

172 *school agreed to keep the team:* Julia Perkins and Matt Eisenberg, "QU Reaches Proposed Title IX Settlement," *Quinnipiac Chronicle,* April 30, 2013, http://www.quchronicle.com/2013/04/qu-reaches-proposed-title-ix-settlement/.

173 *that failing to achieve one goal:* See, e.g., Mancuso v. MIAA, 900 N.E.2d 518 (Mass. 2009). (Massachusetts court declines to find that the Massachusetts

Interscholastic Athletic Association violated a swimmer's rights by ruling she was ineligible for her high school team.)

CHAPTER 19: ADVOCATING FOR A SPECIAL NEEDS CHILD

177 *five key points about the law:* "Five Things to Know About a 504 Plan for K-12 Students," National Center for Learning Disabilities, http://www.ncld.org/students-disabilities/iep-504-plan/five-things-to-know-about-504-plan; see also Section 504 and IDEA Comparison Chart, National Center for Learning Disabilities, http://www.ncld.org/disability-advocacy/learn-ld-laws/adaaa-section-504/section-504-idea-comparison-chart.

178 *qualifies for 504 assistance:* "504 Education Plans," KidsHealth.org, http://kidshealth.org/parent/positive/learning/504-plans.html; "How to File a Discrimination Complaint with the Office for Civil Rights," U.S. Department of Education, http://www2.ed.gov/about/offices/list/ocr/docs/howto.htm.

178 *Individualized Education Programs:* "Individualized Education Programs," KidsHealth.org, http://kidshealth.org/parent/growth/learning/iep.html.

179 *The specifics will vary by state, but will generally include:* "A Guide to the Individualized Education Program," U.S. Department of Education, http://www.ed.gov/parents/needs/speced/iepguide/index.html.

179 *a small group of the parents:* Michael Vasquez, "Broward Parents Demand More Rigor for Special-Needs Students," *Miami Herald*, February 5, 2013, http://www.miamiherald.com/2013/02/05/3219059/broward-parents-demand-more-rigor.html.

180 *these steps for parents:* "Financial Planning for Kids with Special Needs," Kids Health.org, http://kidshealth.org/parent/positive/family/needs_planning.html.

183 *a victory on behalf of the parents:* Florence County School District Four v. Shannon Carter, 510 U.S. 7 (1993).

183 *to mark the win:* Bill Lohmann, "Paradise at End of Road—Champion of Special-Ed Children Still Doing Good While Having More Fun," *Richmond Times-Dispatch*, August 3, 2003, http://www.wrightslaw.com/news/2003/champion.lohmann.htm.

CHAPTER 20: YOUR MISBEHAVING TEENS

186 *an eye-opening list:* "Top 25 Crimes, Offenses and Violations," Global Youth Justice, http://www.globalyouthjustice.org/TOP_25_CRIMES.htm.

188 *number of young women making appearances:* Office of Juvenile Justice and Delinquency Prevention's (OJJDP's) Juvenile Court Statistics 2009, as reported in "Women & Girls in the Criminal Justice System: Facts and Figures," National Criminal Justice Reference Service, https://www.ncjrs.gov/spotlight/wgcjs/facts.html.

188 *authorities to dismiss a case:* Randy Hertz, Martin Guggenheim, and Anthony Amsterdam, "Trial Manual for Defense Attorneys in Juvenile Delinquency Cases," Section 2.01(a), National Juvenile Defender Center, http://www.njdc.info/pdf/2013_Juvenile_Trial_Manual-Updated_Full_Version.pdf.

188 *The court process is not the same:* "Juvenile Justice," National Council of Juvenile and Family Court Judges, http://www.ncjfcj.org/our-work/juvenile-justice.

188 *expunge records for juvenile cases*: See, e.g., "Sealing Juvenile Records," Children's Law Center of Massachusetts, http://www.clcm.org/edsealingrecords.html.

189 *to guarantee that your teen is honest:* Randy Hertz, Martin Guggenheim, and Anthony Amsterdam, "Trial Manual for Defense Attorneys in Juvenile Delinquency Cases," Section 5.03(b), National Juvenile Defender Center, http://www.njdc.info/pdf/2013_Juvenile_Trial_Manual-Updated_Full_Version.pdf.

191 *festival ended a day early:* James C. McKinley Jr., "Overdoses of 'Molly' Led to Electric Zoo Deaths," *New York Times,* September 12, 2013, http://artsbeat.blogs.nytimes.com/2013/09/12/overdoses-of-molly-led-to-electric-zoo-deaths/?_php=true&_type=blogs&_r=0.

191 *a three-step plan:* "What to Do: 3 Steps," Not in My House, Partnership at Drugfree.org, http://notinmyhouse.drugfree.org/steps.aspx.

192 *offers this advice about talking to your child*: "How to Talk to Your Child If You Suspect They're Using," GetSmartAboutDrugs.com, http://getsmartaboutdrugs.com/related_topics/how_to_talk_to_your_child.html.

193 *But beyond the obvious:* "Consequences of Drug Use," GetSmartAboutDrugs.com, http://getsmartaboutdrugs.com/related_topics/consequences_of_drug_use.html.

193 *legalized marijuana for recreational use:* Kurtis Lee, "Denver Council Gives Initial OK to Decriminalizing Pot for Ages 18–21," *Denver Post,* December 16, 2013, http://www.denverpost.com/news/ci_24737489/denver-council-gives-initial-ok-decriminalizing-pot-ages.

195 *if someone is harmed as a result:* Jennifer Levitz, "Party Laws Put Hosts on Hook," *Wall Street Journal,* September 11, 2012, http://online.wsj.com/news/articles/SB10000872396390443571904577631603480250074.

196 *unable to find evidence:* Sandy Brundage, "Burnetts Won't Face Charges for Underage Drinking," *Almanac,* May 17, 2012, http://www.almanacnews.com/news/2012/05/16/burnetts-wont-face-charges-for-underage-drinking.

196 *remind the community to take responsibility:* Christian Nolan, "Teens Held Accountable for Friend's DUI Death," *Connecticut Law Tribune,* December 13, 2013, http://www.ctlawtribune.com/id=1202632985430/Teens-Held-Accountable-For-Friend's-DUI-Death?slreturn=20140213223454.

196 *a powerful case for forbidding alcohol:* Underage Drinking in the Home, Partnership at Drugfree.org, http://socialhost.drugfree.org/.

197 *more than two and a half times:* Charles Toutant, "Social Host's Auto Insurer to Pay Under Assigned-Liability Doctrine," *New Jersey Law Journal,* October 15, 2013, http://www.njlawjournal.com/id=1202623594068/Social-Host's-Auto-Insurer-To-Pay-Under-Assigned-Liability-Doctrine?slreturn=20140213223631.

197 *Benatouil was considering an appeal:* Andrew Keshner, "Judge Upholds Firing of Teacher Over Wine," *New York Law Journal,* January 10, 2013, http://www.newyorklawjournal.com/id=1202583920179/Judge-Upholds-Firing-of-Teacher-Over-Wine?slreturn=20140227083640.

198 *these head-shaking highlights:* Hazel Cills, "Justin Bieber's Wild Decline: A Timeline," *Rolling Stone,* http://www.rollingstone.com/music/pictures/justin-biebers-wild-decline-a-timeline-20140123.

198 *charges were later dropped:* Christie D'Zurilla, "Justin Bieber Assault Charge Dropped in Toronto Limo Case," *Los Angeles Times,* September 8, 2014, http://

www.latimes.com/entertainment/gossip/la-et-mg-justin-bieber-toronto-assault-charge-dropped-limo-driver-20140908-story.html.

198 *The pièce de résistance:* Christie D'Zurilla, "Justin Bieber Deposition Video Clips Paint Unflattering Picture," *Los Angeles Times,* March 10, 2014, http://www.latimes.com/entertainment/gossip/la-et-mg-justin-bieber-deposition-video-selena-gomez-20140310,0,6343488.story.

199 *she can face adult consequences:* "State Laws," Keys2Drive, the AAA Guide to Teen Driver Safety, http://teendriving.aaa.com/NY/supervised-driving/licensing-state-laws/state-laws.

200 *that reduces fines or eliminates points:* Jay MacDonald, "Can a Lawyer Beat Your Traffic Ticket?," Bankrate.com, April 25, 2006, http://www.bankrate.com/finance/auto/can-a-lawyer-beat-your-traffic-ticket--1.aspx.

200 *increased their risk of a crash:* Nicholas Bakalar, "Distracted Drivers and New Drivers a Perilous Mix," Well blog, *New York Times,* January 2, 2014, http://well.blogs.nytimes.com/2014/01/02/distracted-drivers-and-new-drivers-a-perilous-mix/.

200 *adults tell kids not to text while driving:* "43% of Teens Say They Text and Drive; 77% Say Adults Warn Against Risks; but Text and Drive 'All the Time,'" AT&T, May 14, 2012, http://www.att.com/gen/press-room?pid=22834&cdvn =news&newsarticleid=34435&mapcode=.

200 *it's against the law in almost every state:* "Distracted Driving Laws," Governors Highway Safety Association, ghsa.org/html/stateinfo/laws/cellphone_laws .html.

201 *it wasn't clear that Shannon knew:* Kubert v. Best, 75 A.3d 1214 (N.J. Super. Ct. App. Div. August 27, 2013).

201 *to criminalize this conduct:* "Sexting Legislation in 2013," National Conference of State Legislatures, http://www.ncsl.org/research/telecommunications-and-information-technology/2013-sexting-legislation.aspx.

201 *even if a teen sends a photo of herself:* Marsha Levick and Kristina Moon, "Prosecuting Sexting as Child Pornography," *Valparaiso University Law Review* 44, no.4 (2010): 137, http://scholar.valpo.edu/vulr/vol44/iss4/2.

202 *claiming the education program:* Miller v. Mitchell, 598 F.3d 139 (3d Cir. 2010).

202 *The district paid N.N. and her lawyers $33,000:* "ACLU Settles Student-Cell-Phone-Search Lawsuit with Northeast Pennsylvania School District," American Civil Liberties Union, September 15, 2010, https://www.aclu .org/free-speech/aclu-settles-student-cell-phone-search-lawsuit-northeast-pennsylvania-school-district.

CHAPTER 21: CAMPUS SAFETY

205 *White House issued a report on rape and sexual assault:* "Rape and Sexual Assault: A Renewed Call to Action," White House Council on Women and Girls, January 2014, http://iaclea.org/visitors/about/documents/WhiteHouse Council_sexual_assault_report_1-21-14.pdf.

205 *some questions the magazine suggests:* J. T. McBride, "Want to Attend a Safe College? 10 Questions You Should Ask," *Campus Safety,* June 14, 2011, http://

www.campussafetymagazine.com/article/Want-to-Attend-a-Safe-College-10-Questions-You-Should-Ask-Before-You-Commit/P2.

206 *as a happy freshman at Lehigh University:* "Our History," Clery Center for Security on Campus, clerycenter.org/our-history.

207 *the school was not required to tell them, either:* Ken Gross and Andrea Fine, "After Their Daughter Is Murdered at College, Her Grieving Parents Mount a Crusade for Campus Safety," *People,* February 19, 1990, http://www.people.com/people/archive/article/0,,20116872,00.html.

208 *the campus crimes schools must disclose:* "Summary of the Jeanne Clery Act," Clery Center for Security on Campus, http://clerycenter.org/summary-jeanne-clery-act.

208 *Colleges also have begun to release data:* "Understanding the Campus SAVE Act," KnowYourIX.org, knowyourix.org/understanding-the-campus-save-act/.

209 *here is a summary of key tips:* Ibid.

210 *student-on-student sexual assault usually involves acquaintances:* Alyssa S. Keehan, "Student Sexual Assault: Weathering the Perfect Storm," United Educators, http://contentz.mkt5031.com/lp/37886/394531/Student%20Sexual%20Assault_Weathering%20the%20Perfect%20Storm.pdf.

211 *nation's strictest college sexual assault policies:* Caroline Kitchener, "How to Encourage More College Sexual Assault Victims to Speak Up," *Atlantic,* August 23, 2013, http://www.theatlantic.com/national/archive/2013/08/how-to-encourage-more-college-sexual-assault-victims-to-speak-up/278972/; see also Carleigh Stiehm, "Duke Changes Sanctioning Guidelines for Sexual Assault Cases," *Chronicle,* July 9, 2013, http://www.dukechronicle.com/articles/2013/07/09/duke-changes-sanctioning-guidelines-sexual-assault-cases.

211 *guidance for students:* "Parents," Student Affairs, Duke University, http://studentaffairs.duke.edu/conduct/information-for . . . /parent.

211 *types of conduct that could be construed as harassing:* See, e.g., "What Are Some Examples of Sexual Harassment?," Frequently Asked Questions, Sexual Harassment Prevention Office, Northwestern University, http://www.northwestern.edu/sexual-harassment/faq/#one.

211 *to bring a lawsuit against the school:* Title IX and Sexual Assault, American Civil Liberties Union Women's Rights Project and Students Active for Ending Rape, https://www.aclu.org/files/pdfs/womensrights/titleixandsexualassaultknowyourrightsandyourcollege'sresponsibilities.pdf.

212 *Here are just some of the incidents:* Jennings v. University of North Carolina, 482 F.3d 686, (4th Cir. 2007).

213 *they supported their coach:* Associated Press, "Dorrance, Former Player Settle Sexual Harassment Suit," *USA Today,* January 14, 2008, http://usatoday30.usatoday.com/sports/college/soccer/2008-01-14-dorrance-settlement_N.htm.

214 *to see records of your freshman's academic performance:* See, e.g., "FERPA," University of Minnesota, http://www.umn.edu/parent/academics/ferpa/index.html.

CHAPTER 22: ON THE JOB

221 *the Equal Employment Opportunity Commission:* "Teaching with Documents: The Civil Rights Act of 1964 and the Equal Employment Opportunity Com-

mission," National Archives, http://www.archives.gov/education/lessons/civil-rights-act/.

221 *a list offered by Equal Rights Advocates:* "Know Your Rights: Sex Discrimination at Work," Equal Rights Advocates, http://www.equalrights.org/wp-content/uploads/2013/04/KYR_SexDiscrm.pdf.

222 *to keep having sex or else face workplace consequences:* Jennifer B. Rubin, "Understanding and Mitigating Liability for Workplace Romances," *New York Law Journal,* December 26, 2012, http://www.newyorklawjournal.com/id=1202582318205/Understanding-and-Mitigating-Liability-for-Workplace-Romances.

223 *can be an employer's dream:* Ibid.

223 *she didn't have a problem signing the contract:* Ry Rivard, "President's Home or Prison?," *Inside Higher Ed,* January 10, 2014, http://www.insidehighered.com/news/2014/01/10/alabama-university-limits-presidents-love-life.

224 *here's a refresher tutorial:* "Sexual Harassment at Work," Equal Rights Advocates, http://www.equalrights.org/legal-help/know-your-rights/sexual-harassment-at-work/.

226 *Federal law will protect you:* "Coverage of Business/Private Employers," U.S. Equal Employment Opportunity Commission, eeoc.gov/employees/coverage_private.cfm.

226 *Federal law gives you 300 days:* "Sexual Harassment at Work," Equal Rights Advocates.

227 *it's rarely done and almost never successful:* "Frequently Asked Questions About Sexual Harassment in the Workplace," National Women's Law Center, http://www.nwlc.org/resource/frequently-asked-questions-about-sexual-harassment-workplace.

227 *Lilly secured a management post:* "About Lilly Ledbetter," LillyLedbetter.com, lillyledbetter.com/index/html.

228 *implored Congress to correct this injustice:* "Lilly Ledbetter Fair Pay Act," National Women's Law Center, January 29, 2013, http://www.nwlc.org/resource/lilly-ledbetter-fair-pay-act-0.

228 *only 7 percent negotiate the first salary offer:* Shoshana Davis, "Women Still Earn Less 50 Years After Equal Pay Act," CBS News, June 10, 2013, http://www.cbsnews.com/news/women-still-earn-less-50-years-after-equal-pay-act/.

229 *pregnancy-related medical conditions:* "Pregnancy Discrimination," U.S. Equal Employment Opportunity Commission, http://www.eeoc.gov/laws/types/pregnancy.cfm; see also Stephen Smith, "Report: Pregnant Workers Face Routine Discrimination," CBS News, June 18, 2013, http://www.cbsnews.com/news/report-pregnant-workers-face-routine-discrimination.

229 *for at least twelve months:* "Fact Sheet #28: Family and Medical Leave Act," U.S. Department of Labor, Wage and Hour Division, http://www.dol.gov/whd/regs/compliance/whdfs28.pdf.

230 *while pregnant and immediately afterward:* "HCS Medical Staffing Ordered to Pay $148,000 for Pregnancy Discrimination by Owner," U.S. Equal Employment Opportunity Commission, http://www.eeoc.gov//eeoc/newsroom/release/3-2-12.cfm?renderforprint=1.

231 *the company "sought to accommodate [Angela's] needs":* Ames v. Nationwide Mutual Insurance Company, 2014 WL 961020 (8th Cir. 2014).

231 *"Nationwide is fully committed . . .":* Jacob Gershman, "Appeals Court Rules Against Breastfeeding Employee Who Claimed Discrimination," *Wall Street Journal,* March 17, 2014, http://blogs.wsj.com/law/2014/03/17/appeals-court-rules-against-breastfeeding-employee-who-claimed-discrimination/.

231 *Breastfeeding is beautiful:* "Breastfeeding Laws," National Conference of State Legislatures, http://www.ncsl.org/research/health/breastfeeding-state-laws.aspx.

231 *"It's ironic that it's fine . . .":* Liz Szabo, "Airline Settlement Fuels the National Breast-Feeding Fight," *USA Today,* March 14, 2012, http://usatoday30.usatoday.com/news/health/story/health/story/2012-03-14/Airline-settlement-fuels-the-national-breast-feeding-fight/53536674/1.

232 *have to provide a nursing mother with a private space:* "Break Time for Nursing Mothers," U.S. Department of Labor, Wage and Hour Division, http://www.dol.gov/whd/nursingmothers/.

232 *specifically exempt breastfeeding mothers:* "Breastfeeding Laws," National Conference of State Legislatures.

232 *The case settled for an undisclosed amount:* Szabo, "Airline Settlement."

233 *obese workers earn about 2.5 percent less:* Del Jones, "Obesity Can Mean Less Pay," *USA Today,* September 4, 2002, http://usatoday30.usatoday.com/money/workplace/2002-09-04-overweight-pay-bias_x.htm.

233 *said he was "flabbergasted":* Josh Sanburn, "Too Big to Cocktail? Judge Upholds Weight Discrimination in the Workplace," *Time,* July 26, 2013, http://nation.time.com/2013/07/26/too-big-to-cocktail-judge-upholds-weight-discrimination-in-the-workplace/; http://mn.gov/mdhr/education/articles/rs10_2weightlaws.htm.

234 *losing the "irresistible attraction" phrase:* Nelson v. James H. Knight DDS, P.C., 834 N.W.2d 64 (Iowa 2013); Ryan Foley, "Iowa Supreme Court Reaffirms Ruling That Dentist Legally Fired Worker He Found Too Attractive," *Star Tribune,* July 12, 2013, http://www.startribune.com/business/215230521.html.

234 *cannot be fired unless there is good cause:* Wrongful Discharge from Employment Act, Mont. Code. Ann. § 39-2-904 (1987).

235 *you also can leave at any time:* "The At-Will Presumption and Exceptions to the Rule," National Conference for State Legislatures, http://www.ncsl.org/research/labor-and-employment/at-will-employment-overview.aspx.

235 *that requires negotiations you will not want to undertake:* Vivia Chen, "The Careerist: You're Fired!," *American Lawyer Daily,* May 9, 2013, http://www.americanlawyer.com/id=1202598958769/The-Careerist:-You're-Fired-Part-1?slreturn=20140215122157.

235 *suggests looking for an employment lawyer:* "Do I Need a Lawyer?," Workplace Fairness, workplacefairness.org/needlawyer.

236 *when you get that new bill:* "What Is COBRA?," American Cancer Society, December 5, 2012, http://www.cancer.org/treatment/findingandpayingfortreatment/managinginsuranceissues/what-is-cobra.

237 *to enroll in your spouse's group health plan:* "An Employee's Guide to Health Benefits Under COBRA," U.S. Department of Labor Employment Benefits Security Administration, http://dol.gov/ebsa/publications/cobraemployee.html.

238 *include an explanation of benefits:* "The Best Way to Terminate an Employee," Vault, March 31, 2009, http://www.vault.com/blog/workplace-issues/the-best-way-to-terminate-an-employee/.

238 *internships can be unpaid:* "Fact Sheet #71: Internship Programs Under the Fair Labor Standards Act," U.S. Department of Labor Wage and Hour Division, April 2010, http://www.dol.gov/whd/regs/compliance/whdfs71.htm.

238 *Unpaid internships still dominate:* Ibid.

238 *create a formal, paid internship program:* Blair Hickman, "Sandberg's Lean In Called For an Unpaid Intern—and That's Apparently Legal," ProPublica, August 15, 2013, http://www.propublica.org/article/sheryl-sandbergs-lean-in-called-for-an-unpaid-intern-a-position-thats-perfe.

239 *Wang had no rights:* Venessa Wong, "Unpaid Intern Is Ruled Not an 'Employee,' Not Protected from Sexual Harassment," *Bloomberg Businessweek*, October 8, 2013, http://www.businessweek.com/articles/2013-10-08/unpaid-intern-not-an-employee-not-protected-from-sexual-harassment.

239 *New York City Council later passed a bill:* Blair Hickman, "Interns Are Now Protected Against Sexual Harassment in New York," ProPublica, March 28, 2014, http://www.propublica.org/article/interns-are-now-protected-against-sexual-harassment-in-nyc.

240 *filed suits for lack of payment:* Christine Haughney, "Condé Nast Faces Suit from Interns over Wages," *New York Times*, June 13, 2013, http://www.nytimes.com/2013/06/14/business/media/two-ex-interns-sue-conde-nast-over-wages.html?_r=0.

240 *paying them up to $250,000 in back wages and legal fees:* Steven Greenhouse, "'Charlie Rose' Show Agrees to Pay Up to $250,000 to Settle Interns' Lawsuit," *New York Times*, December 12, 2012, http://mediadecoder.blogs.nytimes.com/2012/12/20/charlie-rose-show-agrees-to-pay-up-to-250000-to-settle-interns-lawsuit/.

240 *when interns can work without pay:* Jan Wolfe, "Second Circuit Takes Up Fate of Intern Class Actions," Litigation Daily, *American Lawyer*, November 27, 2013, http://www.litigationdaily.com/id=1202630024477/Second-Circuit-Takes-Up-Fate-of-Intern-Class-Actions?slreturn=20140215125201.

240 *pulled the plug on its internship program:* Lauren Weber, "Condé Nast Ends Internship Program," *Wall Street Journal*, October 23, 2013, http://online.wsj.com/news/articles/SB10001424052702304682504579153961333903066.

CHAPTER 23: HOUSEHOLD HELP

243 *"You pay Betty Shore . . .":* Publication 926, Household Employer's Tax Guide, Internal Revenue Service, http://www.irs.gov/publications/p926/.

244 *". . . Neither John nor his helpers are your household employees":* Ibid.

245 *IRS Publication 15:* Employer's Tax Guide, Internal Revenue Service, http://www.irs.gov/pub/irs-pdf/p15.pdf.

245 *only limited protection under those laws:* "Frequently Asked Questions," U.S. Department of Labor, Wage and Hour Division, http://dol.gov/whd/flsa/companionNPRM-FAQ.htm.

246 *it's hard to justify describing that person:* "Do I Need to Use Form I-9?," U.S.

Citizenship and Immigration Services, http://www.uscis.gov/i-9-central/complete-correct-form-i-9/who-needs-use-form-i-9/do-i-need-use-form-i-9.

246 *the IRS won't call the Department of Homeland Security:* Jacoba Urist, "Should You Be Paying Taxes on Your Babysitter?," *New York Times,* April 14, 2013, http://parenting.blogs.nytimes.com/2013/04/14/should-you-be-paying-taxes-on-your-baby-sitter/.

247 *hired a Peruvian couple:* David Johnston, "Clinton's Choice for Justice Dept. Hired Illegal Aliens for Household," *New York Times,* January 14, 1993, http://www.nytimes.com/1993/01/14/us/clinton-s-choice-for-justice-dept-hired-illegal-aliens-for-household.html.

247 *summarily axed from consideration:* Richard L. Berke, "Judge Withdraws from Clinton List for Justice Post," *New York Times,* February 6, 1993, http://www.nytimes.com/1993/02/06/us/judge-withdraws-from-clinton-list-for-justice-post.htm.

247 *Janet Reno, a Florida prosecutor:* Ruth Marcus, "Clinton Nominates Reno at Justice," *Washington Post,* February 12, 1993, http://www.washingtonpost.com/wp-srv/politics/govt/admin/stories/reno021293.htm.

248 *invites employers to reclassify employees correctly:* "Voluntary Classification Settlement Program," Internal Revenue Service, http://www.irs.gov/Businesses/Small-Businesses-&-Self-Employed/Voluntary-Classification-Settlement-Program.

248 *here are two basic rules:* "Recording Phone Calls and Conversations," Digital Media Law Project, http://www.dmlp.org/legal-guide/recording-phone-calls-and-conversations.

248 *not participating and can't overhear it:* "Can We Tape?" Reporters Committee for Freedom of the Press, Fall 2008, http://www.rcfp.org/rcfp/orders/docs/CANWETAPE.pdf.

248 *consider telling your nanny first:* Brooke Chateauneuf, "Nanny Cam: Yes or No?," Care.com, http://www.care.com/child-care-nanny-cam-yes-or-no-p1017-q21097627.html.

249 *These are its guidelines:* "Take One STEP UP with Hand in Hand!," Hand in Hand: The Domestic Employers Association, http://domesticemployers.org/wp-content/uploads/2011/04/2010_One_Step_Up_Form.pdf.

251 *Let's say you have a personal assistant:* Brendan Pierson, "Lady Gaga Settles Suit with Ex–Personal Assistant," *New York Law Journal,* October 23, 2013, http://www.newyorklawjournal.com/id=1202624697358/Lady-Gaga-Settles-Suit-With-Ex-Personal-Assistant?slreturn=20140215140228.

252 " . . . *when I need you, you're available":* O'Neill v. Mermaid Touring, Inc., No. 11 Civ. 9128(PGG) (S.D.N.Y. September 10, 2013).

CHAPTER 24: ONLINE ESSENTIALS

256 "... *do not put yourself through this nightmare of a contractor":* Justin Jouvenal, "In Yelp Suit, Free Speech on Web vs. Reputations," *Washington Post,* December 4, 2012, http://www.washingtonpost.com/local/crime/2012/12/04/1cdfa582-3978-11e2-a263-f0ebffed2f15_story.html.

256 *missing the point of his own lawsuit:* Ibid.

256 *The case of the competing complaints:* Justin Jouvenal, "Fairfax Jury Declares a Draw in Closely Watched Case over 'Yelp' Reviews," *Washington Post,* February 1, 2014, http://www.washingtonpost.com/local/in-closely-watched-yelp-case-jury-finds-dual-victory/2014/01/31/2d174580-8ae5-11e3-a5bd-844629433ba3_story.html.

257 *"right to be forgotten":* Charles Arthur, "Google Removing 'Right to be Forgotten' Search Links in Europe," *Guardian,* June 26, 2014. *http://www.theguardian .com/technology/2014/jun/26/google-removing-right-to-be-forgotten-links.*

257 *links Google removed in Europe:* See, e.g., Chris Moran, "Things to Remember About Google and the Right to Be Forgotten," *Guardian,* July 3, 2014, http:// www.theguardian.com/technology/2014/jul/03/google-remember-right-to-be-forgotten.

257 *but to see if a reputation management company can help:* Caitlin Gibson, "Your New Boss Is Going to Google You. Make Sure She Likes What She Sees," *Washington Post,* June 10, 2014, http://www.washingtonpost.com/lifestyle/style/your-new-boss-is-going-to-google-you-make-sure-she-likes-what-she-sees/2014/06/10/646124be-f09f-11e3-9ebc-2ee6f81ed217_story.html.

258 *it might use the information:* "Data Use Policy," Facebook, https://www .facebook.com/about/privacy/.

258 *the site's Interactive Tools:* "Interactive Tools," Facebook, https://www .facebook.com/about/privacy/tools.

258 *Enable privacy-protecting settings:* Elizabeth Dwoskin, "Give Me Back My Online Privacy," *Wall Street Journal,* March 23, 2014, http://online.wsj.com/news/articles/SB10001424052702304704504579432823496404570.

259 *Limit the amount of personal information:* Julia Angwin, "Tips for Protecting Your Privacy Online," Moyers & Company, March 13, 2014, http:// billmoyers.com/2014/03/13/tips-for-protecting-your-privacy-online/; Julia Angwin, "Privacy Tools: Protecting Your Kids Online," JuliaAngwin.com, February 23, 2014, http://juliaangwin.com/privacy-tools-how-to-protect-your-kids-privacy-online/; Christina DesMarais, "11 Simple Ways to Protect Your Privacy," Techlicious, *Time,* July 23, 2013, http://techland.time .com/2013/07/24/11-simple-ways-to-protect-your-privacy/.

260 *". . . you open yourself up to potential legal liability."* "Risks Associated with Publication," Digital Media Law Project, June 18, 2011, http://www.dmlp .org/legal-guide/risks-associated-publication.

260 *unless she signed away her rights:* "Can I Use Someone Else's Work? Can Someone Else Use Mine?" U.S. Copyright Office, revised April 2, 2013, http:// www.copyright.gov/help/faq/faq-fairuse.html.

260 *to repost and share those photos without permission:* Steve Eder, "How to Use Pinterest Without Breaking the Law," *Wall Street Journal,* March 13, 2012, http://blogs.wsj .com/law/2012/03/13/dont-get-stuck-by-pinterest-lawyers-warn/.

260 *We are free to reuse federal government publications:* "Fair Use," Digital Media Law Project, August 25, 2008, *http://www.dmlp.org/legal-guide/fair-use.*

260 *Holmes and Dr. Watson still protected property:* Jennifer Schuessler, "Appeals Court Affirms Sherlock Holmes Is in Public Domain," Artsbeat blog, *New York Times,* June 17, 2014, http://artsbeat.blogs.nytimes.com/2014/06/17/conan-doyle-estate-loses-sherlock-holmes-copyright-appeal/.

261 *claimed ownership in a lawsuit:* Ted Johnson, "Court Keeps Candles Lit on Dispute Over 'Happy Birthday' Copyright," *Chicago Times,* October 7, 2013, http://articles .chicagotribune.com/2013-10-07/entertainment/sns-201310071754reedbusivariet yn1200703048-20131007_1_patty-smith-hill-plaintiffs-copyright-claims.

261 *Take a look at the legal guide:* "Legal Guide for Bloggers," Electronic Frontier Foundation, http://www.eff.org/issues/bloggers/legal.

262 *to share images of a recently used emergency room:* Liz Neporent, "Nurse Firing Highlights Hazards of Social Media in Hospitals," abcnews.com, July 8, 2014, http://abcnews.go.com/Health/nurse-firing-highlights-hazards-social-media-hospitals/story?id=24454611.

262 *With limited exceptions, your employer can fire you:* "How Social Media Networks Can Get You Fired," Privacy Rights Clearinghouse, https://www .privacyrights.org/social-networking-privacy-how-be-safe-secure-and-social#socialmediafired, revised May 2014.

262 *your company isn't interested:* John Weber, "Should Companies Monitor Their Employees' Social Media?" *Wall Street Journal,* May 11, 2014, http://online .wsj.com/news/articles/SB10001424052702303825604579514471793116740.

262 *Do not post confidential information:* Ibid.

262 *protect work-related information:* "How to Not Get Fired for Social Networking on Twitter and Facebook," Reputation.com, http://www.reputation .com/reputationwatch/articles/how-to-not-get-fired-for-social-networking-facebook-twitter.

CHAPTER 25: DOMESTIC VIOLENCE

264 *found the following:* "National Intimate Partner and Sexual Violence Survey: 2010 Summary Report," National Center for Injury Prevention and Control, Centers for Disease Control and Prevention, http://www.cdc.gov/violenceprevention/ pdf/nisvs_executive_summary-a.pdf; "Stalking Fact Sheet," Stalking Resource Center, http://www.victimsofcrime.org/docs/src/stalking-fact-sheet_english.pdf ?sfvrsn=4.

265 *30 percent of women worldwide:* "Violence Against Women: A 'Global Health Problem of Epidemic Proportions,'" World Health Organization, http://www.who.int/mediacentre/news/releases/2013/violence_against_ women_20130620/en/.

265 *women are disproportionately victims:* "National Intimate Partner and Sexual Violence Survey: 2010 Summary Report," National Center for Injury Prevention and Control, p. 2.

265 *exposed beautiful best-selling cookbook author:* Elizabeth Sanderson, "I'm Divorcing You, Nigella: Saatchi Breaks News to Wife in Exclusive Statement to the Mail on Sunday and Says He's 'Sorry It's Over' . . . But Insists She Put Her Hand on His Throat, Too," *Mail Online,* July 6, 2013, http://www.dailymail .co.uk/news/article-2357634/Charles-Saatchi-breaks-divorce-news-Nigella-Lawson-exclusive-statement-Mail-Sunday.html.

265 *granted their divorce after a seventy-second hearing:* Sam Jones, "Nigella Lawson and Charles Saatchi Granted Divorce in 70-Second Hearing," *Guardian,* July 31, 2013, http://www.theguardian.com/lifeandstyle/2013/jul/31/nigella-lawson-charles-saatchi-divorce.

265 *Nigella's drug use from two of her former personal assistants:* Peter Wilkinson and Laura Smith-Spark, "Nigella Lawson Faces Police Drugs Investigation," CNN, December 22, 2013, http://www.cnn.com/2013/12/22/world/europe/britain-nigella-lawson/.

266 *to develop and fund protection and prevention programs:* "Factsheet: The Violence Against Women Act," WhiteHouse.gov, http://www.whitehouse.gov/sites/default/files/docs/vawa_factsheet.pdf.

266 *answered more than three million calls:* Ibid.

267 *relationship can range from spouses:* "Definitions of Domestic Violence," Child Welfare Information Agency, https://www.childwelfare.gov/systemwide/laws_policies/statutes/defdomvio.pdf.

267 *suggestions adapted from those offered by Family Tree:* "FAQ Domestic Violence," Family Tree, thefamilytree.org/en/faqs/156.

269 *the person who has the order can call authorities:* "Getting an Order of Protection," American Bar Association Division for Public Education, http://www.americanbar.org/groups/public_education/resources/law_issues_for_consumers/dvprotection.html.

269 *"victims face a dilemma . . .":* "Practical Implications of Current Domestic Violence Research: For Law Enforcement, Prosecutors and Judges," National Institute of Justice, June 2009, https://www.ncjrs.gov/pdffiles1/nij/225722.pdf.

270 *the judge made a firearms ban:* Wolt v. Wolt, 778 N.W.2d 802 (N.D. 2010).

270 *the husband had not been physically violent:* Ficklin v. Ficklin, 710 N.W.2d 387 (N.D. 2006).

271 *A consistent story, well told, is the place to start:* "Getting an Order of Protection," American Bar Association Division for Public Education.

271 *He was charged with stalking, pled guilty:* Justin Jouvenal, "Stalkers Use Online Sex Ads as a Weapon," *Washington Post*, July 15, 2013, http://www.washingtonpost.com/local/i-live-in-fear-of-anyone-coming-to-my-door/2013/07/14/26c11442-e359-11e2-aef3-339619eab080_story.html; "Former Library of Congress Worker Charged in Sex Ad Case," CBS DC, November 15, 2013, http://washington.cbslocal.com/2013/11/15/former-library-of-congress-worker-sentenced-in-sex-ad-case/.

272 *"a course of conduct directed at a specific person . . .":* "Stalking Fact Sheet," Stalking Resource Center, http://www.victimsofcrime.org/docs/src/stalking-fact-sheet_english.pdf?sfvrsn=4.

272 *6.6 million people are stalked every year:* Ibid.

272 *shot to death by an obsessed fan:* Lambers Royakkers, "The Dutch Approach to Stalking Laws," *Berkeley Journal of Criminal Law* 3 (2000):8, http://scholarship.law.berkeley.edu/cgi/viewcontent.cgi?article=1073&context=bjcl.

272 *California passed the first antistalking law in 1990:* Domestic Violence, Stalking, and Antistalking Legislation, U.S. Department of Justice National Institute of Justice, April 1996, https://www.ncjrs.gov/pdffiles/stlkbook.pdf.

272 *stalking is a crime in every state:* Status of the Law, Office for Victims of Crime, https://www.ncjrs.gov/ovc_archives/bulletins/legalseries/bulletin1/2.html.

272 *So let's review some concrete advice:* "Stalking Response Tips," National Center

for Victims of Crime, http://victimsofcrime.org/docs/src/tips-for-victims.pdf
?sfvrsn=2.

273 *thirteen states have passed laws:* "State 'Revenge Porn' Legislation," National
Conference of State Legislatures, September 2, 2014, http://www.ncsl.org/
research/telecommunications-and-information-technology/state-revenge-
porn-legislation.aspx.

274 *The federal government has offered grants:* "Grant Programs," U.S. Department
of Justice, ovw.usdoj.gov/ovwgrantprograms.htm.

275 *A data point suggests it does:* Rachel Louise Snyder, "A Raised Hand," *New Yorker,*
July 22, 2013, http://www.newyorker.com/reporting/2013/07/22/130722fa_
fact_snyder.

CHAPTER 26: TAKING CHARGE I: MEDICAL DECISIONS AND POWERS OF ATTORNEY

280 *In a* living will, *you offer guidance:* "Living Wills and Advance Directives for
Medical Decisions," Mayo Clinic, http://www.mayoclinic.org/healthy-living/
consumer-health/in-depth/living-wills/art-20046303.

281 *By granting* health care power of attorney: "Giving Someone a Power of Attorney for Your Health Care," American Bar Association Commission on Law and
Aging, 2011, http://www.americanbar.org/content/dam/aba/administrative/law_
aging/2011/2011_aging_hcdec_univhcpaform_4_2012_v2.authcheckdam.pdf.

281 *comprehensive checklist of patient preferences:* Brittany Hargrave, "New Form
Adds Some Teeth to End-of-Life Care Preferences," *USA Today,* August
5, 2013, http://www.usatoday.com/story/news/nation/2013/08/04/polst-
paradigm-end-of-life-care-form-expanding-reach/2595889/.

282 *Karen was removed from her respirator:* In re Quinlan, 355 A.2d 647 (N.J.
1976); Julia and Joseph Quinlan, "Karen Ann Quinlan's Parents Quietly
Mark a Decade of Watching and Waiting," *People,* April 15, 1985.

283 *Nancy's parents found that evidence:* Cruzan v. Director, Missouri Department
of Health, 497 U.S. 261 (1990); Tamar Lewin, "Nancy Cruzan Dies, Outlived
by a Debate Over the Right to Die," *New York Times,* December 27, 1990,
http://www.nytimes.com/1990/12/27/us/nancy-cruzan-dies-outlived-by-a-
debate-over-the-right-to-die.html.

283 *Other laws were passed:* Abby Goodnough, "Schiavo Dies, Ending Bitter Case
Over Feeding Tube," *New York Times,* April 1, 2005, http://www.nytimes.com/
2005/04/01/national/01schiavo.html?pagewanted=1&contentCollection=
General&version&action=click&region=TopBar&module=SearchSubmit
&url=http://query.nytimes.com/search/sitesearch/?action=click&pgtype=Blogs.

284 *A handful of states allow terminally ill patients:* Erik Eckholm, "New Mexico
Judge Affirms Right to 'Aid in Dying,'" *New York Times,* January 13, 2014,
http://www.nytimes.com/2014/01/14/us/new-mexico-judge-affirms-right-
to-aid-in-dying.html.

285 *What can your agent do for you?:* "Durable Power of Attorney," BB&T, bbt.com/
bbtdotcom/wealth/retirement-and-planning/trusts-and-estates/durable-
power-of-attorney.page/.

286 *summarizes four core fiduciary duties:* "CFPB Releases Guides for Managing
Someone Else's Money," Consumer Financial Protection Bureau, October 29,

2013, http://www.consumerfinance.gov/newsroom/cfpb-releases-guides-for-managing-someone-elses-money/.

287 *a guardian operates under court supervision:* "What Is Guardianship?," National Guardianship Association, http://guardianship.org/what_is_guardianship.htm.

288 *an octogenarian widow:* Ralph Blumenthal, "A Family Feud Sheds Light on Differences in Probate Practices from State to State," *New York Times,* December 28, 2005, http://www.nytimes.com/2005/12/28/national/28probate.html?pagewanted=print.

288 *even after Lillian died in 2011:* Beth Fitzgerald, "New Jersey Considers Law to Prevent 'Granny Snatching,'" NJSpotlight.com, May 21, 2012, http://www.njspotlight.com/stories/12/0520/2037/.

288 *thirty-seven states and the District of Columbia:* Adult Guardianship and Protective Proceedings Jurisdiction Act, Uniform Law Commission, http://www.uniformlaws.org/Act.aspx?title=Adult+Guardianship+and+Protective+Proceedings+Jurisdiction+Act.

CHAPTER 27: TAKING CHARGE II: ESTATE PLANNING

291 *fewer than half of American adults:* Scott James, "Dying Alone Intestate Places Burden on the County," *New York Times,* July 22, 2010, http://www.nytimes.com/2010/07/23/us/23bcjames.html.

291 *The basic rules for creating a valid will:* "Writing a Will," USA.gov, http://www.usa.gov/topics/money/personal-finance/wills.shtml.

292 *If you have complicated plans:* Sienna Kossman, "Estate Planning Tips for People Under 40," *US News & World Report,* September 19, 2013, http://money.usnews.com/money/personal-finance/articles/2013/09/19/estate-planning-tips-for-people-under-40.

292 *If the prospect of estate planning seems daunting:* Rande Spiegelman, "Why You Need an Estate Plan," Charles Schwab, January 29, 2014, http://www.schwab.com/public/schwab/resource_center/expert_insight/personal_finance/estate_planning/leave_less_to_the_irs.html.

295 *A revocable living trust is popular:* "Revocable Trusts," American Bar Association Section of Real Property, Trust, and Estate Law, http://www.americanbar.org/groups/real_property_trust_estate/resources/estate_planning/revocable_trusts.html.

295 *Trusts also suit people who require privacy:* "Ten Things You Should Know About Living Trusts," *AARP Bulletin,* http://www.aarp.org/money/estate-planning/info-09-2010/ten_things_you_should_know_about_living_trusts.htm.

295 *Trusts do not work unless they contain assets:* "Understanding the Differences Between a Will and a Trust," Elder Law Answers, January 28, 2013, http://www.elderlawanswers.com/understanding-the-differences-between-a-will-and-a-trust-7888.

296 *When set up properly, a special needs trust:* "Special Needs Estate Planning Guidance System," National Alliance on Mental Illness, http://www.nami.org/template.cfm?section=Special_Needs_Estate_Planning.

296 *has to meet specific criteria:* Robert M. Freedman, Barry I. Lutzky, and Lauren I. Mechaly, "Analyzing the Unique Duties and Obligations of

Special Needs Trusts," *New York Law Journal,* September 16, 2013, http://www.newyorklawjournal.com/id=1202618858674/Analyzing-the-Unique-Duties-and-Obligations-of-Special-Needs-Trusts.

296 *parents also should draft a letter of intent:* "Letter of Intent," *Voice,* Special Needs Alliance, July 2013, http://www.specialneedsalliance.org/the-voice/letter-of-intent-3/.

297 *then went to court when Yahoo declined:* Paul Sancya, "Yahoo Will Give Family Slain Marine's E-mail Account," *USA Today,* April 21, 2005, http://usatoday30.usatoday.com/tech/news/2005-04-21-marine-e-mail_x.htm?POE=TECISVA.

297 *Yahoo eventually granted the Ellsworth family permission:* "Yahoo Terms of Service," Yahoo, http://info.yahoo.com/legal/us/yahoo/utos/terms/.

297 *Facebook's policy, by the way, is to "memorialize" the account:* "Report a Deceased Person," Facebook, http://www.facebook.com/help/408583372511972.

297 *Facebook also allows immediate family to contact the site:* "How Do I Submit a Special Request for a Deceased Person's Account on the Site?," Facebook, http://www.facebook.com/help/265593773453448/.

297 *"Inactive Account Manager":* "About Inactive Account Manager," Google, support.google.com/accounts/answer/3036546?hl=en.

298 *make an inventory of your online assets:* Paul Hyl, "From Jewelry to JPEGs: Planning in the Digital Age," *New York Law Journal,* January 28, 2013, http://www.newyorklawjournal.com/id=1202585773856/From-Jewelry-to-JPEGs%3A-Planning-in-the-Digital-Age; Anne Eisenberg, "Bequeathing the Keys to Your Digital Afterlife," *New York Times,* May 25, 2013, http://www.nytimes.com/2013/05/26/technology/estate-planning-is-important-for-your-online-assets-too.html.

298 *to ensure your pet's happy future:* "Taking Care of Your Four-Legged Companion After You're Gone," *USA Today,* May 11, 2013, http://www.usatoday.com/story/money/personalfinance/2013/05/11/pets-trust-will/2150943/.

299 *the trustees at a local bank:* Lyneka Little, "Chicago Bank Steps In to Save Boots the Cat," ABC News, July 5, 2012, http://abcnews.go.com/blogs/business/2012/07/bank-steps-in-to-save-boots-the-cat/.

299 *". . . I don't want her to go unloved":* James R. Hagerty, "A Woman's Will Provides for Trusty Houseplant upon Her Death," *Wall Street Journal,* May 4, 2014, http://online.wsj.com/news/articles/SB10001424052702303939404579530311915386326.

299 *founding father left 1,000 pounds each:* Fox Butterfield, "From Ben Franklin, a Gift That's Worth Two Fights," *New York Times,* April 21, 1990, http://www.nytimes.com/1990/04/21/us/from-ben-franklin-a-gift-that-s-worth-two-fights.html.

300 *Brophy may be best known for his starring role:* "Kevin Brophy," Internet Movie Database, http://www.imdb.com/name/nm0112403/.

300 *Barton played the title role:* "Peter Barton," Internet Movie Database, http://www.imdb.com/name/nm0059228/.

300 *both actors had written:* Dave Bakke, "Broadwell Man Leaves Estate to Actors He Never Met," *State Journal-Register,* February 8, 2013, http://www.sj-r.com/x766863855/Broadwell-man-leaves-estate-to-actors-he-never-met?zc_p=0.

301 *made several suggestions:* Mark Accettura, "18 Recommendations for Minimizing Inheritance Conflict," *AAII Journal,* April 2012, http://www.aaii.com/journal/article/19-recommendations-for-minimizing-inheritance-conflict.

302 *It disinherits a beneficiary:* T. Jack Challis and Howard M. Zaritsky, "State Laws: No Contest Clauses," American College of Trust and Estate Counsel, March 24, 2012, http://www.actec.org/public/Documents/Studies/State_Laws_No_Contest_Clauses_-_Chart.pdf.

302 *it's very difficult to disinherit your spouse:* "Writing Your Will," American Bar Association Division for Public Education, http://www.americanbar.org/groups/public_education/resources/law_issues_for_consumers/wills.html.

302 *Putting your decision in writing:* Geoff Williams, "Disinheriting Someone Is Not Easy," Reuters, January 31, 2013, http://www.reuters.com/article/2013/01/31/us-retirement-wills-disinheriting-idUSBRE90U10K20130131.

302 *that they want to maintain property as separate:* Liz Moyer, "Estate Plans and Prenups," *Wall Street Journal,* November 15, 2013, http://online.wsj.com/news/articles/SB10001424052702304868404579194383854 68263.

302 *four legal arguments that might overturn a will:* Nancy Mann Jackson, "Where There's a Will . . . ," *AARP Bulletin,* August 17, 2011 http://www.aarp.org/money/estate-planning/info-08-2011/contesting-wills.html.

303 *former Playmate of the Year:* Dan P. Lee, "Paw Paw and Lady Love," *New York,* http://images.nymag.com/news/features/anna-nicole-smith-2011-6/index.html.

304 *ur-text about a ruinous inheritance fight:* Adam Liptak, "Anna Nicole Smith's Estate Loses Supreme Court Case," *New York Times,* June 24, 2011, http://www.nytimes.com/2011/06/24/us/24smith.html; Dawn C. Van Tassel, "Supreme Court Decides *Stern v. Marshall,*" American Bar Association Section of Litigation, September 15, 2011, http://apps.americanbar.org/litigation/committees/trialevidence/articles/fall2011-supreme-court-decides-stern-marshall.htm.

304 *sanction the estate of Marshall's son:* Associated Press, "Anna Nicole Smith's Estate Loses Bid to Obtain Late Husband's Millions," *Dallas Morning News,* August 20, 2014, http://www.dallasnews.com/entertainment/celebrity-news/headlines/20140820-anna-nicole-smiths-estate-loses-bid-to-obtain-late-husband-s-millions.ece.

304 *Anna's own will was a tangled mess:* Susan Candiotti, "Anna Nicole Smith Leaves Everything to Dead Son," CNN, February 22, 2007, http://www.cnn.com/2007/LAW/02/16/smith.ruling/index.html?section=cnn_latest.

CHAPTER 28: MANAGING MOM, DAD, AND OTHER OLDER LOVED ONES

306 *rebranded May as Older Americans Month:* S. Res. 137, 113th Cong. (2013), http://thomas.loc.gov/cgi-bin/query/z?r113:S09MY3-0045:.

308 *home health aides now qualify for minimum wage:* Steven Greenhouse, "U.S. to Include Home Care Workers in Wage and Overtime Law," *New York Times,* September 17, 2013, http://www.nytimes.com/2013/09/18/business/us-to-include-home-care-workers-in-wage-and-overtime-law.html.

309 *who cannot live alone but don't require constant medical care:* NCHS Data Brief: Residents Living in Residential Care Facilities: United States, 2010; http://cdc.gov/nchs/data/databriefs/db91.htm.

309 *almost 40 percent of residents:* "Residents Living in Residential Care Facilities: United States, 2010," National Center for Health Statistics, http://cdc.gov/nchs/data/databriefs/db91.htm.

309 *These facilities are not federally regulated:* "Assisted Living Regulatory Review," National Center for Assisted Living, March 2013, http://www.ahcancal.org/ncal/resources/Documents/2013_reg_review.pdf.

309 *CCRCs are not federally regulated:* "Your Guide to Choosing a Nursing Home," Centers for Medicare and Medicaid Services, U.S. Department of Health and Human Services, May 2011, http://medicare.gov/pubs/ebook/pdf/Guide%20to%20Choosing%20a%20Nursing%20Home%2002174.pdf.

309 *Patients who stabilize sometimes find themselves discharged:* Paula Span, "Bounced From Hospice," New Old Age blog, *New York Times,* January 7, 2014, http://newoldage.blogs.nytimes.com/2014/01/07/bounced-from-hospice/; see also Peter Whoriskey and Dan Keating, "Hospice Firms Draining Billions from Medicare," *Washington Post,* December 26, 2013, http://www.washingtonpost.com/business/economy/medicare-rules-create-a-booming-business-in-hospice-care-for-people-who-arent-dying/2013/12/26/4ff75bbe-68c9-11e3-ae56-22de072140a2_story.htm.

310 *medical professionals can share a patient's health information:* "A Patient's Guide to the HIPAA Privacy Rule," U.S. Department of Health and Human Services, hhs.gov/ocr/privacy/hipaa/understanding/consumers/consumer_ffg.pdf.

311 *AARP offers some commonsense suggestions:* "Assisted Living: Weighing the Options," AARP, http://aarp.org/relationships/caregiving-resource-center/info-09-2010/ho_assisted_living_weighing_the_options.2.html.

312 *patients to pay for it themselves at first:* Nadia Taha, "Medicaid Help Without Falling into Poverty," *New York Times,* November 19, 2013, http://www.nytimes.com/2013/11/20/your-money/medicaid-help-without-falling-into-poverty.html.

312 *a senior trying to qualify for Medicaid:* Ibid.

312 *If a spouse is heading to a nursing home for more than thirty days:* "Spousal Impoverishment," Medicaid.gov, medicaid.gov/Medicaid-CHIP-Program-Information/by-Topics/Eligibility/Spousal-Impoverishment-Page.html.

313 *any senior money transfers should be carefully reviewed:* Patricia Barry, "Paying for Nursing Home Care: The Different Roles of Medicare and Medicaid," *AARP Bulletin,* September 30, 2010, http://www.aarp.org/health/medicare-insurance/info-09-2010/ask_ms_medicare_question_89.html.

313 *They will each be responsible for the other:* Craig Reaves, "Ask an Elder Law Attorney: Late-Life Marriage," New Old Age blog, *New York Times,* June 16, 2011, http://newoldage.blogs.nytimes.com/2011/06/16/ask-an-elder-law-attorney-late-life-marriage-issues/.

314 *hold children responsible for their parents' sky-high bills:* Jane Gross, "Adult Children, Aging Parents and the Law," New Old Age blog, *New York Times,* November 20, 2008, http://newoldage.blogs.nytimes.com/2008/11/20/unenforced-filial-responsibility-laws/.

314 *A judge held John liable for the bill:* Health Care and Retirement Corp. of America v. Pittas, 46 A.3d 719, (Pa. Super. Ct. 2012).

314 *If you don't have that authority:* "Should You Sign a Nursing Home Ad-

mission Agreement?," Elder Law Answers, November 26, 2013, http://www.elderlawanswers.com/should-you-sign-a-nursing-home-admission-agreement-6360.

315 *to sue a nursing home for wrongful death:* See, e.g., Pisano v. Extendicare Homes, Inc., 77 A.3d 651, (Pa. Super. Ct. 2012).

316 *one-third of telemarketing victims are age sixty or older:* "They Can't Hang Up," Fraud.org, http://www.fraud.org/learn/older-adult-fraud/they-can-t-hang-up.

316 *The National Council on Aging offers a good one:* "Top 10 Scams Targeting Seniors," National Council on Aging, http://www.ncoa.org/enhance-economic-security/economic-security-Initiative/savvy-saving-seniors/top-10-scams-targeting.html.

317 *teaches older adults how to avoid financial scams:* "Protecting What's Yours," Consumer Financial Protection Bureau, http://consumerfinance.gov/older-americans/protecting-whats-yours/.

CHAPTER 29: HIRING A LAWYER, OR DOING IT YOURELF

322 *". . . ten thousand stages of an endless cause . . .":* Charles Dickens, *Bleak House,* Project Gutenberg e-book, chap. 1.

323 *Thus you have Paul Nardini:* Debra Cassens Weiss, "Lawyer Sues over Bad Google Plus Review," *ABA Journal,* September 20, 2013, http://www.abajournal.com/news/article/lawyer_sues_over_bad_google_plus_review.

323 *posted fake positive reviews about his own firm:* Patrick Clark, "Yelp's Newest Weapon Against Fake Reviews: Lawsuits," *Bloomberg Businessweek,* September 9, 2013, http://www.businessweek.com/articles/2013-09-09/yelps-newest-weapon-against-fake-reviews-lawsuits.

323 *feared the accolades could be misleading:* Henry Gottlieb, "N.J. Supreme Court Eases Restrictions on 'Super Lawyer' Advertising," *New Jersey Law Journal,* Law.com, http://www.alm.law.com/jsp/article.jsp?id=1202435211682.

323 *they should comply with its rules:* Mary Pat Gallagher, "Groupon Deals on Legal Services Get ABA Ethics Panel's Wary Nod," *New Jersey Law Journal,* October 22, 2013, http://www.njlawjournal.com/id=1202624714196/Groupon-Deals-on-Legal-Services--Get-ABA-Ethics-Panel's-Wary-Nod?slreturn=20140215235216.

324 Breaking Bad's *Saul Goodman:* "Saul Goodman Quotes," Breaking Bad Saul Goodman, http://www.amctv.com/shows/breaking-bad/cast/saul-goodman#anchor.

326 *And consider these questions:* "Questions to Ask Before Hiring a Lawyer," North Carolina State Bar, http://www.ncbar.gov/public/questions.asp.

328 *your complaint could get a lawyer disbarred:* "When You Need to Lawyer Up," *Consumer Reports,* September 2011, http://www.consumerreports.org/cro/money/consumer-protection/when-you-need-to-lawyer-up/overview/index.htm.

329 *conflicts of interest, candor, and professional behavior:* J. Randolph Evans and Shari L. Klevens, "Sex with Client Is Flirting with Disaster," *Daily Report,* September 24, 2013, http://www.dailyreportonline.com/id=1202620431509/Sex-With-Client-Is-Flirting-With-Disaster?slreturn=20140215235758.

329 *A jury awarded the cuckolded ex $1.5 million:* Pierce v. Cook, 992 So.2d 612 (Miss. 2008).

330 *"I knew I was going to get screwed":* Leigh Jones, "Affair with Former Client's Wife Costs Attorney $1.5 Million," *National Law Journal,* August 20, 2008, http://www.alm.law.com/jsp/article.jsp?id=1202423908229.

330 *The Texas Legal Service Center:* TexasLawHelp.org, http://texaslawhelp.org/.

330 *jealous guardians of their licensed profession:* Jennifer Smith, "Rivalry Grows Among No-Frill Legal Services," *Wall Street Journal,* December 3, 2012, http://online.wsj.com/news/articles/SB1000142412788732371700457815541 349310.

BIBLIOGRAPHY

American Bar Association. *The American Bar Association Guide to Wills and Estates.*
    4th ed. New York: Random House Reference, 2012.
——. *Legal Guide for Women.* New York: Random House Reference, 2004.
Doskow, Emily. *Nolo's Essential Guide to Divorce.* 4th ed. Berkeley, CA: Nolo, 2012.
Hauser, Barbara R. *Women's Legal Guide.* Golden, CO: Fulcrum, 1996.
McGee, William, and Sandra McGee. *The Divorce Seekers.* St. Helena, CA: BMC,
    2004.
Morris, Virginia. *How to Care for Aging Parents.* 3rd ed. New York: Workman, 2014.
Silverman, Rachel Emma. *The Wall Street Journal Complete Estate Planning Guide-
    book.* New York: Crown Business, 2011.
Steingold, Fred. *The Employer's Legal Handbook.* 11th ed. Berkeley, CA: Nolo, 2013.
Weisman, Steve. *A Guide to Elder Planning.* Updated and revised ed. Upper Saddle
    River, NJ: FT Press, 2013.

ACKNOWLEDGMENTS

I confess.

Throughout this book, I've warned you about a host of scary legal problems you either never considered or hoped to ignore, nagged you to sign daunting documents, and even urged you to contact more lawyers for still more discussions of these unpleasant (though important and unavoidable) topics.

You may have concluded that I'm a cold, heartless, hyperrational woman who prefers quiet time with a copy of *Black's Law Dictionary* to the warmth of human contact.

And, sure, that's often true—just ask my family.

But it's not the case when it comes to my affection for the dear friends and family who made *On Your Case* possible. While flaws in the book are mine alone, these busy, successful, and altogether impressive people made time to support its creation, iron out its wrinkles, and make sure it traveled a straight and true path into your hands. I cannot repay their kindness and generosity, so let me at least share my gratitude to:

Esteemed members of the bar: Craig Bloom, Lorraine Cooper, Joseph Fein, Robin Freimann, Ed Hernstadt, Michael Markhoff, Susan Sawyer, and Sam Talkin.

Researcher extraordinaire: Emily Wolf.

Superagents: Amy Hughes and Betsy Lerner.

Publishing wizards: Cassie Jones, Sharyn Rosenblum, Liate Stehlik, Kara Zauberman, Lynn Grady, Jennifer Hart, Tavia Kowalchuk, Kaitlin Harri, Emily Homonoff, Laura Cherkas, Jamie Kerner, Adam Johnson, and Marta Durkin.

Indispensable colleagues: John Hearn and John Hodder.

Wise advisers: Brandy Bergman, Yolanda Cartusciello, Jean Chatzky, Jamie Gangel, and Bill McGowan.

Impeccable hosts: Cathy Bacich and Ed Schallert Robert Boyd and Amy Kaufman; and Nevine Michaan and Steven Michaan.

True friends and stalwart supporters: Amy Glickman, Lisa Goodman, Mark Goodman, Jean Harper, David Laufman, Judy Laufman, Elena Nachmanoff, Matt Saal, Antoine Sanfuentes, Michele Willens, and Alex Witt.

Soul sister: Esther Fein.

Sisterhood of the Traveling Running Injuries: Esther, Laurie Hays, and Elisabeth Rosenthal.

Ever-tolerant family: Howard Green, Marie Green, Jeff Leighton, Sharon Leighton, Jayne Stein, Richard Stein, my beloved mother, Pearl Green (who missed her calling; she would make an outstanding litigator), and my father of blessed memory, Jack Green. Dad, I miss you every day. And though I indulge here in double dipping, since this book is dedicated to them, my children, Andrew and Claire, were exceptionally patient and good-humored, not to mention responsible for some of the livelier anecdotes that populate the book. My respect for the mother-child privilege means others won't ever be published, promise.

And finally: the exception that proves the rule. Behind every successful women's empowerment book, there ought to be a smart, handsome, loving, and indefatigably support- ive man. In my case, the book's true inspiration is the in- comparable Eli Gottlieb, of great talent and bigger heart. None of this—not a single word—would have been possible without him.

INDEX